ANTES

Stories From The Past
Rural Cuba, New Mexico, 1769–1949

For my dearest Amina,
I will always remember
you and love you.
Fondly,
Esther May
12/3/11

ANTES

Stories From The Past
Rural Cuba, New Mexico, 1769–1949

Esther V. Cordova May

SANTA FE

Photo credits. All photographs not otherwise attributed
are from the author's personal collection.

Sunstone books may be purchased for educational, business, or sales promotional use.
For information please write: Special Markets Department, Sunstone Press,
P.O. Box 2321, Santa Fe, New Mexico 87504-2321.

Book and Cover design ✦ Vicki Ahl
Body typeface ✦ Book Antiqua
Printed on acid free paper

Library of Congress Cataloging-in-Publication Data

May, Esther V. Cordova, 1936-
  Antes : stories from the past : rural Cuba, New Mexico, 1769-1949 / by Esther V. Cordova May.
     p. cm.
  Includes bibliographical references and index.
  ISBN 978-0-86534-840-0 (softcover : alk. paper)
  1. Cuba (N.M.)--History--Anecdotes. 2. Country life--New Mexico--Cuba--History-
-Anecdotes. 3. City and town life--New Mexico--Cuba--History--Anecdotes. 4. Community life--New Mexico--Cuba--History--Anecdotes. 5. Cuba (N.M.)--Social life and
customs--Anecdotes.
  6. Folklore--New Mexico--Cuba. 7. Cuba (N.M.)--Biography--Anecdotes. I. Title.
  F804.C95M39 2011
  978.9'57--dc23
                              2011036082

WWW.SUNSTONEPRESS.COM
SUNSTONE PRESS / POST OFFICE BOX 2321 / SANTA FE, NM 87504-2321 /USA
(505) 988-4418 / ORDERS ONLY (800) 243-5644 / FAX (505) 988-1025

~ Contents ~

~ Preface ~

In October of 2007, the late Betty Jane Curry, then acting editor of the *Cuba News*, contacted me to see if I would be interested in writing a series of articles on the history of Cuba. We agreed that they would be limited to the period before World War II and the few years immediately thereafter; a time when Cuba was transformed quite rapidly from a village that had gone largely unchanged for nearly two hundred years to a community with all of the amenities of any other town of its size anywhere else in the country. The articles would be called *Antes* (pronounced AHN' tace and meaning *before,* or *in the past*).

In accepting Mrs. Curry's invitation to write for the *Cuba News,* my commitment was to relate stories about events, people and folklore of this area. I especially wanted to write about whatever it was that made *antes* such a special and memorable time, recalled with passion by so many people even today. I believed that if the articles were to be well received, I had an obligation to assure local readers that this would not be a gossip column. Furthermore, under no circumstances would I knowingly publish any information that would cause embarrassment or injury to any family or individual's name. Having known people of several generations in this community over my lifetime, I felt they needed this assurance in order to gain their cooperation and contributions to this effort.

The first *Antes* article was published in the November 2007 issue of the *Cuba News.* Articles have appeared in every issue of this monthly newspaper since then. During this time I have been supported continuously by members of the community. Local people have provided details, and entire new stories, photographs and, most importantly, strong and consistent encouragement for my efforts. Together, we have been able to reconstruct a far more complete and comprehensive picture of our ancestral home and the people who have made it the unique place that it has been. With their help, my own understanding of this dear place has been expanded far beyond anything I would have imagined at the outset of this project.

I was born in the town which is the center of the story of *antes*. My ancestors have lived here or in nearby communities for at least five generations. I am familiar with this history from personal experience and have maintained a long and close connection with my community for more than seventy years and feel strongly that this history needs affirmation.

From very early in my childhood I became increasingly curious about the meaning of my mother's family name, which was *DeLaO*. It literally means *of the O* and even for northern New Mexico it is an unusual name. I would repeatedly ask my grandfather what the *O* stood for and he would always give me the same response: he did not know. This was an answer I was not willing to accept. Being a child, I still believed that there were answers to all the questions that arose in my mind and that an adult would have these answers. As I grew older, it became a personal, private and passionate goal of mine to learn my own history and the history of my community by whatever means were available to me. Furthermore, I believed that this history needed some outward expression. Ultimately, this book is the product of my passion for this history.

I recall a time, perhaps in the third grade, reading in our history book about the early English settlements in New England. As I read this, I knew even then that the history of those Pilgrims and Puritans had very little to do with me. I knew I was not a Pilgrim, nor were my classmates or my family.

Some chapters later, we started reading about the *Conquistadores* in the southwest. I started to pay more attention. I was able to relate to the familiar place names and people's names that I could recognize as being like our local names. As well, I became aware that I was a part of this story. Only later did I realize that the history of the southwest began well before the history of the Pilgrims in New England. I decided to follow these early historical fragments until the whole picture emerged of who I am and how the people around me lived and how our community came to be as it was.

As I grew up I became increasingly proud of my history. However, my passion and pride got me into a lot of trouble in school. I did not survive a single Spanish class in junior high school or high school. The reason for this had to do with my consistently defending our northern New Mexico dialect from teachers who were trying to teach standard Spanish to students who shared this New Mexico dialect. Furthermore, either directly or by implication, they were telling us that our Spanish was inferior to that spoken elsewhere. Perhaps if these teachers had said that New Mexico Spanish evolved differently from Spanish spoken elsewhere, I might have been more open and accepting of their efforts. Instead, I was simply transferred out of the classes.

In college, I studied Spanish and loved every class I took and excelled, especially in literature. Fortunately, my first Spanish professor was a young woman who, although born in California, was a descendent of the Pino family of New Mexico. This family included Don Pedro Bautista Pino, New Mexico's first delegate to the newly created *Cortes Constituyentes* (constituent assembly from all of Spain's colonies) reporting to the King of Spain in 1810. This professor was able to help me understand the relationship between my Spanish and the Spanish of the rest of the world. She also added to my understanding of the unique history of the northern New Mexico Spanish dialect.

During the years I lived away from Cuba, I returned many times, maintaining contact with the people and the practices of my community. In 1972, during my collegiate experience, I was awarded a grant from Mills College to do an oral history project here in Cuba. I spent the entire summer conducting interviews with numerous elderly individuals still living in the community. Furthermore, over the past thirty-five years I have been researching and collecting materials related to Cuba with the specific intent of writing its history.

My materials up to now include approximately fifty recorded tapes of the interviews which I conducted in 1972 along with many photographs which people have shared with me over the years simply because they knew I had an interest in such materials. I also have my own photographic collection and reams of notes on the general topic of the history of the village of Cuba and the surrounding area. Over the years, I made academic visits to Mexico and Spain where I pursued my interest in the history of the Spanish colonial period of Mexico and New Mexico. As well, I have had academic training and the experience to conduct serious and responsible historical research.

In 1980, my husband and I left our community college teaching positions and returned to Cuba to manage the family cattle ranch and to teach in the local schools. Since that time I have continued to add to my storehouse of verbal accounts and photographs for the period before World War II: the world of *antes*.

As I have listened to stories about my community, I have learned that we are a community of interrelated families who have helped each other in good times as well as in the worst of times. This interdependency allowed us to survive into the modern world with a measure of dignity and the will to determine our own destiny, whether right here in Cuba or wherever else we might live today.

As for my question regarding the origin of my mother's name, according to *Origins of New Mexico's Families* by Fray Angélico Chávez, José Santiago DeLaO arrived in New Mexico in approximately 1807 as the armorer of the Presidio of Santa Fé. José was the son of Tiburcio DeLaO and Maria Josefa Herrera and had been born at the Presidio of Guajoquilla in New Biscay. This Presidio was located between Chihuahua and Durango, Mexico. These locations had been formed into a distinct region known as New Biscay. According to Fray Angélico Chávez, the DeLaO's were among the soldiers and officers who decided to remain in New Mexico permanently rather than return to Mexico. Given Fray Angélico Chavez' information, the O was already in place before the early 1800s. This O may have been an abbreviation for a place name or some other descriptor of those early soldiers. Whatever it referred to has been totally lost to history and had ceased to be known well before my grandfather's time. It is no wonder that he did not know and could not tell me what that O stood for, despite my insistence.

We will probably never know how that name came into being but we do know that this family has had a long and interesting role in the history of New Mexico as well as a part in the history of the village of Cuba.

Today, Cuba remains a small town but it is definitely tied to the wider world. Our businesses are linked to the rest of the world by high-speed internet connections and we have a modern four-lane highway running through town that connects us to major population centers elsewhere. Our schools have produced students who have gone on to become doctors, engineers, mathematicians and other professionals. Many of our homes are filled with the same electronics as homes elsewhere and our children use their cell phones to text their friends. In these ways, we have become a community very much like many others across the nation. It is not our present or our future that make us different in any significant way from other communities. It is only our past that is different and it is particularly that part of our past that we call *antes* that makes us different from other places and unites us because we have this special history that is shared only by the people of northern New Mexico.

—Esther V. Cordova May
Cuba, New Mexico
2011

~ Acknowledgments ~

Sincere thanks to the staff of the *Cuba News* for allowing the dawning of *Antes*. They allowed the *Antes* articles to flow interactively between the readers and me so willingly and without limitations of any sort. This staff also graciously accommodated *Antes* as it began to take on a life of its own. Their support has been constant and generous.

I am especially grateful to the late Betty Jane Curry, formerly editor of the *Cuba News* for offering me the opportunity to write the *Antes* series. I regret that she did not live to see *Antes* in book form. I believe she would have been proud of the outcome. It was Betty Jane Curry that really provided the motivation to commit to contributing an *Antes* article each month. In all humility, if it had not been for Mrs. Curry, a life-long friend of my parents, this project might very well never have gotten on paper. This was a commitment I intended to uphold.

The stories I have written were all here and have been repeated many times over. I, like so many of the readers, have heard many of these stories since early childhood. Luckily the *Cuba News* accorded the incentive to write them down least they be forgotten. There are certain individuals who deserve special mention for their sincere help in making this book a reality through continuous interest, support and encouragement. Foremost, my beloved friends George and Emma Casaus deserve mention. Over the years they have provided me with a wealth of reliable information related to people's names, places and events that occurred before my lifetime. These two formerly close friends of my parents, now in their declining years, have enriched my life and expanded my knowledge of our community through many hours of conversation over a cup of tea and a few cookies.

I thank them both for their sincere friendship as well as for their store of knowledge. Many other members of the community, too numerous to name individually, have also taken hours of their own time (and more tea and cookies) over many years to share their stories and their photographs with me as well. While they have shared their memories with me for years, they have been especially helpful since the *Antes* articles began to appear.

Special thanks to all the members of my family, other community members and individuals and organizations outside the community who have been urging me to publish the original newspaper articles in book form and have provided their generous support.

Given today's electronic world, it has been through the untiring efforts of my devoted and most technically competent husband, Don Moore, that I was able to meet the paper's deadlines at least ninety-nine percent of the time. He also provided frequent and insightful editing assistance. Our dear friend Diddy Greacen agreed to join our book venture and contributed her amazing technical and editing skills and experience as well. I could not have had a better team to bring this project to fruition. Thank you Don and Diddy. Your hard work has paid off.

Finally, I want to thank Mr. Jim Clois Smith and his staff at Sunstone Press in Santa Fé for their kind and generous support in bringing this project to completion. Their gentle guidance has helped to turn a series of individual and often disconnected articles into a relatively coherent overview of life as it was in our tiny village.

Today, with the help of so many people both here in Cuba, former residents and others who have contributed material and guidance, we have something tangible to share with those for whom *antes* would otherwise be little more than a myth retold by an old *abuelita* (grandmother) or some long-lived *tío* (uncle). Everyone can now know that *antes* was a real time in a real place, now known as Cuba but previously called Nacimiento.

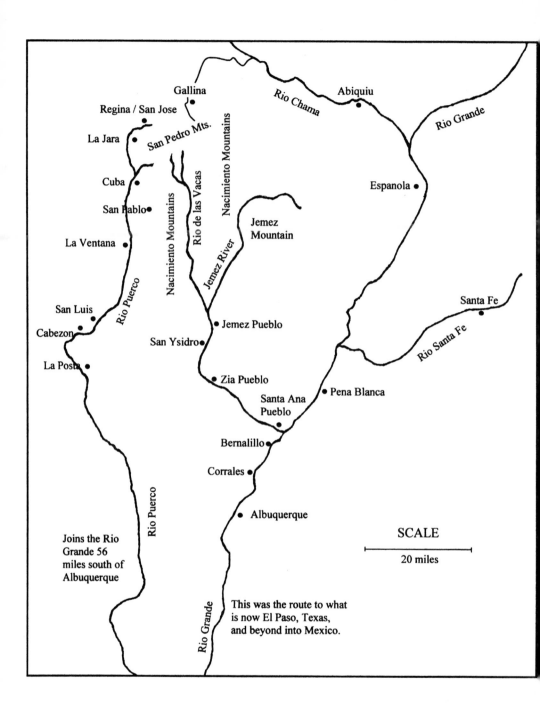

Gallina

Regina / San Jose

La Jara

San Pedro Mts.

Rio Chama

Abiquiu

Rio Grande

Cuba

Nacimiento Mountains

Rio de las Vacas

Nacimiento Mountains

San Pablo

Espanola

La Ventana

Jemez
Mountain

Nacimiento Mountains

Rio Puerco

Jemez River

San Luis

Cabezon

Jemez Pueblo

San Ysidro

La Posta

Santa Fe

Rio Santa Fe

Zia Pueblo

Pena Blanca

Santa Ana
Pueblo

Bernalillo

Corrales

Rio Puerco

Albuquerque

SCALE

20 miles

Joins the Rio
Grande 56
miles south of
Albuquerque

Rio Grande

This was the route to what
is now El Paso, Texas,
and beyond into Mexico.

The Wider World

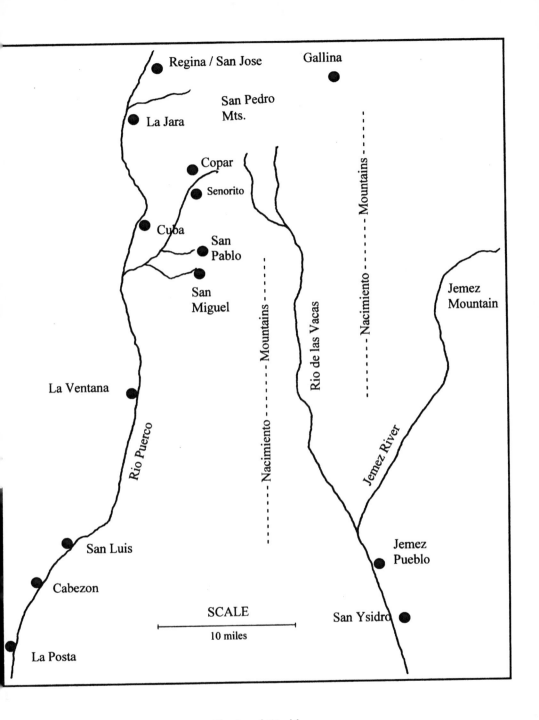

The Local World

− Introduction −

A*ntes* (pronounced AHN' tace) in Spanish means "before" or "in the past." Before what? Before when? For the local Spanish-speaking people of Cuba and our neighbors in surrounding communities, *antes* refers to a time before our communities changed, or were changed for us. It was a time before significant events changed our life styles, traditional customs and values that had been in place for over two hundred fifty years. The reference is always implied to mean the way things happened in our world before the changes that followed World War II.

In some instances, these changes occurred for reasons few if any of us still alive remember or understand. In the local vernacular, when people here speak of *antes*, the "what" and the "when" are implied. One frequently hears people in conversations say, "*Antes*, we used to have to do such and such in a particular way;" or, "*Antes*, people here had such and such." The time frame is understood by both the speaker and the listener. A Spanish-speaking outsider overhearing such a conversation would be left with the questions of before when, and before what? But the people of Cuba know and understand the implied "what's" and "when's".

We have become aware in recent years that the Hispanic history of northern New Mexico and southern Colorado is long and filled with activities and attitudes not shared or well understood by the mainstream culture of the United States. There are many interesting points about this history that are largely unknown by many people in our own state and across the nation but reflected upon fondly by those who lived in that time in this community and elsewhere across the Southwest.

Cuba, New Mexico, originally known as Nacimiento, was first

settled in 1769. It was located on the very northwestern edge of the Spanish colonial empire. After several attempts, a permanent settlement was established. It was isolated and the people who eventually settled Cuba seldom travelled to other areas due to the lack of roads and the distances between settlements. Isolation was simply something the people of Cuba accommodated and endured.

As a consequence of this isolation, Cuba retained many of the traditions and practices of the early colonial period until the middle of the twentieth century. It also retained many of the language traditions of that period while also utilizing words from native languages, as well as creating some of its own to fit the local circumstances.

Only after World War II did this area emerge from its colonial traditions and begin to acquire amenities like those of other towns elsewhere in the nation. Different from many other small towns, it did not change because of the coming of a railroad, a new industry or a new highway. Nor did it change because of the influx of some large group of people from some other part of the country. Cuba changed because of the actions of a small group of people who had been away during World War II and had come back wanting more of the modern conveniences that were commonplace in other communities. They wanted these amenities in their own communities rather than moving away to some other place that already had such modern conveniences. Certainly communities everywhere have changed through time. What makes this story unusual is that the traditional ways of doing things lasted so late in history and changed so quickly that there are still people living who remember how things were done and can help document this story.

The material for this book originated as a series of more than forty newspaper articles written over a three year period and published in the local monthly newspaper, *The Cuba News*. They describe substantial details of life as it was from the earliest settlement of the Cuba area up to just after World War II. They include celebrations such as weddings and feasts as well as simply coping with life without running water or electricity or decent roads. They describe the games children played and the music and dances people enjoyed and the foods they ate. They also include descriptions of religious events and activities of ordinary day-to-day life. Some parts are quite serious while others are rather humorous. They constitute a montage of many of the attitudes and practices that made up authentic rural northern New Mexico village life. The book ends just after World War II because that is when many of the older practices were supplanted by more main-stream ways of life.

The purpose of this book is to illustrate the history of this community and others like it through this series of vignettes, both for serious scholars of New Mexico history as well as for those who grew up here and only dimly recall their own history. It is also intended for the many people who have moved into New Mexico over the last half-century who would like to know more about this place they have come to live in and to love. As well, there is a substantial exile group who originally came from Cuba and wants to continue to stay in touch with the community and reminisce about their *antes*. It is also meant to provide a glimpse into a past that may be quite different from that which many readers may have experienced or read about from some other parts of northern New Mexico. The book contains many old photographs both from my own collection along with some loaned by other members of the community. These photographs also bring back memories of that way of life that no longer exists.

1

─ Early history ─

Las Herencias de Idiomas
Our Language Inheritance

The people of northern New Mexico and southern Colorado speak a language which is in many ways unique. Various historical and cultural circumstances have led to the development of a language which has been drawn from a range of sources and is rather different from modern standard Spanish.

This unique linguistic treasure-trove began with conquest in the New World and separation from the Old World. This linguistic inheritance grew and gained in wealth in the same way it began: at the point of a sword along with religious ideology. The language of *antes* developed largely because of the type of people who were involved in these campaigns. These were generally soldiers, normally drawn from the ranks of the common people. Usually these men were young and not well educated. As well, they were energetic, adventurous and willing to go anywhere.

A second reason the linguistic treasure-trove grew as it did was that the people involved were separated and isolated from their mainstream societies. As a result, they were forced to accommodate to the local linguistic and cultural environment or, conversely, to impose their own language and culture on the conquered peoples in order to survive. (This happened in much the same way as what happened when the Romans invaded Spain and Latin became the official language of that part of the Roman world.) There were many compromises along the way that resulted in accommodation by both the conquerors and the conquered. As a result of this interaction, the Spanish speakers of this region speak in the uniquely rich regional dialect we inherited from our various ancestors and from those around them over a period of hundreds of years.

This local language was derived originally from sixteenth- and seventeenth-century Spanish. For purposes of comparison, this would be similar to the English language of Shakespeare and the King James Version of the Bible! This part of the language is indeed archaic. In the sixteenth century, when Spanish explorers and settlers began coming to the new world, Spain had been unified politically for less than a hundred years. Furthermore, Spain was not then (nor is it today) a strictly monolingual country. Even though Castilian Spanish has been the official language of Spain since 1492, there have always been many other sources of language in that country.

Among the language sources in sixteenth century Spain, there were probably still Ladino speakers, despite the expulsion of the Jews from Spain in 1492. Ladino, also called Judeo-Spanish, is a Romance language of the Sephardic Jews based on archaic Spanish and written in Hebrew script. There are reports that as late as the nineteenth century there were Spanish speakers in New Mexico for whom Ladino was one of their languages. Besides Ladino, there were many other archaic Spanish words that date back to the days of the expedition of Juan de Oñate y Salazar in 1598. For instance, there is the term *pelizcar*. In modern Spanish, this word has evolved into *pellizcar* (to pinch). The double-l spelling calls for a rather different pronunciation than the original. Here we still say *pelizcar*. Other such ancient words used here include *alverjon* (peas), *arrollar* (to lull to sleep), *camalta* (a high bed), *¡curre!* (run!), and *empeloto* (stark naked). These are but a few of the archaic words still in use here which are understood perfectly well by those who still speak the language of the *Conquistadores*. However, these are not words generally used in the rest of the Spanish-speaking world and might not be understood even by Spanish speakers in Texas or California.

These archaisms are few compared to the more than four thousand Arabic words that became incorporated into the official Spanish language after the unification of Spain. Spain was invaded from North Africa in 711

A.D. and was almost completely occupied for the next several centuries. Spanish, Jewish and Arabic cultures flourished socially, intellectually and economically (in some places together) throughout much of this time, but the Arabs were finally expelled after their defeat at the battle of Granada in 1492. Linguistic sources state that the Arabic element in the Spanish language is second only to that of Latin in the number of words and their importance. There are a tremendous number of Arabic words inherited by Spanish speakers all over the world. Many of these words are related to agriculture and therefore very familiar to the people of Cuba and throughout northern New Mexico. The following are just a fraction of what could be included. Among the most widely used terms of Arabic origin in this area: *acequia* (irrigation ditch), alfalfa (no translation needed), *alazan* (sorrel horse), *jinete* (horseman, or rider), *noria* (water well), *albaricoque,* (apricot), *jara* (sandbar willow), *almouada* (pillow), *alfiler* (pin), and *aguja* (needle). Here we say *albarcoque* instead of *albaricoque* and *abuja* instead of *aguja* reflecting more of the regional variation that makes northern New Mexico Spanish unique.

The names of some of our herbs are also of Arabic origin. These include *alhucema* (lavender), *albahaca* (basil) and *ajenjibre* (ginger). In modern Spanish, the name for ginger has become *jengibre.* And, of course, who would be willing to live without *azúcar* (sugar)?

Among the most interesting words inherited from the Arabic are place names related to rivers, brooks or washes. The Arabic word for such landmarks is *wadi*. In Spanish, *wadi* has become *guada* and from there we get *Guadalajara* (river of willows), *Guadalope* or *Guadalupe* (river of the wolf) and *Guadalquivir* (Great River or *Rio Grande*).

Without being aware of it, local Spanish speakers use words derived from Latin, Arabic, Ladino and Sephardic languages, all brought to the New World from Spain with the earliest Spanish soldiers and settlers.

But the story goes on and the language continued to grow. In 1521, just sixty years after the Arabs and Jews were expelled from Spain, the young Hernan Cortés and a few men in metal armor, armed with swords and on horseback, conquered and destroyed the beautiful capital city of the Aztec empire known as Tenochtitlan. At that time a new and different chapter began for the Spanish speaking world. This was especially true for what came to be the poor, isolated colonists eking out a living in the northern-most frontiers of New Spain, what we now call New Mexico and southern Colorado.

Following the conquest of the Aztec empire, the Spanish language of the New World would acquire countless words from the Na'huatl language. Na'huatl is a Uto-Aztecan language spoken by over half a million people, mostly in central Mexico, including the Aztecs. When looking up Na'huatl words in a Spanish dictionary, the source is usually given as "from Mexican Spanish."

In northern New Mexico, many of these words became fully integrated into the day-to-day vocabulary. Even today, as these familiar words are used, most people assume they are as Spanish as *Don Quixote de la Mancha*. It is very likely that if a local Spanish-speaker were asked what the Spanish word for a ladle or dipper is, they would answer *jumate*. In Na'huatl, the word was *xumatl*, meaning a ladle or dipper made from a gourd or shell. (The English sound represented by an *x* in Na'huatl is variously translated as *h*, *sh* or *ch*.) In standard Spanish, a ladle is a *cucharón* or a *cazo. Cazo* is sometimes used here but the most common word for ladle is *jumate*.

Another common local word is *chapulín* (little grasshopper). In Na'huatl, the word is *chapul*. For any reader who has visited Mexico City, you likely visited Chapultepec Park. This would be "the place of the grasshoppers." European Spanish-speakers refer to a grasshopper as a *langosta* or a *saltamonte* or just as a *salton* (a hopper). The Na'huatl word for coyote is *coyotl* and the word for *capulín* (chokecherry) is *capulí*. Then there is *ocote* (piñon wood or sap), which was originally *ocotol* in Na'huatl.

For reasons unknown at this time, the next two words were totally confused by northern New Mexicans. An *ajolote*, according to linguistic sources, is a tiger salamander or a water dog. This is a fairly common amphibian that lives in and around local ponds and streams. Here in most of northern New Mexico we refer to water dogs and such animals as *guajalote*, which in Mexico is the word for a turkey. *Antes*, local children were kept from getting into stagnant ponds of water because our mothers and grandmothers had warned us all that these ugly *guajalotes* in the ponds would go right up our rectums if we dared to play in such water. The warning worked very well! The fear of such a creature going up our "behinds" kept most of us out of the ponds. Had we known that a guajalote was actually a turkey, things might have been different.

Lastly, out of the many Na'huatl words our ancestors appropriated for their own use, there are the words *atole* (blue cornmeal mush) and *chili* which were lifted out of Na'huatl without any change at all. These were probably among the earliest words everyone had to learn in order to survive in this unforgiving land of ours and is also the reason they are still so widely used today.

The linguistic contributions from New Mexico's native languages come primarily from the middle Rio Grande Pueblos. These were the pueblos where the Spanish and native people had more contact with each other due to continuous threat of raids on any of their communities from more nomadic tribes. According to the Laws of the Indies, the Spanish were forbidden to establish themselves within the limits of Indian settlements. Yet, the words acquired primarily from the Tewa-speaking pueblos are still in common use here in Cuba. A word most people will recognize is *osha* (wild celery), a widely-used medicinal plant. We also have *chimaja* (wild parsley) and *aguapá* (cat tail). Another word of Tewa origin is *cunques* (sediment). We still use the word *cunques* for coffee grounds. We use the word *teguas* (buffalo-hide shoes) for moccasins which our ancestors very likely also learned to make from these people. *The word teguas* is still used widely to describe the hide moccasins people used to make and wear all through this area. This name may simply be an adaptation of the name of the Tewa people used to describe this important product.

There are two words which became place names that would be easily recognized by most readers. The first one is *Chimayó*, originally meaning obsidian flake and the other *chiquil*, which became *chiquilé*, meaning a dale or meadow. The list of words from Tewa is not very long and some of the words derived from that language are rarely used any more. For example, we used to use the word *chaquegue* (a thick, blue cornmeal mush) that few around here make or eat anymore. This is also true of the word *tasayes*, which became *tasajo* (sun-dried strips of pumpkin). Again, hardly anyone makes *tasajo* anymore and so these words are being lost from the local vocabulary from lack of use.

With all these sources, the Spanish language of northern New Mexico has become extremely rich and somewhat different from Spanish spoken elsewhere. Our isolation here allowed our local vocabulary to evolve separately from the rest of the Spanish-speaking world and to remain intact until sometime in the twentieth century.

There is yet another story related to the language contributions made primarily by the people of Mexico who have been coming into the southwestern United States over an extended period of time. Unlike the Spanish spoken in northern New Mexico, the Spanish spoken in Mexico and the rest of Latin America continued to evolve along the same lines and with the same rules as what became modern standard Spanish. Furthermore, these people brought with them books, newspapers and other written materials in Spanish, something that had been lacking in the rural parts of this area. In addition to the impact of standard Mexican Spanish, there is now an overwhelming influence from English on the local language.

Despite our linguistic wealth, there is a measure of sadness related to the lack of appreciation and pride among many of the heirs of this marvelous linguistic past. It is hoped that this article helps to explain why it is that speakers of modern, standard Spanish have difficulty understanding the Spanish spoken in this area. This is the language of ancient conquerors as well as the languages of the conquered. It is a unique language that, like many others around the world, is being lost through lack of use and through influences from outside of this area. *Y asi es como se an perdido las herencias siempre.* (And this is how inheritances have always been lost.)

Las Hijas de los Colonistas
The Daughters of the Colonists

The four women in this article were born in or around the village of Nacimiento, Nuevo Mexico (the Territory of New Mexico), in the middle to late nineteenth century. That place, of course, is now the village of Cuba, in the State of New Mexico. These women were part of the first or second generation of families who had successfully migrated and permanently settled into the upper Rio Puerco valley, mostly from the middle Rio Grande valley. Some families came from such places as Peña Blanca, Sile and La Cienega. Others came from places as close as the San Luis and Cabezon areas of the middle Rio Puerco valley. These women's families were herdsmen and farmers looking for arable land to plant their crops and pastures for their animals. Above all, they were looking for dependable sources of water.

Other families with women of this generation came from the north. These were the families forced out of the San Luis Valley in Colorado by the Anglo invasion from the east earlier in the nineteenth century. These families first migrated back into the Abiquiu area and from there went to such places as Coyote, Capulín and Gallina. From these villages they crossed into the area drained by San José Creek, which empties into the Rio Puerco near Cuba. Along the way, they formed communities such as San José (now Regina), La Jara and Los Pinos.

These four women are just a few examples of many women of their generation. They are representative of many others in that they were born here and lived in Cuba their entire lives, or at least during the most productive parts of their lives. These women and many others like them shared a lifestyle and experiences that made them outstanding role models for modern women. They were physically strong, adaptive to change and resilient in the face of hardship, sorrow and death.

Generally speaking, the women of this generation were married early in their teens and frequently married to men much older than themselves. During their childbearing years they endured many pregnancies, some as many as fourteen or more, with many of these pregnancies ending in miscarriage, stillbirth or infant mortality. Nonetheless, they might still end up with families of eight to twelve children who survived into adulthood.

Of those who did survive into adulthood, many would die young. The young women might die in childbirth or from illness. Dozens of young people, as well as older members of the community, died in the influenza epidemic of 1918. Boys and young men died from farm or ranch accidents or from communicable diseases. The losses these mothers suffered were tremendous, particularly in comparison to the relative comfort and safety enjoyed by young people today.

Another thing that makes these women interesting but not unusual for their time, is that they were each widowed for many years before their deaths, leaving them to be cared for by their children or other members of their extended families. Yet in spite of all their hardships, these women kept their faith, their sanity and sensitivity and above all, a vibrant spirit and dignity. They were also known in this community as competent and tireless workers. Perhaps this is why they are remembered today with so much fondness and respect.

The earliest of these *pobladoras* (settlers) was actually a generation older than the others being written about. Her name was *Doña* Petra Vigil C de Baca. She was born on April 24, 1866. She was the oldest of eight surviving children born to *Don* Francisco Vigil and *Doña* Eugenia Montoya Vigil.

According to an ancient little piece of blue paper on which *Doña* Petra's birth was recorded, the family feared this baby was not going to survive. The priest was present to baptize the baby and to give her last rites. The *padrinos* (godparents) are named. *Doña* Petra was baptized by her aunt, *Doña* Martina Montes, who was probably present at the house when the birth occurred, and a gentleman named *Don* Santiago Blea. Regardless of *Doña* Petra's condition at her birth, she survived and lived to be ninety years old.

Doña Petra's family had migrated to Las Lagunitas (now the southwest part of Cuba) from Sile, a tiny Hispanic community on the west bank of the Rio Grande near Peña Blanca. She was married to *Don* Facundo C de Baca who was from Peña Blanca. Although he was related to the other C de Baca family members here in Cuba, his immediate family apparently stayed in Peña Blanca. When he married *Doña* Petra, he joined the family operation of his father-in-law, Don Francisco Vigil in Las Lagunitas where he and *Doña* Petra lived and raised their family.

Doña Petra may have had as many as fifteen pregnancies. There is a record of at least ten children having survived infancy, some into adulthood.

Among the children that *Doña* Petra gave birth to was a hydrocephalic girl who lived to the age of puberty. Hydrocephalus is an abnormal condition characterized by increased amounts of fluid in the cranium. Lay people referred to this as having "water on the brain." This excess amount of fluid causes an enlargement of the child's head and the child is sometimes unable to walk. Again, according to family folklore, this girl was kept in a baby buggy and cared for by the family until she died.

There is no record or verbal account of what might have happened to at least five of the other children who had apparently survived infancy. There is a photograph taken around 1912 in which *Doña* Petra and *Don* Facundo are pictured with three of their adult daughters and their youngest daughter, Maria Natividad, who was born on September 8, 1907.

The three adult daughters, *Doña* Genara, *Doña* Josefina and *Doña* Deluvina married and had children. By 1918, *Doña* Josefina had three children, *Doña* Deluvina had one and *Doña* Genara had three. In the winter of 1918, *Doña* Petra and *Don* Facundo lost their beloved *Doña* Josefina and *Doña* Josefina's young daughter Margarita in the influenza epidemic, leaving *Doña* Josefina's husband *Don* Onofre Garcia with two very small motherless boys needing care. That same winter, *Doña* Deluvina also died in the deadly influenza epidemic, leaving her five-year-old son Tomas motherless and in the care of his father, *Don* Raphael Aragon.

Family stories tell that no fewer than ten members of the extended family of *Don* Facundo and *Doña* Petra died from the influenza epidemic. Those who witnessed this disastrous event said that the family had difficulty making enough coffins to bury their dead while they were trying to take care of those who were still alive but very sick. It is hard to believe that the world-wide influenza pandemic could have had such an effect on families such as this one in such an isolated place as Cuba.

In today's world, it also seems unimaginable how families could and did come through pain and loss of this magnitude. Yet, we know that somehow the children were taken care of and survived into adulthood. We also know that the pain and memories lingered on. As *Doña* Petra's family is followed down to the present, one can see that *Doña* Josefina was never forgotten. There are at least four women named Josefina in the next four generations following the loss of *Doña* Petra's daughter.

This generation of women was resilient in the face of hardship, sorrow and death. This is well demonstrated in the case of *Doña* Petra. By 1929 she and *Don* Facundo were having a hard time maintaining their ranch and *Don* Facundo's business as a blacksmith. Things were changing too rapidly and resources, including irrigation water, were scarce for everyone in the Rio Puerco basin. Making a living had become nearly impossible for anyone. *Don* Facundo had no sons who survived to adulthood. His sons-in-law were off working on their own to keep their families fed. *Don* Facundo's neighbors, who in the past might have planted, irrigated and harvested together had either died, moved away or, like *Don* Facundo's sons-in-law, were away working for wages. *Don* Facundo and *Doña* Petra found themselves with only their very young grandson Tomas to help run the ranch. His primary job was to tend the small goat herd the family still had for milk and meat. Apparently in late 1929, the stress became too much for *Don* Facundo. He suffered a complete mental breakdown. *Don* Facundo's condition became serious enough that *Doña* Petra, with the help of her daughter *Doña* Genara, arranged with one of *Doña* Petra's nephews, *Don* Frank Vigil, who had a car, to take *Don* Facundo to the State Mental Hospital in Las Vegas, New Mexico. Luckily, the nephew could read and write because neither *Doña* Petra nor *Doña* Genara spoke English. Try to imagine these women's pain in having to take this previously successful and loving patriarch of their family to such a far-away place and leaving him there for the rest of his life!

Given the lack of transportation, it is unlikely that any family members went to see *Don* Facundo after he was taken to Las Vegas. The family simply prayed a lot because that was what they always did in such situations.

Don Facundo C de Baca died on November 17, 1930, in Las Vegas, about a year after he had been taken there. Somehow the family managed to bring the body back home for burial in the Cuba Catholic Cemetery. There, he is now surrounded by the graves of his wife *Doña* Petra, his oldest and youngest daughters, two sons-in-law, grandchildren and great-grandchildren, very much as he had been in life.

Doña Petra was widowed for twenty-six years. She was left without financial resources of her own and only two surviving daughters. The rest of the resilient *Doña* Petra's life was spent lovingly taking care of her youngest daughter Maria's ten children as well as Tomas, Deluvina's son. In return, she was lovingly cared for in the home of her daughter *Doña* Maria and Maria's husband *Don* Raphael Aragon.

Her other surviving daughter, *Doña* Genara and her family, all visited her at the Aragon home as did her beloved Garcia grandsons, Facundo and Mariano, from La Jara. She was lovingly known as *Mamá* (grandma) Petra to all of her grandchildren and great-grandchildren. As the younger members of this extended family became more proficient in English than in Spanish, she also became known as *grammita Petra.*

Doña Petra died on May 20, 1956, in a world that bore no resemblance to the world she had been born so precariously into back in 1866. Throughout a lifetime filled with hardship and loss, she retained her love and caring, as well as her enduring strength and resilience. She became an example of a woman who triumphed over her personal misfortunes to focus on the most precious gifts of life, her grandchildren.

The next of the women to be portrayed in detail was unquestionably one of the female pillars of this community. Her name was *Doña* Lázara Vigil Aragon. She was born on January 17, 1887. She was nearly twenty years younger than her oldest sibling. She was only fourteen in 1901 when her father, *Don* Francisco Vigil died. Unlike her older siblings, *Doña* Lázara had been sent to school at the Loretto Academy for girls in Bernalillo. Her older brother *Don* Rumaldo had wanted her to have an education. More than anything else in the world, Lázara had also wanted this. This desire to learn would become one of her strongest personality traits as an adult. She never missed an opportunity to learn for herself or to teach someone else a new skill.

Unfortunately, upon the death of her father, her formal education came to an end. Being the youngest member of the family and unmarried, she was assigned to remain at home and take care of her mother, Eugenia, until she married.

In 1913, *Doña* Lázara married the young, tall, handsome *Don* Celestino Aragon from the nearby community of Cubita. *Don* Celestino was one of the sons of *Don* José Francisco Aragon and *Doña* Porfiria Gonzales Aragon. Atypically, *Doña* Lázara married a man who was five years younger than herself. Remarkably, she and *Don* Celestino never had any children of their own. After several years of marriage, *Doña* Lázara and *Don* Celestino informally adopted Edwina DeLaO. Edwina was their god-child and by then the second child of *Doña* Genara and *Don* Eduardo DeLaO's rapidly growing family. *Doña* Genara was *Doña* Lázara's niece and *Don* Celestino and *Doña* Lázara had been *Don* Eduardo and *Doña* Genara's wedding *padrinos* (best man and matron of honor) in 1914. These two women were not only related by blood but the couples were double *compadres,* as wedding *padrinos* and as *padrinos de pila* (baptismal god-parents) for Edwina. This relationship provided a very strong bond between the families and made Edwina the most appropriate choice among the DeLaO children to go to live with her *padrinos.* They raised Edwina as their own child until she married but Edwina always referred to them as *mi madrina* (my god-mother) and *mi padrino* (my god-father), not as mother and father.

Having had a basic education, *Doña* Lázara apparently continued to study and learn everything she could. She spoke and read English well enough that, as a young woman, she worked for Mrs. John Young at the Young's Hotel. There she learned non-traditional ways to prepare and preserve foods. She became an excellent baker and a most competent and creative cook. There was not a vegetable, an overripe plum or wilting apple that would escape her ability to make into something delicious. She was also a meticulous housekeeper and a kind and gentle hostess to everyone who visited.

Doña Lázara was a devout Catholic and wanted to attend daily mass. However, she and *Don* Celestino lived so far from town that getting to Sunday mass was usually all they could manage. Being the intelligent woman that she was, in 1931 *Doña* Lázara persuaded her dear husband to sell his share of the ranch in Cubita (a nearby settlement west of Cuba) and move closer to the church in town. Eventually she and *Don* Celestino purchased property very close to the church where an old gambrel-roof barn still stands. They also built a house on the upper part of the property where they lived and ran the local dairy.

Doña Lázara's wish had come true with the move to Cuba. She was now living only a few hundred yards from the church and was able to attend mass every day. Furthermore, she and *Don* Celestino became ardent supporters of the church and tireless in their efforts to support the work of the nuns at the convent. They were viewed by the community as being closely associated with the church and people frequently honored them by requesting them to be god-parents of countless children in the community. This was an honor and an obligation that they both took very seriously throughout their lives. Along with their many god-children, they each had numerous nieces and nephews and were known to half of the town as *Tía* (aunt) Lázara and *Tío* (uncle) Celestino.

In 1958, both *Doña* Lázara and *Don* Celestino became sickly and were having a difficult time keeping up with their work. As well, two of Edwina's sons who had for years helped with the demands of the dairy and all of the animals were growing up and went to join their parents, first in Los Alamos and then in Albuquerque. *Don* Celestino and *Doña* Lázara sold their house and the dairy and moved first to Bernalillo, where they lived on their own for a while. Ultimately, they moved to Albuquerque to live with Edwina and her family.

Don Celestino died in 1963 but the Rock of Gibraltar, *Tía* Lázara lived for twelve more years. She was five years older than her husband, yet strong enough to outlive him for more than a decade. During the twelve years that she was widowed, she was cared for by her beloved god-child Edwina, and her husband *Don* Patricio Montoya as well as their six children. *Doña* Edwina's children always referred to these two devoted people as "grandpa" Celestino and "grandma" Lázara while their mother continued to refer to them as her *padrinos* (god-parents). Ultimately those children had inherited the gift of three sets of grandparents, ironically, being closest in every way to the grandparents who were said to have been childless. *Don* Celestino and *Doña* Lázara Aragon, although childless themselves, ended up having more children in their family than almost anyone else in the community.

Another highly admired and remarkable daughter of the *colonistas* was *Doña* Julia Cebada Cordova. *Doña* Julia was born on December 16, 1893. She was one of two daughters born to *Don* José Maria Cebada and *Doña* Epifania Archibeque Cebada. *Doña* Julia and her sister *Doña* Juanita Cebada Archuleta were born in San Pablo at the Cebada ranch, where their father had a general merchandise store and ran the local Post Office.

According to the local folklore, *Don* José Maria wanted *Doña* Julia to go to school and to get an education so that eventually she would take over the family business. *Doña* Julia did go to school. She attended the Allison James Girls' School in Santa Fé, as did her aunts *Doña* Tomasita and *Doña* Petrita Cebada. As a result of this education, *Doña* Julia, like *Doña* Lázara, was an English speaker and could read and write in English as well as Spanish.

Doña Julia married *Don* José Julian Cordova, a man who was seventeen years older than she was. *Doña* Julia and *Don* Julian had nine children, three girls and six boys. They lived in Los Pinos, in part of what had been land homesteaded by *Don* Julian's father, *Don* Pasqual Cordova.

Life in Los Pinos, as elsewhere in this area, could be described as hard work followed by more hard work. There were animals to care for, crops to plant and harvest, wood to cut for winter and always children to attend to. Beside all this work, there were Sunday morning trips into town by wagon to attend services at the Cuba Presbyterian Church. Both *Doña* Julia and *Don* Julian were dedicated members of this church, which they helped to build. On many Sundays following church, they would spend the day visiting members of their extended families who lived in town. Through it all, *Doña* Julia remained one of the most genteel women in our community.

It is said that *Don* Julian Cordova was impatient, short tempered and demanding of everyone around him because there was always so much work to do. The family's herd of sheep demanded that he be away from home tending these sheep for long periods of time. *Doña* Julia, on the other hand, was known to be even tempered and genuinely kind to everyone. She also possessed a great sense of confidence which is illustrated in the following story.

Sometime while she was already in her nineties, *Doña* Julia wanted to go to Delta, Colorado, to visit her sister *Doña* Juanita. She asked various members of her family if they would drive her up to Colorado for this visit. At the time *Doña* Julia was asking for help for this trip, it appeared that everyone in the family had commitments and no one was able to drive her. So gentle, but very determined *Doña* Julia, got herself a bus ticket to Delta. When the family found out about what she had done, they all made quite a fuss about how she couldn't possibly go to Colorado by herself on the bus and that if she would only wait a little while; someone would be available to take her. She listened to all the fuss and the proposals offered to her and then finally said to all of them, "I want all of you to know that I am only going to ride in this bus as a passenger and I am not going to drive the bus." She did ride the bus, on her own terms, and had a wonderful visit with her sister (pers. comm.). Another interesting story about *Doña* Julia has to do with a now-faded photograph of her taken in 1980. At the age of 87, *Doña* Julia was photographed wearing her wedding dress from approximately seventy years earlier!

    Doña Julia died at the age of 103, loved by all who knew her. When she died, she had fifty-two grand-children, one hundred-ten great grandchildren and twenty-two great-great-grandchildren. She had no nieces or nephews of her own, having had only the one sister who was childless. Nevertheless, the entire Cordova clan in every generation, including in-laws, regardless of degree of relationship always referred to this wonderful woman as *mi Tía* Julia (my aunt Julia).

    Tía Julia was widowed for twenty-five years following the death of her husband in 1970. During part of that time she lived next door to her son Pablo's family in Albuquerque. In about 1980 she decided she wanted to return to Cuba. She returned to Cuba and lived on her own until close to the age of one hundred. At that time, she moved into her daughter *Doña* Carmelita's home, near where she had previously lived. This was a place *Tía* Julia enjoyed very much because there were always so many young people coming and going. *Tía* Julia always treated children with respect, giving each child her full attention when engaged with them. *Tía* Julia was among Cuba's ultimate role models and a woman many aspired to emulate in every way.

De las hijas de los colonistas de antes, among the most assertive and self-assured of the four women described here was *Doña* Sophia Lobato Martinez. She was born on February 10, 1893 to *Don* Pablo Lobato and *Doña* Marcelina Garcia Lobato. By then they were living near the community of Cuba, in the territory of New Mexico. According to family sources, *Doña* Sofia had at least five siblings who survived to adulthood and like her, were members of this community.

The youngest and only surviving of *Doña* Sofia's children, Mrs. Liva Martinez Lucero, believes that of *Doña* Sofia's five siblings, she was second to the youngest. Unfortunately, Mrs. Lucero does not know how old her mother was when she married, nor does she recall in what year her parents married. However, *Doña* Sofia married *Don* Anastasio Martinez, a gentleman who was ten years older than herself. Over the course of their marriage, *Doña* Sofia endured thirteen pregnancies, but only six children survived into adulthood. One daughter was in her teens when she died. As well, she and *Don* Anastasio adopted one more child, thus having a family of at least seven children.

Like the majority of women of her generation, *Doña* Sofia did not attend school. However, she had a male cousin who did go to school. *Doña* Sofia, being as assertive as she was, pestered the cousin to teach her what he was learning in school. This was a sort of "peer tutoring" that was made use of long before modern schools adopted the practice.

According to family lore, *Don* Pablo Lobato (*Doña* Sofia's father) did not want his daughters to learn to read and write because he did not want them corresponding with young men. *Don* Pablo wanted to make sure that any young men his daughters communicated with were ones he approved of.

It is said that *Doña* Sofia's husband, *Don* Anastasio and one of his sisters, *Doña* Bersabé had attended one of the Indian Schools in their youth. During the few years he attended this school, *Don* Anastasio learned to read and write and also learned to speak some English. Mrs. Lucero says that even while she was growing up, her father would instruct *Doña* Sofia, especially on matters of business. According to Mrs. Lucero, her father's family migrated to this area from the San Luis Valley in Colorado. In those days, when *Don* Anastasio would have been of school age, there were schools being set up for the Native people, such as the neighboring Utes of southern Colorado. It is likely that *Don* Anastasio and *Doña* Bersabé would have gone to such a school.

Previously, I said that the women of *Doña* Sofia's generation seemed outstanding compared to their offspring. These women were truly stronger physically than we are and were far more adaptive to change and resilient in the face of hardship, sorrow and death. In the case of *Doña* Sofia, it also seemed that she was far ahead of her time compared to other women of her own generation. She was so self-assured in her actions that people simply accepted what she did without censure or comment.

One of the things *Doña* Sofia did differently from other women in the community was to wear men's trousers when she had a job to do that was made easier by such attire. Wearing trousers made sense to her and that is what she did. However, when Sunday morning came, she would attend mass dressed like all of the other women of the time and, like them, had her head covered.

She regularly would gallop into town on horseback from the highest part of Vallecito where the Martinez family lived. It was obvious that she needed to get to town to attend to business as quickly as she could and riding a horse was the quickest way to do that. Hitching up the horses to a wagon, as other women might have done, and slowly maneuvering the terrible road from Vallecito to Cuba would have taken all day. On horseback, *Doña* Sofia not only saved time but avoided the use of the wagon and only needed one horse instead of two.

Doña Sofia's daughter, Mrs. Lucero, related the following story that occurred when *Doña* Sofia was pregnant with Mrs. Lucero (pers. comm.). Apparently *Doña* Sofia came galloping into town one day, looking obviously pregnant. It happened that Mrs. Annie Parsons was at the post office when *Doña* Sofia arrived. Mrs. Parsons was a jolly, roly-poly woman who knew everyone in town but reprimanded *Doña* Sofia for riding on horseback while she was pregnant. She asked, "Sophia, what are you going to do if that baby girl is born while you are on horseback?"

Doña Sofia answered Mrs. Parsons by saying, "I will carefully put the baby in the saddle bag and take her home and take care of her." Mrs. Lucero pointed out that no one knew that this baby was going to be a girl but apparently Mrs. Parsons had decided that it would be. In fact, *Doña* Sofia had lost twin boy babies before getting pregnant with this child. In all likelihood, Mrs. Parsons would have known about this and was cautioning *Doña* Sofia about the possible danger of losing yet another child. At the time baby Liva Martinez (Lucero) was born in 1933, her remarkable mother was forty years old.

Among the reasons that *Doña* Sofia had been such a tireless and ambitious worker was that *Don* Anastasio was away from the ranch in Vallecito for long periods of time. *Don* Anastasio and his sister *Doña* Bersabé had a ranch in San Miguel, south of Cuba, where they had flocks of sheep, herds of cattle and horses to care for. Until *Doña* Sofia and *Don* Anastasio's sons became old enough to help with the heavy lifting, *Doña* Sofia largely ran the ranch in Vallecito by herself.

In 1963, *Don* Anastasio died. By then he was eighty years old and had worked hard all his life. Doña Sofia was widowed for eight years before her death in 1971. During those eight years that she survived her husband, she stayed at her home in Vallecito where she still exercised some authority over her grown children as she had always done. When she became sickly, *Doña* Sofia was cared for in her home, primarily by her youngest daughter *Doña* Liva and her husband, *Don* Climaco Lucero. During those years, they moved into *Doña* Sofia's house to attend to her.

By the time of her death, *Doña* Sofia had become a legend in her own time and served generations of younger local women as a valuable role model. I end this mere sketch of *Doña* Sofia's life with a personal story related to the impact she had on other females such as me.

When I was growing up, my family lived on the side of town closest to the road from Vallecito. In the summertime when I was outdoors playing, I would frequently hear a galloping horse coming down the hill. I would drop whatever I was doing and run toward town to see whether *Doña* Sofia was going to continue south into town or come north to the post office. If *Doña* Sofia was coming north, I would run really fast so I could be at the post office when she got off her horse. *Doña* Sofia Martinez was one of my idols and I wished I could be like her. I regret that she never knew how much I admired her.

This woman, along with others of her generation, taught me that one can be an honorable woman while also getting a job done and protecting what is rightfully ours. Different from other widows of *Doña* Sofia's generation who often ended up landless and without resources for themselves and their children, this woman managed to hold onto her family's resources. What commonly occurred was that some fast-talking business man would come to the widows and tell them that their husbands owed them money for loans or supplies or they owed stock from a *partido* (partnership) agreement. Most of these women had no idea whether the debt was as the merchant described since most women were never informed about such gentlemen's agreements. The business man would suggest, or in some cases demand, that land be handed over to resolve the debt. It is very likely that the ranchers did have outstanding accounts or debt with merchants and businessmen. However, it is very unlikely that such debts exceeded the value of the properties that were taken over from so many women who had fallen victim to such schemes.

This did not happen to *Doña* Sofia. She had always been involved in the decision-making process and when her husband died, she apparently knew exactly what her family's financial situation was. *Doña* Sofia had been known to be outspoken (something else I admired as a child and learned to emulate) but apparently she had also learned some math and some business practices from her tutors. A member of the family related that upon *Doña* Sofia's death, each of her children inherited an equal amount of land of approximately equal value.

Doña Sofia was really ahead of her time and by the standards of her generation, a true trail blazer. The trail may only have extended between Vallecito and Cuba, yet there is no doubt that *Doña* Sofia became a role model even for many of us who could merely watch her from a distance.

Doña Petra Vigil C de Baca with her youngest child, Maria Natividad C de Baca. *Doña* Petra was 41 years old when Maria Natividad was born. Photo taken circa 1908.

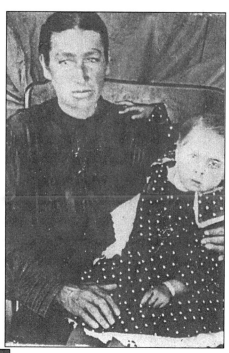

Don Celestino Aragon and *Doña* Lázara Vigil before their wedding, circa Summer, 1912. Courtesy of *Doña* Celia Chavez and Tim Chavez.

Mr. and Mrs. Celestino
Aragon, circa Winter, 1956.
Note their beloved church and
convent in the background.

Doña Julia Cebada Cordova in her
late eighties or early nineties.
Courtesy of Amelia Crespín Aragon.

Los que por Cuba Pasaban
Those who Passed through Cuba

(This article was originally written for a December issue of the *Cuba News*. Given the continuous media commercialization of Christmas, which seems to happen earlier each year, the following was an effort to divert attention from the usual December themes related to the holidays. Thus, the reference to "given the season" in the following paragraph.)

Given the season, some among you will perhaps be expecting to read that a "Wise Man" or two once came through Cuba some time during our *antes*. As for shepherds, you are already aware we had shepherds aplenty who watched over their flocks by day and by night anywhere between San Luis and Abiquiu. So these *pastores* were not among the infrequent visitors who came through Cuba, *antes*. However, the closest we ever got to the Magi were the obligatory visits from the bishop of the diocese.

There really weren't any good roads to travel on, even for the bishop. The bishop did not come to Cuba very often given the lack of communication in places as isolated as this. In fact, it is probable that no bishop ever visited Cuba prior to 1850. After that, the local priest would have been notified by letter informing him of this important visit and more than likely a date would have been set. At this point, the priest, with the help of the *mayordomos* and everyone else in the parish, would begin the preparations for this momentous visit. During the bishop's brief visit, he would have to inspect the parish records, make recommendations to the parish priest before signing off on the church register, and confirm eligible parishioners who up to that time had not been confirmed. These visits were very significant as well as highly ritualistic and festive. All of this required a great deal of community cooperation, preparation and prayer. Prayers were especially offered on behalf of the confirmation candidates, lest they not meet the bishop's expectations and embarrass their families. As well, heaven only knew when the next time the bishop would be back through Cuba for the next round of confirmations,

Among the most fascinating rituals related to this weighty visit from the bishop was his arrival. Not having any way to keep the priest and the participating parishioners informed of the exact time of his arrival, some of the men from the parish, led by one of the *mayordomos,* would ride their best horses ten miles out in the direction from which the bishop was expected and wait for him there. When the bishop's carriage was spotted, a rider would be sent back to Cuba to announce that the guest of honor was on his way. The people would gather and all would be made ready. The bishop would be greeted, welcomed and escorted into town by this impressive entourage of riders, dressed in their best attire and riding their finest horses. Once in town and at the church, the mass would begin and the festivities would follow. Rare as the bishop's visits were, they were a welcome change of pace and cause for considerable celebration.

Bishops were not the only visitors to our town. Quite a variety of groups and individuals came to visit us from time to time. Some were unwelcome, mysterious and down-right scary. Fortunately, the arrival of the *Turcos* was infrequent but unforgettable. The word *Turco* goes back to the colonial New Mexico Spanish period and is one of our regionalisms unique to northern New Mexico. It seems that the rest of the Spanish speaking world refers to these people as *Gitanos,* which means gypsies. For purposes of this article, the word *Turco,* which literally means Turk, will be used. Whether these people were indeed Turks, Gypsies or something else, no one really knows. They did not stay around long enough for formal introductions or casual conversation. After writing the original newspaper article, I have discovered that many people from this and other communities across northern New Mexico remember visits of such people. In all cases, they were referred to by the same name.

The day a caravan of *Turcos* would appear in our town, as if from nowhere, would be remembered long after their departure. *Antes, y mucho mas antes,* the caravan was made up of several covered wagons, but unlike the covered wagons we were accustomed to seeing. Once seen, everyone knew we were in trouble; word spread all over town and an effort was made to warn the more isolated family compounds. Apparently because the *Turcos* travelled in these caravans of several wagons followed by, or led by a few people on horseback, they tended to stay off the more travelled roads. They would appear unexpectedly from some side road or come down from the mountains somewhat quietly in the middle of the day when people were focused on their work in the fields or at home. People were caught by surprise and were understandably frightened.

Once on someone's property, the band would spread out and would start taking anything and everything they pleased. Among the first things to go were the chickens, the rabbits and any other small animals that were around the barnyard or house. The *Turcos* worked swiftly outdoors, while others tried to get into the house. Getting into a house was the worst of scenarios because they could easily and swiftly clean out the whole place.

As word got out that the *Turcos* were near, the local families would try to lock themselves in their houses. The children would hide because it was rumored that the *Turcos* took children. To my knowledge, none were ever taken from here. However, the rumors were enough to keep every child for miles around close to home and behaving very well, long after the caravan had moved on to their next destination.

One can assume that one of the reasons these bands would steal was because the merchants would not trade with them. In fact, the merchants, along with everyone else that could, would lock up their stores and try to protect their livestock and households. Once supplied, the caravan would move on and no one bothered to ask where they had gone, just so they were far from here.

As late as 1949 or 1950, a caravan of *Turcos* came through Cuba. By then they were in cars, but still travelling in a caravan. According to the folklore, the caravan was escorted out of town by one of our law enforcement officers long before they could get out into the countryside. I don't think they would have taken any of our chickens or our goats by then. After all, where do you put a goat in a car full of people?

For those who lived here *antes* in the humble way we did, there were times when an interruption of the monotony of daily chores was welcome. While those visitors just described were most unwelcome, others were colorful, interesting and came to entertain. Like other visitors, these were unexpected and unannounced and their visits were short and infrequent.

Up until the 1930s, there were people who came here with small troupes of vaudeville-like stage performances called *maromas*. The term *maroma* literally means somersault but can also refer to acrobats or the circus. The performers were called *maromeros*. Performances by these groups were apparently negotiated around town upon arrival of the troupe. Then one of the dance halls would be designated as the venue. This would either be *la sala de la sociedad* (the hall of the society), which was at the south end of town or *la sala de arriba* (the hall at the north end of town). Then the word would spread all over town and into the *Vallecitos* (valleys or hamlets) and even as far as La Jara that there would be *maromas* that night.

Everyone would hurry up to get their chores done with the hope that they, too, would get to the show. All tools would be put away carefully and all creatures great and small fed so that by early evening the adults and the young males would be ready to attend the event. *Maromas* were not considered "wholesome family entertainment" by some of the more religious or conservative families. Therefore, the children, and the unmarried and young females would remain at home with grandmother and, in many cases, even Mom would stay home.

The shows couldn't have been very elaborate, given the limited amount of space available. Yet, there were singers, colorful dancers, magicians and probably even some acrobats. The jokes were new and funny (at least they were new to the local population), and town folk would repeat them to each other for days or tell them to the unlucky folks who did not make it to the show. Besides being entertaining, these *maromeros* were important to our isolated community in other ways. They introduced new songs and different music as well, new styles of dress and perhaps even a new hair style to the ladies who were allowed to attend.

Most of the audience had to stand to watch the show since the dance halls only had wooden benches along two walls and a small stage in the front for the band. The benches along the walls were usually reserved for the women, so the men must have stood in the back of the hall during the performances. There must have been an admission fee for the audience but, given the lack of money here in those days, it couldn't have been very much. Whatever the price of admission, it would have to be enough to pay for the hall and some profit for the *maromeros*. By early the next day, the only sign of the *maromeros* having been here would be the jokes or a new tune that someone was trying out on a guitar. These visitors had gone just as they had come, moving on to some other place and another audience. In the meantime, the local people had enjoyed a break from their work routine and at least had something new to talk to their neighbors about.

In addition to the bishop, the *Turcos,* and the *maromeros* that passed through Cuba during *antes,* there were *los Arabes* (the Arabs). These were peddlers who usually came through town during late summer or early fall. They were men who carried big suitcases full of dry goods and went door to door selling their merchandise. Whether or not they were Arabs I don't know, but that was what the local people called them. It is probably the case that at least some of them were Arabic. Certainly, there are Arabic businessmen in New Mexico today and there likely were during our *antes* as well. As with some of the others who passed through our village, these men simply appeared one morning and they would walk along the side roads, stopping only where they were allowed entry.

Always polite and not overly friendly, they were simply very business-like in showing what they had to offer. The women and children would gather around to see what was available and at what price. The items these men carried were mostly beautifully embroidered shawls, small tapestries and small decorated bags. They also carried rugs which, of course, had to be small enough to carry along with the suitcases. Many local families did buy these items and they were used as decorative pieces in their homes.

How much money was made by these traveling salesmen, given the tremendous amount of time and effort they invested, is hard to determine at this late date. However, it must have been worth the trip because either the same people or different ones kept coming back, not regularly but not infrequently. I suppose that when it was no longer profitable for them to make the trip to Cuba, these interesting men with suitcases full of lovely things to sell simply stopped coming.

In the meantime, like some of the other colorful people who passed through here, they introduced us to new and different things from faraway places. In retrospect, all of these people enriched our *antes* and added to our storehouse of the memories that make our *antes* special.

Antes, los Casorios eran Sinceros y Serios
In the Past, Weddings were Sincere and Formal

Prior to the beginning of World War II, weddings here in Cuba and throughout northern New Mexico were so formal in structure and in expectation, one could say they were formula weddings. Several steps were involved in the process with specific time spans between the steps. The entire process could take many weeks (or months) and there were very specific roles for the prospective bride and groom, their families and for other members of the community.

Weddings from the colonial period until the mid-twentieth century were not so much about love as they were another of the efforts to build alliances and strengthen bonds between families. These alliances, in many instances, were motivated by the need to protect property, irrigation rights and/or to maintain class status among families who valued their Spanish pedigree.

In modern times these motives for marriage may seem demeaning to the couple getting married but it was actually quite the opposite. Keep in mind that under the colonial system of inheritance, which people here still abided by, all children of landowners inherited equally. Therefore, a young woman from a landed family would inherit the same as her brothers, whether older or younger than they, thus making such a woman "a fine catch." This was especially important for young men who were landless or were otherwise trying to gain social status. The advantage to the young woman's family was that they would increase the labor force by another strong, healthy young man. Today, we might call this "a win-win situation," or perhaps "a marriage made in Heaven."

The age of the bride-to-be varied, given the resources of the families who were arranging the marriage. Some records show that among families with few resources, the marriages of their daughters occurred when they were somewhat older relative to the daughters of families with better means. Nonetheless, it was not unusual for girls as young as fourteen to be married off to men who were frequently older and perhaps more settled. In many instances, this "settled" man might have been married before and needed a young, strong woman to look after his children.

As interrelated as families were, one would expect that the bride and groom would have known each other, yet in the local folklore there are stories about women whose marriages were arranged to men they had never met. In one such case, it is said that the girl was peeking through a curtain and asking the other women in the room with her which of the men, among the many of the groom's relatives who had come to arrange the marriage, she was to marry.

This formal visit by the groom's family was the first step in the process and was called *el pedimento*, the ceremony of asking for the girl's hand. In some cases, where the young people did know each other and were in love, the young man would go to his father or head of his family and ask for permission to marry. Having agreed to that, the girl's family would have to be notified that the young man's family would be making this formal call. In many instances, the young man's *padrino* (godfather) would carry the message and set the date and time for the *pedimento* with the girl's family.

Following the *pedimento*, the groom's family had to wait eight days for a response. If the girl and her family agreed to the marriage, a message would be sent to the groom's family telling them of the acceptance. On the following three Sundays, the banns were read in church and, if there was no opposition to the marriage, arrangements for the wedding would begin. On the other hand, in the case of refusal, it was said, *se le daba calabazas* (colloquially, to give him pumpkins instead of a bride). Indeed, there were times when young suitors did "get the pumpkins."

Following the *pedimento* and the acceptance of marriage, the wedding date would be set and the groom's family would either go to Mexico or send for the bride's *donas* (trousseau), which would arrive in a huge trunk. Frequently, the Mexican gold filigree jewelry that would be given to the bride was purchased along with the *donas*. No engagement ring was used. The jewelry usually consisted of earrings and necklaces.

Some families have managed to pass down some of these pieces, especially the earrings.

However, neither the *donas* nor the jewelry would be presented to the bride until the *prendorio* (the joining of the families, a pledging ceremony). Here in Cuba, this ceremony usually took place one week before the wedding. In some places, it was not until the day before the wedding. At this point in the series of rituals, the groom's parents and relatives would be invited to the bride's home for a banquet of sweets, pastries and wine, called *el brinde* (a toast, or an offer). The primary reason for this highly ritualistic ceremony was to present the bride and groom to their respective families. This was also the time when gifts were presented to the bride, including the trunk containing the trousseau and as much jewelry as the groom and his family could afford.

At this ceremony the family would eat together, socialize, and sing and dance to the music of local musicians who would have been in attendance throughout the day. The *prendorio* was truly the coming together of the families, the sealing of the agreement. Following these festivities, the bride's mother would turn her kitchen over to the groom's family. The groom's mother and her relatives would begin preparation for the wedding feast, which was their responsibility to provide, making use of food they had brought with them to the *prendorio*.

The day of the wedding was in large measure the responsibility of the *padrinos*, the best man and the matron of honor. They would have been the ones to make sure that everyone got to church on time and that all the little details had been attended to. In those days, wedding parties were usually small, consisting only of the bride and groom and the *padrinos*. Occasionally there would be two sets of *padrinos*, but not as a rule. The choice of *padrinos* was yet another way in which family loyalty was demonstrated and relationships between families was solidified. The *padrinos* may have been chosen because they were close friends of one or the other family or older cousins of the bride or groom, or even an aunt and uncle of one or the other. For some, the *padrinos* at a wedding could have been the baptismal *padrinos* of the bride or groom. In any case, the *padrinos* would have been a highly respected and a very responsible couple. (If conflicts were to arise between the bride and groom later in their marriage, it was the responsibility of the *padrinos* more than the parents to resolve the problems.)

The wedding itself was celebrated with a high mass, communion and blessings. *Antes, mucho mas antes, arras* were presented to the bride by the groom. *Arras* were literally thirteen coins which served to formalize the matrimony and make it official. It is difficult to say when this custom was dropped from the wedding ceremony here in Cuba, or if it was replaced by the exchange of wedding rings by the couple, as occurs now.

As the wedding couple walked out of the church after the ceremony, the musicians would start playing and the newly-weds would follow the musicians as they marched out into the street, followed by the parents, relatives and friends. If the bride's parents lived nearby, the march would continue to their home where a feast awaited the wedding party. If the family lived on the outskirts of the village, the wedding party would be driven to the bride's home either by horse-drawn wagon, or later in cars that the *padrinos* would have arranged for. The wedding feast was an all-day event consisting of eating, some drinking, dancing and singing.

In the evening, most of the guests would leave to get ready for the dance. Wedding dances would begin when the wedding party arrived. A local couple experienced in leading *la marcha* (the grand march) would have been designated before the event to lead this long, intricate march. They would lead the bride and groom, their immediate families, other significant relatives and, finally, other members of the community in an array of interwoven circles and lines so that the whole community would have seen the bride and groom and all of their relatives and friends accompanying them. Following the grand march, the dance would begin and go on until right before midnight, when the last phase of the formalities would take place.

This last phase was called *la entriega*, the ceremony that returned the wedding couple to their parents for one last time. It was the *padrinos* who, having fulfilled all of their responsibilities to the families as assigned, returned the couple to their parents and then were relieved of further wedding duties. The *entriega* is actually a process conducted through a song with as many verses and variations as the group would tolerate. These verses admonished the couple regarding the sacredness of marriage and the vows the couple have committed themselves to. The *padrinos* didn't normally do the singing. The verses were sung by a local poet or, in some cases, the same couple that led the grand march. There are literally hundreds of *entriega* verses that have been collected in northern New Mexico and, with few exceptions, seem to be specific to this area and southern Colorado. *Antes*, there was no *luna de miel* (honeymoon). When the dance ended, customarily the wedding couple returned to the bride's home for at least eight days. Thereafter, the newly-weds would begin to set up housekeeping either near the groom's family or near the bride's family where they could help, and be helped by, both families.

Wedding of *Señorita* Petrita Cebada and *Don* Alejandro Jaquez, circa 1914. Courtesy of *Doña* Dolores Crespín Casaus and son, Harry James Casaus.

2

− Day-to-Day Life −

No Teníanos Dinero
Living Without Money

Prior to the mid-twentieth century Cuba had very little or no money. This can be attributed in part to several historical events. Although seemingly removed from here, these events had a tremendous impact on the severity of people's experiences here and in nearby towns.

By the turn of the twentieth century the people of northern New Mexico had lost their long and desperate struggle to retain titles to their privately owned lands within the major land grants. These included the grants in the Chama Valley, the San Luis Valley (in what became southern Colorado) and of particular interest to us, the loss of the *San Joaquin del Nacimiento* land grant which included Cuba. The grantees' descendants' final plea for title had been rejected in 1889, following more than ten years of fierce struggle in the courts and the Land Claim Offices.

Among the results of the losses of clear title to private land holdings were big shifts in population within the boundaries of New Mexico. People were displaced from land they had legally occupied for generations under Spanish and Mexican law. Many of these people moved to other settlements where they had relatives or knew of unoccupied land where they might be able to resettle. With each of these moves people became poorer and less able to recover from their losses.

Following the end of the American Civil War in 1865, there was a huge migration of people from the eastern United States who had been displaced by the war and wanted land. By then the Homestead Act of 1862 was in full operation and prompted westward expansion, especially for agriculture, adding to the pressures on the people in New Mexico to move off the land they had previously occupied.

Within the boundaries of the *San Joaquin del Nacimiento* grant, land was made even more attractive due to the discovery copper in *Copar* (in the mountains just east of Cuba) in the mid 1880s. Coal deposits were obvious at *La Ventana* (about 15 miles south of Cuba). The outsiders, seeing the potential of these resources, but not yet knowing how rich they might be, were not about to let the descendents of the thirty-four families of the *San Joaquin del Nacimiento* grant retain the land.

In addition to the people's losses in the courts and Land Claim Offices, the United States government designated much of the land within this grant (and other grants) as public lands. These included a portion of the Carson National Forest and the Santa Fe National Forest. As well, the government had imposed strict restrictions on grazing on these public lands, especially the grazing of herds of sheep and horses. These large herds of sheep, which in some instances numbered in the thousands, had been for many northern New Mexicans their only source of livelihood. Having no place to graze the sheep, the herds were minimized or sold off completely.

Following the loss of their land and their livestock, some of these people petitioned for unoccupied land under the Homestead Act (one hundred sixty acres per family) and retreated into the farthest corners of the territory where there was some water for irrigation and a few acres to farm. Thereafter, these families focused on surviving under a new and difficult authority that spoke a language they did not comprehend. The rules had changed in ways these people did not understand. Our *abuelitos* (grandparents/elders) would say, "That is our burden to bear," *y Dios que les ayude* (and may God help them) for taking away what had been ours.

Loss of land through these changes in the rules was not the only reason people here remained poor. Under American law, taxes were levied on land and livestock measured in dollars rather than as a portion of the production from the land. There was always the threat of losing land because of delinquent taxes, which happened more frequently than we care to recall. Recently, while reviewing a title abstract, I noticed that a local family had lost title to eighteen acres of land that had been in their family for generations. The tax bill amounted to less than two dollars! At that time no one had the two dollars to pay the property tax. In this case, the family lost their land and, again, had to move elsewhere, making them even poorer than they were before.

Given today's standard of living, it may be difficult to impress upon readers the severe impact of having no money and little opportunity to earn any. The following is an illustration of just how little money was available in this or other nearby communities. In 1931 my father, Ruben Cordova, was offered a job as a teacher. However, he needed fifty cents to pay for the state license. Neither he nor his father had any cash money at all. Given no other alternative, he got on his horse and rode all day from one relative's house to another, where some were able to lend him a nickel, a dime or a few pennies until he collected the fifty cents to pay for the teaching license. He was then able to teach for several years in places such as La Jara and Ponderosa. Many people learned basic reading, writing and mathematics and to adopt more progressive farming practices because of his teaching.

Antes, families here in Cuba and surrounding areas, having no other options, were almost entirely involved in subsistence farming which provided only meager resources in terms of food, clothing and shelter needed by the immediate members of their families as well as some members of their extended families. There were no luxuries, no running water and no sympathy for any member of the family who did not do his or her part.

Children were taught to work from early on and every child had chores and was responsible for the care of some of the animals, for younger siblings or for older members of the family. Children grew up as working, responsible and contributing members of their families and communities.

People had very few clothes. Most of what they had would have been home-made, and if anyone outgrew a garment, it was simply handed down to someone else that could wear it until it wore out completely.

There were few if any toys for children and, like the clothing, they would have been made at home. As well, there were few tools and the tools people had were highly valued and cared for with devotion. *Pobre de ti* (Woe be unto you) that the ax be left out in the rain or a shovel left out in a field. Such irresponsible acts likely did not happen more than once (if at all) since such behavior could have threatened the survival of the entire family, and these people were about surviving, basically *sin dinero* (without money).

Interpersonal relationships between members of extended families, neighbors and friends provided safety nets for the survival of children. The skill sets that were engrained in children from early on served the same purpose. Everyone knew how to milk a cow or a goat, how to kill and dress out a chicken, skin a rabbit, hoe weeds in a garden and store and preserve food to last through the winter. Men, women and children chopped and gathered wood. Oh, and don't forget the *palitos* (kindling). Even toddlers knew about *palitos* because everyone knew how to build a fire and how to keep it going at the most efficient level.

In a society that had little means or opportunity to earn cash money, the people bartered, shared and simply helped each other in times of need. A youngster who knew how to work could be sent out to work off a debt or reciprocate for labor that the family had received in an earlier time of need. Men, when they found wage-paying jobs, worked a whole day for a dollar, while women might earn fifty cents for a day's work.

Witnessing the horrendous losses among their relatives and neighbors, without having any control over their own destinies, *Los Abuelitos* counseled their young above all, to feed their families and manage their livestock *con cuidado* (kindly, with care), to attend to the duties and responsibilities of their church, to avoid debt and to listen to but not to trust anyone they did not know.

It would be years before people here would be able to earn money through wages in government programs such as the Works Progress Administration (WPA) and Civilian Conservation Corps (CCC), and finally in the 1940s, in World War II defense jobs and military service. Until then, *no teníanos dinero*, but we had been taught how to survive in this unforgiving land that we still love and call home.

Los Fleteros
The Overland Freight Haulers

Antes, the *fleteros* (freight haulers) were the lifeline of New Mexico's first Spanish colonial settlers, soldiers and missionary priests. *Fleteros* were the men who transported all the merchandise, tools, ammunition, dry goods, mail and a few luxury items overland. Originally, these goods were brought from locations in Mexico to the far reaches of the Spanish northern frontier in New Mexico and elsewhere. The *fleteros* accomplished these journeys using horse-drawn wagons, ox-carts and pack mules.

As Spain continued to expand its northern frontier, these *fleteros* became progressively more important as they hauled goods between settlements throughout the northern part of the empire and Mexico's *Nueva Vizcaya* (New Biscay). These carefully planned and generally successful expeditions to and from places such as Zacatecas, Durango, Culiacán and Chihuahua allowed New Mexico's colonial population to survive for approximately two hundred and fifty years. These routine treks did not vary until around the time Mexico gained its independence from Spain in 1821.

Supplying the northern frontier colonies of New Spain during the seventeenth and eighteenth centuries was a laborious and extremely dangerous operation. Transportation and communication were difficult because of the long distances, the lack of roads and the crude equipment possessed by the settlers and the *fleteros.* Horses, mules, donkeys and the primitive *carretas* (originally large wooden carts with two large, solid wooden wheels) were the earliest means of transportation, later replaced by horse-drawn wagons. *Carretas* were most effectively drawn by oxen, but oxen are slower than either horses or mules. Given the limited size of *carretas,* even fully loaded they would not hold a large amount of goods.

It is reported that *Don* Juan de Oñate's expedition in 1598, had brought thirty-two wagons for his troops and missionaries in addition to the many *carretas* brought by the settlers for transporting their own belongings. Following that influx of goods, missionary caravans which originated in

Mexico City, consisting of no fewer than thirty-two wagons, brought in what the Franciscan missionaries needed for their own use along with those items they provided to their Native converts. The Franciscan missionaries really came here to Christianize the Native population and did little to serve the Hispanic settlers who had accompanied the military and missionary expeditions. These caravans also supplied resources for the upkeep and expansion of the churches built for Native people. However, these missionary caravans did not begin operation until 1610, some twelve years after the arrival of the Oñate expedition. Very likely, this was also the time when the commercial *fleteros* first began their hazardous occupation to provide for the needs of the settlers. These *fleteros* transported virtually everything possible to sustain the non-missionary population of New Mexico. Beyond locally-grown crops, livestock and game and other local foodstuffs, this was the only source of material goods available to the early settlers.

A missionary supply caravan was usually scheduled to arrive from Mexico City every three years. Given the uncertainties of weather, the lack of roads, the rough terrain and the ever-present danger of Indian attacks, it was not uncommon to wait four or five years for these caravans to return. In modern terms, this would be roughly equal to a trip to Mars and back, in terms of both time and hazard.

For the settlers in New Mexico, the arrival of a missionary caravan was an event of tremendous excitement and joy. Cargo on these caravans would include church supplies, building hardware and clothing for the missionaries. There might be new settlers, priests and government personnel that came with the supply trains. There might also be long-awaited and much anticipated mail, even though the news contained could well be five years old when it arrived. Along with these supplies, there might even be a few luxury items for those few isolated settlers who could afford them.

Since the commercial *fleteros* brought goods explicitly for the settlers, they were met with even greater enthusiasm. Having arrived safely at the distant northern frontier, the *fleteros* would begin to organize a return trip to Mexico. Originally a return trip would be a difficult task to put together, primarily because the settlers had so little of value to send back to Mexico to trade for things they needed so badly here. Still, on these return trips, the *fleteros* would take hides, piñon nuts, wool and woolen blankets woven here in New Mexico as they were available.

As sheep herds increased, there was much more wool to trade, as well as live sheep. Herds of sheep were driven southward with the caravans to be sold in the mining communities in Chihuahua and Zacatecas. The original *Churro* sheep brought into New Mexico travelled extremely well but try to imagine how old and in what shape any surviving sheep would be when they arrived in Zacatecas! These caravans were frequently attacked by raiding parties of Indians. These raids resulted in great losses of sheep, horses and supplies, even though they were being guarded by the military escorts.

By the early seventeen hundreds, following the Pueblo Revolt of 1680 and the reoccupation of New Mexico, the Spanish colonists successfully developed their irrigation systems. This development resulted in some improvement in what had been a subsistence economy based on crop production and sheep. With this advancement, trade between northern Mexico and New Mexico grew due to the increases in both crop yields and sheep herds. Now settlers had much more wool to sell as well as more and better quality woven blankets. Piñon nuts and buffalo jerky were still highly desirable trade items among the miners of northern Mexico. The fine wine being produced by this time in the middle Rio Grande valley was a valuable addition to what the commercial *fleteros* could take on their more frequent trips southward.

By the eighteenth century, the *fleteros* had helped to develop several trade routes to the different commercial centers in northern Mexico and to some extent, the *corporales* (leaders or wagon masters) could choose their destinations following their safe arrival in *El Paso del Norte* (now, El Paso, Texas). Depending on their cargo, the *corporales* could decide whether to go directly south into Chihuahua or to go southwestward to Culiacán or beyond that to Durango or even as far south as Zacatecas. Some even went as far as Mexico City. Depending on which and how many of these places they visited, the trip could be extended by weeks, months or perhaps as much as a year.

An interesting sidelight on this period of commerce has to do with the wide-brimmed woven straw hats that people here wore to protect themselves from the harsh summer sunlight. Locally, these hats were always known as *sahuaripas*. In fact, *Sahuaripa* was one of the last villages any of these expeditions would have visited before crossing the desert into New Mexico. It is likely that the *fleteros* bought straw hats in this village and put them on top of the rest of their cargo so they would not get crushed in the journey northward. The name we came to know these hats by was simply the name of the village from which they had come.

During this time of a growing economy on the northern frontier, trade was limited to a north-to-south direction. In an effort to protect its territories, the Spanish Crown had explicit restrictions against foreigners trading anywhere within Spanish territorial boundaries or trade from within those boundaries with any foreign interests. These laws were strictly enforced until Mexico's independence from Spain.

During the Mexican period (1821–1848) the former Spanish restrictions on trade were abandoned. The newly formed independent government in Mexico had not realized in advance just how great the trade opportunities with the outside world would be. Nor had the Mexican officials understood how badly the needs of the people along the northern frontier had gone unmet by the trade restrictions of the colonial period.

In 1821, the first wagons loaded with commercial goods arrived in Santa Fé over the Santa Fé Trail. These wagons brought merchandise from far-away Independence, Missouri, over the hazardous Raton Pass and down into Santa Fé in the Mexican territory of *Nuevo Mexico.* This new trade route was the direct result of the newly-formed Mexican government lifting restrictions on foreign trade within its territorial boundaries, a restriction the Spanish government had enforced very strictly. At this time, *fleteros* needed to travel no farther than Santa Fé to trade or sell goods from places like Cuba and return with merchandise brought out along the Santa Fé Trail.

Once the Santa Fé Trail opened for trade in New Mexico and northern Mexico, the direction of trade changed. Commerce was now dominated by east-to-west flow with a smaller portion of flow going as far south as Chihuahua. The volume of trade coming into Mexican territory far exceeded the government's expectations or its ability to control. The cheaper goods provided by American merchants in the east broke the monopoly that the Chihuahua merchants formerly had over trade in New Mexico. Previously, Chihuahua merchants had controlled the value of goods coming from New Mexico as well as the price of what came back to the north. This monopoly had never been to the advantage of the people living on the northern frontier. With the opening of the Santa Fé Trail, the Americans controlled the prices of goods moving both in and out of this area.

Originally, the port of entry on the Santa Fé Trail from the United States was at the village of Taos. However, within a short period of time, Santa Fé became the port of entry as well as the center of trade in New Mexico. With this new trade center and with the expanding level of commerce, the local *fleteros* now had more opportunities and a growing market. Merchants buying goods in Santa Fé were now looking for experienced *fleteros* to transport their goods to stores in towns and remote villages all over northern New Mexico. As compared to their previous journeys into Mexico, trips in and out of Santa Fé were far shorter and less hazardous.

These local *fleteros* were expert horsemen and teamsters. They knew the terrain and they knew where to find springs with fresh water tucked away on otherwise long stretches of arid landscape. They also knew where the rivers were located and where (or if) they could safely cross during periods of high water. This was especially true of the Rio Grande, the Rio Puerco and the Rio Chama. These were the sort of experienced *fleteros* the merchants looked for and depended upon to get their goods from Santa Fé to people who were anxious to buy, barter or trade. The *fleteros* transported such goods as various kinds of cloth, manufactured clothing, shoes and gloves. There were also badly needed tools, metal kitchen utensils, different foods, spices and such novelties as baking powder. Among the most cherished items village people now had available were paper, ink and books, as well as new kinds of medicines.

During the Spanish colonial period, as well as during the Mexican era, there was such a dearth of essentials throughout the Spanish colonial frontier that people became accustomed to endure without or to invent alternatives. The demand for all the new kinds of merchandise from the United States opened such an active market that it was not infrequent for the merchants bringing goods over the Santa Fé Trail to sell their wagons and all but enough horses to get back to Missouri right there in Santa Fé. Their wagons were better crafted than what was available locally. They had wheels with metal rims and there was always a need for a few more horses. In such cases, the traders and drivers would return to Independence, Missouri, on horseback with only a few pack horses for what they hoped would be a quick turn-around and a second trip to Santa Fé before winter set in. Harsh weather all along their route, especially the high snows on Raton Pass, brought travel to an end by late fall each year.

The impact of the Santa Fé Trail would only be surpassed by the coming of the railroad in 1880. Like the opening of the Santa Fé Trail, The arrival of the railroad in New Mexico greatly increased the demands on these tireless and adventurous *fleteros*. By this time, there were many more kinds of cargo to transport and more small communities to be served. These *fleteros* arduously brought tons of freight up and down the mountains from our remote villages to Santa Fé and later to Albuquerque. All of this freight continued to move on carts and on mule-back until early in the twentieth century. By then, some of the *fleteros* were able to replace their wagons with newly available trucks to haul cargo.

The history of New Mexico railroads is interwoven with the successful history of the Atchison, Topeka and Santa Fé Railroad. This rail line connected New Mexico to both the Pacific and to the Midwest. The Atchison, Topeka and Santa Fé Railroad crisscrossed New Mexico, going from El Paso to Raton and from Gallup to Clovis. Of course it went much farther than that; but this was the first time that goods from all parts of the state could be interchanged.

Because of its mountainous location, Santa Fé was not on the rail line and lost its position as the center of trade in the region; a position it had held since 1821. Albuquerque's central location, along with its lower elevation and smoother terrain, made it the new hub of commercial activity in New Mexico. Albuquerque is generally accessible from all directions and was very attractive to the highly competitive and rapidly growing railroad industry.

Fleteros continued to carry goods back and forth from isolated communities to the railroad in Albuquerque. For the *fleteros* of the Cuba area, having the center of trade move from Santa Fé to Albuquerque was a huge advantage. The routes between Cuba and Albuquerque were well known to the *fleteros*. In good weather, the trip down the hill could be made in only five days. On the downhill trip, they carried loads of wool, wheat, hides and pelts. The trip back could be longer, depending on the kinds of freight they had picked up in Albuquerque for the local merchants who had hired them. Elsewhere I have described early merchants and stores in the Cuba area. These were among the merchants involved in the commerce described here.

As in the past, the *fleteros* would follow a well-travelled path to San Ysidro, crossing *El Rio Salado* in the area of San Ysidro as the modern highway does and then moving along the base of *Mesa Colorada* (Red Mesa) where fresh-water springs are located. From there, they would stay close to the base of the mountains before attempting to climb the grade at *los bancos* (now called Warm Springs grade). From *los bancos* they would remain close to the foothills where there was pasture for their animals and water in streams such as *Rito de Semilla* and *Ojo del Espiritu Santo* (Holy Ghost Spring). Their trip continued on to San Miguel, San Pablo, Señorito, Copár or Cuba. The *fleteros* who were hired by the San Pablo merchant, *Don* José Maria Cebada, would unload their wagons into his warehouse there. Those *fleteros* who had loads going on to Señorito, Copar or Cuba would likely rest at San Pablo before completing the last leg of their journeys.

The *fleteros* bringing goods to *La Posta* (Cabezon) and perhaps on to Cuba would leave the other route at San Ysidro and head northwest to the Rio Puerco. This possibly involved one "dry camp:" a night without water for the animals or the drivers. Once on the Rio Puerco, they would have had grass and water for the horses the rest of the way to Cabezon and on to Cuba. Such a wagon or caravan would have to cross the Rio

Puerco at some point. The name of this stream actually means "murky" river. It has a notoriously muddy channel that could only be crossed in a few specific places without getting a loaded wagon stuck. This was an old and established route for horse and wagon traffic and the experienced *fleteros* knew exactly where to cross without getting stuck.

A different group of local *fleteros* headed northward. The Denver and Rio Grande Railroad ran to Chama and had a spur that went west from Chama to Lumberton and Dulce. At either of these points the *fleteros* delivered goods from here (mostly wool) and picked up merchandise to bring back to Cuba and other local communities. Again, this territory was relatively familiar to the *fleteros.* They knew where the water sources were and where they could rest and graze their animals. In some cases, they had relatives living along the route.

In an effort to illustrate the enormous risks *fleteros* took and the tremendous amount of time they were expected to be away from home, a custom was practiced here when heads of families were about to leave home on one of these journeys. Just prior to the patriarch's departure, he would give his family *la santa bendición* (his last blessing).Every member of the family would kneel in a circle and pray for the safe return of the head of their family as well as other members of the family who would be going with him. When the prayers were ended, the head of the family and the other travelers would go around the circle and give each person what might be their last blessing and their last moments together. Everyone would remain kneeling until all the family members being left behind had been blessed and then they would all tearfully say their goodbyes.

Here in Cuba, this custom remained in practice well into the twentieth century. Very likely this form of parting began during the colonial period or even before, when men would go off to war or any other type of campaign without any assurance that they would ever return from their dangerous missions. So it was with our *fleteros;* the dangers being so great that their families never knew if they would ever see them again.

Today, given the ease with which our local citizens travel from Cuba to Albuquerque, Santa Fé, Farmington and beyond, it is difficult to impress upon people how prominent and important the role of the *fleteros* has been in New Mexico. These men formed the lifeline of our isolated and underdeveloped frontier. These trustworthy men risked their lives, their animals and their equipment and were separated from their families for long and undeterminable periods of time. They did this to transport the basic necessities that allowed people to remain in our villages. It would take the building of hundreds of miles of roads and the coming of trucks and regular trucking delivery routes to finally bring this honorable league of *fleteros* to the end of their careers.

Las Casas de Antes
The Houses from the Past

The traditional *casas de antes* in Cuba and throughout northern New Mexico evolved through their lifetimes. Until very recently, due to limited resources of all kinds, very few houses were built completely at one time. Most of our houses have an original room or two somewhere within the structure which still shows the scars of the additions attached to it as the family grew into, and sometimes out of *las casas de antes*. As one looks around Cuba at some of the older houses, of which there are many, one can trace the evolution of these landmark buildings by looking at the various types of building materials used for each addition attached to the original one-room module.

Another common characteristic is that the additions were frequently at different levels, accommodated by steps, both inside and outside the house. Except for some ranch style houses of the mid-twentieth century, this is a feature not usually seen in modern houses.

The areas in which our *casas de antes* were located determined what type of foundation, if any, these structures would have. Until the mid-twentieth century, cement was not readily available to build a modern type of foundation. However, a foundation could have been built out of cut stone extending two or more feet above ground or constructed in a trench a foot or more deep and the width of the wall, filled with stones and sand. There is, for example, a house beside *Rito de Leche* that was built on a foundation of neatly cut slabs of sandstone stacked at least three feet above the ground. It is assumed the reason for this ambitious effort was the location of the house on a sandstone outcrop that runs from *Rito de Leche* northward approximately a mile and a half. When this house was built in the early 1930s, there was no way builders could have dug a trench into the sandstone. Because the sandstone was immediately available, they used the stone slabs. Houses were generally built in higher areas around what is now Cuba in order to avoid flooding during spring runoff and summer flash floods.

Some of the old houses in the area were built on trenches filled with field stones and sand for foundations. This happened in areas that were somewhat rocky but not as solid as the exposed stone near *Rito de Leche*. In fact, some adobe houses were built directly on the ground. These houses would likely have had earthen or mud floors instead of wood floors.

Adobe brick was the preferred material for constructing homes among the Hispanic population of this area. However, making enough adobe bricks for a house was labor-intensive and very time consuming. Furthermore, there was always some urgency to get a house built and closed in before winter, so people frequently chose options other than adobe for that first stage of home construction. This would likely have been *jacal* (logs, five to eight inches in diameter, placed on end, side-by-side in a trench.) The tops of these logs were trimmed into a wedge shape that fit into grooved cross beams. Other first-stage houses were built of horizontal planks *(vigas)* with lath and earthen plaster to fill the cracks. These were called *fuertes* and were roughly similar to log cabins built in other parts of the country.

Long before Spanish settlers came to this area; their ancestors had learned about making adobe bricks from the Arabs during their seven-hundred-year occupation of Spain. This adobe brick making differs from the Pueblo "puddle adobe" building in that it requires wooden molds for the bricks. The molded bricks gave the *albañil* (mason) walls that were straight and more consistent in width. The molded bricks also make it easier to construct walls at right angles as well as openings for doors and windows with straight sides.

Once a family had a roof over their heads in their one-room *jacal,* they could settle into a place while waiting to make enough adobe bricks, perhaps several thousand of them, to begin the second stage of their evolving house. Traditionally, adobe bricks were made by placing well-mixed, moistened earth into wooden molds. Straw was usually added to the mixture to help keep the mud together, to facilitate even drying and to prevent cracking. When the mud was dry enough, the molds were removed. After about two days the bricks were stood on end to dry further. After another week, the adobes were stacked on edge for at least a month of baking in the sun. Given the small number of molds available, one can imagine how long it would take to make the several thousand bricks needed to add a large room or two to the original *jacal* house. Under favorable weather conditions and with sufficient water, enough bricks could be made over a period of one summer for construction the following year. However, neither favorable weather, nor sufficient water nor time away from other chores was ever guaranteed.

In addition to *jacal* or adobe bricks, people around Cuba frequently constructed the original module out of what was called *relleno. Relleno* literally means "stuffed" or "filled." In construction, it is a type of frame made of vertical planks with lath attached to both sides of the uprights. This form would then be filled with mud and straw to create a rather solid wall. These walls would have at least two layers of *enjarre* (mud or clay plaster) applied both inside and out. There were many houses in Cuba either completely or partly built out of *relleno*. Given the time it took to make enough adobe bricks to build a house of two or three rooms, one can understand why *relleno* construction was attractive.

Late in the nineteenth century, when milled lumber became available to local residents, an interesting treatment to the outside walls of *relleno* houses began. Instead of plastering the outside walls, builders would nail *orillos* (rough-sawn pine slabs) directly onto the uprights and lath, giving the house the appearance of a log cabin. *Orillos* were probably inexpensive and plentiful during the early days of the lumber industry in this region. Furthermore, since women did all of the mud and clay plastering, the *orillo* siding saved the women in the family from having to plaster the outer walls. *Orillos* would break down after a few years so this treatment to outer walls didn't survive as long as *enjarre* (mud or clay plaster).

Originally, *las casas de antes* would have had flat roofs in the tradition of early New Mexican architecture. However, like the evolving construction of rooms in houses, roofs also evolved. As resources became more plentiful, a family home would have gone from a *zotea* (flat, packed dirt roof over *vigas*) to a standard double-pitched roof, especially if the house developed as a series of additions in a single row. However, pitched roofs did not become popular here until after 1880 when the railroad came into Albuquerque. With the coming of the railroad, different building materials and better tools became more available. Among the building materials that improved the construction of houses were corrugated metal roofing and framed windows and doors. These were items hauled to Cuba by the local *fleteros* (freighters).

Pitched-roof construction on local houses was one of those advances that truly improved the quality of life for families in this area. A pitched roof allowed the home-owner to have a *tejaván* (attic) that did not leak and which could be ventilated at both ends. These attics provided families with added dry storage space and extra sleeping space when cousins from far away appeared at the door and stayed for indefinite periods of time. In these ventilated attics, food could be spread out to dry more safely than outdoors. Lines could be strung to dry jerky and green chili. Furthermore, since these evolving houses already had *zoteas* (flat mud-packed roofs), the families very likely put in another layer of adobe mud on top of the existing mud pack to level the attic floor and to make it smooth for better and more varied uses.

Among the most important benefits a pitched roof provided was that rain water could be collected off the roof and stored in cisterns for household use. This water would have been cleaner, closer at hand and more closely guarded, given the valuable resource water has always been here.

Eventually, local carpenters learned to build dormers, with windows in them, projecting out of the pitched roofs. With the added light from these dormer windows, *las casas de antes* were greatly improved and began to take on a very different appearance, both inside and out. A *zotea* roof had to be kept up and no matter how carefully people tried to keep such an earthen roof from leaking, they usually did leak during rainy seasons. Snow was also a continuous problem in winter and had to be removed from the tops of the houses after any heavy storm. The pitched roofs allowed for the interior walls of the houses to remain cleaner. These walls were carefully coated with *enjarre* (mud or clay plaster) and then whitewashed with quicklime (cal) to last longer and to look better. Again, these roof improvements gave women in these families a break from the annual chore of repairing the interior walls of the house.

There are two other features that make our *casas de antes* distinct. One is that as the houses evolved, they did so in one of two ways. Some houses became L-shaped and more likely than not, had an enclosed porch inside the L. The other common option was that the house became relatively square with a hip roof. These roofs had sloping ends and sides and a porch was added onto one or more sides of the house.

As more and better building materials became available to families in the area, house designs changed slightly and improved. However, with few exceptions, the size of houses did not change remarkably. A large house was simply too difficult to heat in the winter.

Following World War II, when natural gas and electricity became available, we began to see other changes in *las casas de antes.* Lights and some electric appliances could be installed. Natural gas could be used to heat both water and the house.

Another real change occurred once Cuba had running water. With running water, everyone had to find a place to add a bathroom. The solution to this problem in older houses usually happened in one of two ways. One solution was to close in one of the porches that had been added to the square or L-shaped house. The other solution was simply to add a small room off one side of a bedroom. These little rooms usually had a shed roof that was not connected to the main roof on the rest of the house. Thus, the modern bathroom became yet one more part of the evolution of *las casas de antes.*

Ultimately, as has happened in small towns all across the country,

mobile homes and manufactured houses began to replace *las casas de antes.*
Today, many of the really old houses are abandoned and still standing
but the families have moved into more modern houses or mobile homes
nearby.

Las Enjarradoras
The Women Plasterers

Antes, women did the plastering of all adobe structures and of
other kinds of structures, such as *jacal* (a structure with walls consisting of
rows of vertical poles filled in between with mud). Once the men had built
the walls and put the roof on a house, the women would begin their work.

One of the interesting things about adobe plastering is that you
can't just get dirt from any field or hillside to prepare this special mud.
There were very specific places around Cuba where people would dig out
and haul wagon loads of dirt in order to have the exact quality of mud
for plastering purposes. Unfortunately, we no longer know where these
places were or what the quality of the dirt was that made it special and
appropriate *para enjarrar* (for plastering).

The men and boys of the family would haul the dirt into the yard
next to the building to be plastered. An experienced man would also
help mix the mud under the watchful eye of the expert woman who was
directing the plastering.

For buildings that had not been plastered before, the process
was quite involved. On a newly constructed adobe building the exterior
walls were plastered promptly to weatherproof them before winter. This
was especially true if the house had been closed in during late summer or
early fall. This was very likely to occur in Cuba because of our very short
summers.

Once the adobe walls were dry and all the cracks were sealed, a
rough coat of special mud was slapped onto the adobes, but not smoothed
out. The first coat would stick to the dry adobes and was allowed to dry
in the sun for several days. This rough coat of plaster allowed the women
to seal all the cracks around the doors, windows and roof line. After the

rough coat of mud was dry the women were ready to begin applying the smooth coat of mud onto the building. The mud was put on by hand, again under the watchful eye of the older, experienced women. The older women and young girls would also help haul the fresh mud to the ones who were applying the plaster. The mud had to be of just the right consistency, neither too dry nor too wet. This required the mud to be hauled in relatively small amounts to the plasterers to keep it from drying out.

On a previously plastered structure, plastering was usually done in late summer before *las fiestas* (the feast day on September 8th) or before a special family event such as a wedding. On a building such as is seen in one of the photographs that follow, where people are plastering the 1915 Catholic Church before the 1938 fiestas, no rough coat was required. However, a certain amount of sealing of cracks around the doors and windows would be done. There would also be repairs to the weathered wood, which is what appears the man on the scaffold on the far upper right of the same picture is doing. The youngish-looking woman on the highest part of the ladder is plastering, but only she and another young woman in the middle of the photograph are wearing trousers. All the other women are wearing dresses. An older woman in a black dress and black head scarf is hauling fresh mud in buckets to the *enjarradoras* (plasterers).

In one of the other photographs, there are many more men involved. However, they seem to be mixing mud and adjusting the scaffold while the women are doing the actual plastering. For this part of the process, the women needed to carefully apply the mud to the wall by hand and then use their *cuchara de enjarra* (trowel) to smooth out the mud evenly. Here we called this pointed metal trowel a *cuchara*, which is a spoon. The rest of the Spanish-speaking world calls a trowel a *trulla*, a *paleta* or a *llana*. It was at this stage in the process that expertise was really required. The women knew exactly how much mud to apply so the entire wall would be smooth and not have bumps where too much mud had been applied.

At the time these three photographs were taken in the late summer of 1938, the Catholic Church and its attached rectory was the second largest building in Cuba. The only building larger than this was the three-story convent next door. In the final photograph there are between forty and forty-five people involved in plastering the church. Even with this number of people involved, it would have taken many days to plaster the entire church as expertly as women did back in those times. Add to the immense effort shown in these photographs the general lack of modern tools, the lack of adequate lumber for proper scaffolding and the work involved in digging dirt and hauling water to the church and you can appreciate the love and dedication the people of this community put into this project. Keep in mind as well that this process was generally repeated every year!

Once the exterior of an adobe building was sealed and plastered, the women would begin plastering the interior. It was in the interior part of the building that the women would take the greatest care in their craft. It would be the interior which would be inspected by their friends and *comadres* and in which the best family *enjarradora* could take the greatest pride. Once the interior plastering was completed and sufficiently dried, the walls would be ready for the final touch, called *encalar. Encalar* literally means to apply *cal*. In English, *cal* is called quicklime. The material used here and called *cal* was probably brought from Mesa Blanca, near the community of San Ysidro. Today, that site is a gypsum mine. The Spanish word for gypsum is *yeso* and that material was used for purposes other than whitewashing the interiors of buildings. It is possible that there are limestone deposits at Mesa Blanca, along with the gypsum and that *cal* was made from that limestone or a combination of limestone and gypsum.

Eighty-eight year old *Don* Antonio Lucero, a life-long resident of Cañon de Jemez, recalled that in his youth he would be sent to Mesa Blanca to get a wagon load of *cal* (pers. comm.). This was the material his mother and grandmother used when they were preparing to do their annual whitewashing of the interior walls of their homes. Given the prevalence of the practice of *encalar* here in Cuba, someone must have brought wagon loads of material from Mesa Blanca in order to keep the local women happy and in style.

The material brought here was roasted in outdoor ovens which would produce quicklime from the limestone and possibly from the gypsum. Following the roasting, they would grind it into a fine powder using *metates* (grinding stones) and sift out the remaining pieces of stone. They would mix the fine powder with just enough water so that it could be applied onto the walls with small pieces of sheep skin. This would have the effect of whitewashing the walls, but would also seal the adobe plaster when it was completely dry. Incidentally, the interior of the Catholic Church shown in the photographs was also whitewashed very likely using the same process women used in their own homes.

Sometime in the early-to mid-1930s, local merchants started bringing a product known as calsomine into Cuba. This product was a commercially prepared form of whitewash, rather like what had been called *cal* here for many generations, except it was sometimes mixed with other minerals to produce pale tones of pink, blue, green and perhaps yellow. Imagine the popularity of such a new product. Furthermore, Calsomine (locally called *Calsaman*), was ready to mix into water and could be applied with a brush (also carried in local stores) instead of patches of sheepskin. Calsomine came in boxes of four to five pounds and was not very expensive. Within a short period of time following the introduction of this product the whole process of whitewashing with *cal* the old-fashioned way came to an end, thus eliminating the hauling of *cal,* the roasting and the laborious grinding and sifting processes. The women still plastered but the new calsomine was so much easier to use that the old practice disappeared entirely. Besides, much to our mothers' delight, they could now have different colored interiors in their houses.

Some women would also paint household items with something called *maque*. According to my sources, *maque* is a kind of lacquer. At least locally, it seems that *maque* only came in lapis blue and the pieces that were painted with it seem to have been meant to outlast the painter and several generations of descendents. Few people still alive remember *maque* and now the source of this material is probably lost.

As an aside for readers who appreciate the unique qualities of the local Spanish dialect, the subject of this article is further evidence of our unusual language history. The word *enjarrar* is not a Spanish word. In standard Spanish the word for plaster is *yeso, emplasto* or *estuco.* The term *yeso* is used here but it applies only to gypsum and not to whitewash. A plasterer such as our *enjarradoras* is a *yesero* and the process of plastering is referred to as *revocar* or *enlucidir*.

There is an Arabic word, *jarrar*, originally pronounced *jaharrar* which means to apply plaster or mortar to a wall. That word may have survived in this isolated area for close to five hundred years in our everyday vernacular while the rest of the Spanish-speaking world moved on to other terms. Those of us who continue to retain and practice this unique language of ours have every right to be proud.

These three photographs were a gift to the author from Father Leo Phiffer in 1972. Father Leo served in Cuba during the 1930s and 1940s and photographed many of the events at the Catholic Church and the Convent School during his tenure. These photographs vividly illustrate the plastering process from *antes*.

Annual plastering of the church. Women apply plaster as a man repairs woodwork.

Men are mixing plaster and adjusting scaffold as women carefully apply plaster to the church walls.

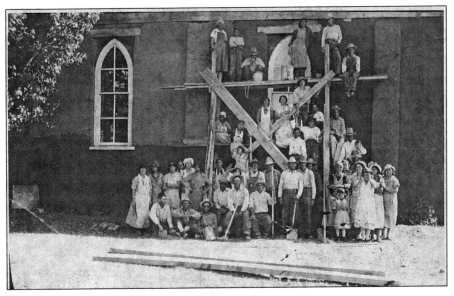

The church plastering crew of 1938 showing their rustic scaffold and tools.

Hijas que eran Mujerotas y Buenas Mandadas
Competent and Obedient Daughters

It is frequently assumed that among patriarchal families the pride of the family is the oldest son or sons in general. This notion is not necessarily true as it relates to families here in Cuba or in the immediate surroundings. In many cases, there is simply a misconception of where family pride is most abundantly bestowed.

Antes, here locally and in the neighboring settlements, a family that could truthfully claim to have *hijas mujerotas y buenas mandadas* (daughters who were competent and obedient)was looked upon with admiration and perhaps good-hearted envy. The family was also considered blessed.

In the first place, what makes this local situation interesting is that the word *mujerota* does not appear in most dictionaries of standard modern Spanish. Secondly, even Dr. Ruben Cobos, in his life-long study of New Mexico and Southern Colorado Spanish, translates the term *mujerota* as "hard-working or brave female (a lot of a woman)." (Cobos 1983, 115) Yet, this definition does not really delineate the term as used here.

The term *mujerota* loses its meaning and nuances when it is translated literally into English as a "big woman." Historically, it appears that the local people have amplified the word *mujer* into *mujerota* to fill their needs in describing their most competent, useful, able daughters and other female family members. These were females of such abilities and willingness to contribute their utmost efforts on behalf of the family's survival and success that they would rise to any occasion.

In a subsistence society, such as our *antes*, the expectations for these *hijas mujerotas* were no less challenging than those for their male siblings. The expected skills varied little. True, the women did most of the cooking, but cooking was only a fraction of the total range of jobs young women were expected to learn and to do well.

For instance, women almost exclusively did all of the gardening. It was the young women, under the well-trained, watchful eye of older women, who did all of the mud plastering of the adobe houses. As well, during those times the family's house was being expanded, women willingly helped make adobes so the addition could be closed in before the next winter. During haying season, it was not at all unusual for the young women to pitch hay onto the *guadaña* (hay wagon or loft) which was several feet above their heads. Many of these *mujerotas* also rode horses as well as any male, continuously hauled water and did innumerable loads of laundry by hand, something no young man was ever expected to do.

In addition to the many outdoor chores these local women performed, they were also taught to sew, mend and do some kinds of decorative stitchery, embroidery or crocheting. A young woman who truly showed talent in these endeavors would be encouraged to become a creative seamstress. This was a difficult occupation, given that there were few if any resources such as sufficient thread or new fabric with which to complete a project. If a young woman preferred baking to sewing, she might become the family baker. This would become one of her jobs, because she could bake the perfect *bizcochitos* (anise-flavored cookies) or the best *pan de levadura* (yeast bread), and the family would point out to everyone that this daughter *tiene buena mano para el pan* (has a light hand necessary for making leavened bread).

Conversely, the true curse for a large family with a gaggle of girls and few males was to have *una hija inútil* (a useless, fearful, incompetent daughter). Again, translation for the term *inútil* as used locally is difficult. In translation, what it implies is that an *inútil* person simply didn't measure up. Furthermore, such a woman was a burden in so far as she couldn't be depended upon to do a task as thoroughly as it needed to be done. Even a sickly woman was not good to have around, but could be tolerated. If there were daughters inclined to get sick, someone else, one of the *mujerotas*, would have to pick up the slack when, early in the morning, it was announced that, *¡Mamá, Rosita tiene bascas!* (Mother, Rosita is nauseated and sick to her stomach!) At that point, *manzanilla* tea would be prepared for Rosita (or whatever her name) and one of the other women would be instructed to hurry in doing her own chores and make sure Rosita's outdoor chores were also done. Yet, this was not the worst scenario for a family to endure while trying to survive. The worst possible situation was to have *una muchacha sin sentido* (a silly, brainless girl). This was the type of woman who wouldn't milk the family's docile cow because she was afraid of the beast. Such a woman would also let a newborn goat kid or lamb freeze to death because she didn't like the smell of the goats or sheep. Such women were not only a burden but a liability to the entire family and were really looked down upon for their silliness.

Given the obvious differences between *las hijas mujerotas, las inútiles y las sin sentido,* it is not difficult to understand why *las hijas mujerotas* were the recipients of high praise from all members of the adult community and how it was that they became overachievers and perfectionists. These were the kinds of women other families sought to be the wives of their most eligible sons and the mothers of the family legacy.

However well this system worked for some local families, there were problems that existed in this survival strategy. A conflict existed between what young women were expected to do in the reality of living in a preindustrial, agrarian society and the ideal traditional behavior deemed appropriate for all young women. On the one hand, these *mujerotas* were being praised for being the go getters that could slop the pigs, milk the cow in the muck and mire while on the other hand they were told that there were more lady-like behaviors expected of them while out in public. Mothers were constantly cautioning the family *mujerotas: "no anden de adelantadas,"* (don't be forward or assertive), or *"no vallan andar tontiando"* (above all, don't be silly or loud).

The message was that, while it was desirable and essential for women to be able to perform at a high level of skill and, at times, substantial physical effort at home, it was not appropriate to do so beyond those safe boundaries. In cases where these women were really intelligent and even outspoken, many a candle was lit on their behalf to the patron saint so that such a young woman would not embarrass the family by asking questions or expressing her own opinions. Worse yet, perhaps she might show that she was brighter and more able than a young man who might be showing interest in her as a suitor. Locally, there was a mother who would reprimand her inquisitive and outspoken daughter by calling her *la abogada* (the lawyer). This mother's greatest fear was that her daughter would become an attorney. The mother's thinking was that this daughter would put off any possible suitors, never marry and thus become an embarrassment for the family.

Being competent and outspoken, and also being polite and passive at the same time was not always easy. There could be severe consequences associated with trying to maintain both roles. There are many well-known cases where whole productive, successful estates and homesteads were lost in families lacking male leadership following the death of a patriarch. When asked how these losses could be explained, the women would respond by saying that it would not have been appropriate for them to be so forward and assertive as to stand up to a man in defense of their properties and their inheritance. Ultimately, the women from such families became destitute, displaced from their homes and totally dependent.

Conversely, the women who did assert themselves were able to keep title to their properties and continued to be *mujerotas* in every sense of the word. In some cases these women went so far as to remove their long lady-like skirts and put on men's trousers in order to work more efficiently and successfully. Most importantly, these women rose to the occasion demanded of them without fear of the stigma of being thought of as *adelantadas* (forward and outspoken).

Antes, the path these *mujerotas* could tread between praise and reprimand was very narrow, yet their contributions to their families' success had to be recognized. After all, it was these women's obvious competence that maintained the family's resources for the next generation.

This photograph, taken in front of Young's Store in Cuba, circa 1931, is included for you the readers to decide whether this woman was a *mujerota, una muchacha sin sentido, o una mujer adelantada.* It is obvious from what we see, she was not *inútil.*

3

– Family Life and Artistry –

Nuestra Gente Apreciába Las Artesanías
Our People Appreciated Craftsmanship

*A*ntes, craftsmanship was highly valued by the local people as were the artifacts created by the artisans. Yet today, as we look around our homes, our churches, places of business or in our communities at large, there is little remaining evidence of the *artesanía* (craftsmanship) that once existed here. Ironically, it is in large measure this very artisan factor that has made northern New Mexico a Mecca for tourism. The extent of this *artesanía* is also the reason that one of our own New Mexico Museums (The International Museum of Folk Art in Santa Fé) was able to exhibit just a part of its collection of over five thousand pieces of Northern New Mexico traditional artifacts in 1992. This exhibit was in commemoration of the *Quintocentenario Colombiano* (the five-hundredth anniversary of Columbus' first visit to our continent, otherwise known as the discovery of America).

This particular exhibit contained items from the colonial period through the end of the nineteenth century. On display were some of the finest pieces of religious art, such as *santos* (carved and painted wooden sculptures of saints), *retablos* (religious paintings on flat pine surfaces used as altar pieces) and beautifully decorated crosses. There were also fine *tejidos* (textiles) such as the now famous Rio Grande style of hand-woven blankets, along with rare pieces of furniture and some of the finest examples of *hojalatería* (tin work), handmade farm implements, jewelry and scores of household utensils.

It seems obvious that the local populations of northern New Mexico had been correct in their appreciation of these hand-crafted items. Furthermore, our forefathers and mothers were also right in holding their local artisans in high esteem. After all, they were the ones who had crafted these items with care, love and devotion. These items were unequivocally valuable, otherwise why would so much of what was once part of our homes and churches end up on display in museums? Why else are these items parts of the collections of the Archdiocese of Santa Fé, The Society of Hispanic Colonial Arts, Inc. and the museums of New Mexico?

In looking at these vast collections and their places of origin, which are the remote villages of northern New Mexico, a *Norteño/a* (northern New Mexican) at some point must ask, how did all these beloved and ancient treasures get here?

Consider, for example, the renowned Rio Grande style blankets as well as the other *tejidos* (textiles). These blankets were woven from the wool of the Churro sheep brought here during the colonial period. These sheep produced very long-stranded wool, making it very desirable for weaving heavy *frezadas* (blankets) as well as rugs. These *frezadas* were a part of every northern New Mexico home and it is very likely that every adult member of the family had at least one of his or her own *frezadas*. These *frezadas* were woven on treadle looms which had also been brought here early in the Spanish colonial period. These looms were part of many homes and both men and women were involved in the weaving.

Due to the loss of land and the ever-changing grazing laws that occurred in the nineteenth century, the number of sheep that people were able to keep was drastically reduced as was the amount of wool available for weaving. Eventually the looms fell into disuse, the skilled artisans got old and died and interest in weaving among the young was lost. At some time in the late nineteenth or early twentieth century, the local people were convinced that these hand-woven blankets were old fashioned and they gradually disappeared from our homes either because they were worn out, traded away or lost. They were replaced by store-bought blankets. These new blankets were added to the hand-made quilts our mothers made to keep us warm. Yet, in 2005, the United States Post Office regarded these same archaic *frezadas* historically important enough to publish a series of commemorative postage stamps with a dozen examples of these blankets on each sheet of thirty-seven-cent stamps. With few exceptions, these blankets no longer grace our homes. The Postal Service must have gone to museums to get the different examples shown on their stamps.

Prior to the late nineteenth century, especially during the colonial era, a northern New Mexico house was sparsely furnished. The few pieces of furniture that have survived from the eighteenth and nineteenth centuries were chests, a few chairs and *trasteros* (cupboards). Given the lack of tools and the great effort with which pine wood was worked into a piece of furniture, one can understand why such pieces were so deeply appreciated and so rare. Following 1821 and the opening of the Santa Fé Trail, tools became more available and the artisans' work became easier and more refined. However, the needs of the people remained relatively simple. The artisans continued to make the same kinds of furniture they made before, except they could now add tables to the list. However, storage chests and *trasteros* were always in demand, as were *banquitos* (small benches) and *tarimas* (long benches).

Again, these were items that were in every household regardless of economic status. As with the blankets, up to the mid-twentieth century these handmade furnishings gradually lost their places in our homes and, with few exceptions, no one in the family remembers what happened to them. Some people will remember replacing these pieces with store-bought, modern furniture but in most cases cannot account for what happened to the old, hand-made articles.

By the later twentieth century, these everyday furnishings were transformed into exotic and unique pieces to accent modern homes. People went searching for them even right here in Cuba. A sharp observer could see that the high-end, expensive catalogs were featuring *trasteros, banquitos* and *tarimas,* just like grandma's. Regardless of how peeled or cracked the paint on these items might have been, the prices being charged for these treasures was far beyond what they might have been purchased for originally.

Following the opening of the Santa Fé Trail in 1821 and especially after 1846, when New Mexico became a territory of the United States, a new craft developed in northern New Mexico. The new craft was *hojalatería* (tin work). This craft is an example of a people's pragmatism and imaginative creativity. With the military occupation of New Mexico there came many soldiers requiring supplies from the east. Many of the supplies these soldiers received were in tin cans which they promptly discarded as useless. In New Mexico, metal had always been in short supply. Suddenly there were tin cans of various sizes that could be utilized so creatively that a new art form emerged for the people of this region, with tinwork artisans in nearly every village.

Interestingly, people here had been decorating leather for generations and had a few tools that were very appropriate for that task. Tin was soft enough that many of the same tools used to work leather could be used to work their new and abundant supply of tin. Following the end of the Civil War in 1865, even more troops were dispatched westward and with them came an even greater supply of tin for the local artisans.

The local artisans soon discovered that they could make elaborate frames for the religious prints that by then were being strongly promoted by Bishop Lamy of Santa Fé to replace the old *retablos*. They also crafted beautiful *nichos* (three-dimensional hanging or standing niches) to hold the older hand-carved *santos*. These *nichos* generally had a hinged glass door across the front so the *santo* could be changed or the interior space decorated with dried or paper flowers on special occasions.

Sometimes these *hojalateros* (tinsmiths) made small crowns for their *santos* or crafted elaborately decorated crosses to hang on the humble adobe walls of our homes. Among the more common non-religious objects made of tin by tinsmiths were sconces, or candle holders. The tin sconces quickly replaced the earlier wooden ones (which burned rather easily) so we can assume there must have been many of these sconces around.

Unfortunately the demand for tinwork declined in the early twentieth century as frames for prints and family photographs were being shipped in by railroad. Coal-oil lamps replaced candles and the new plaster statues of the saints being promoted by the church didn't seem to require a *nicho*. Shortly after the tinsmiths stopped working, the surviving tinwork, like the *frezadas* and the handmade furnishings began to disappear from peoples' houses. Either these items were relegated to the *dispensas* (storage rooms) or simply gotten rid of or given away to someone who liked them or showed an interest in them. Whatever the case, our homes were soon denuded of these unique and decorative objects, only to be replace by a calendar decorated with a Currier and Ives lithograph or something else similarly inappropriate. Very few of these tin pieces remained in peoples' homes. This is interesting given how abundant these items had been.

Here in Cuba, our local artisans continued to work with the few tools they had available. For example, many households still preferred to use *escobitas de popote* (grass stalk brooms) as can be seen in a photograph that follows. Originally these brooms were of various sizes and had different uses. The larger brooms were used to sweep the earth-packed floors in the old adobe houses or to sweep the patios. Others were used to clean the hearths and fireplaces. A special broom was set aside to clean the inside of the *horno* (outdoor adobe oven) which was used to bake bread and to roast other foods. These brooms became obsolete as people replaced earthen floors with wooden floors and brooms with long handles were made readily available in our local stores.

Families also took great pride in the hand-crafted cemetery grave markers made to honor the memory of loved ones. These markers were made with as much creativity as could be achieved. There were decorative fences around the grave sites, as well as elaborately decorated wooden crosses made with no two of the markers looking alike. As people were able to afford commercial headstones and metal rails for their graves, the old hand-crafted pieces were allowed to weather and deteriorate and finally disappear.

Our local artisans also crafted altar pieces and pedestals for the *santos* and little tabernacles which were storage hutches for the consecrated host, as shown in the middle of the altar seen in one of the following photographs. These pictures were taken here in Cuba in 1972, showing what was left of the devotional pieces made by local artisans. They were situated on what was left of the then abandoned altar in the *oratorio* (chapel for use by the *Penitientes*) which was located west of the Catholic cemetery.

Despite the official objections of the church during the entire nineteenth century, we had at least one *santero* (a craftsman who carved wooden statues of saints) among our local artisans. Locally, there are at least six *santos* that were crafted here in Cuba and these *santos* are still loved and appreciated with great devotion.

Today, we still have so much of our past to be thankful for and to appreciate, even if much of our *artisanía* is behind glass walls in a museum where they can be appreciated by more people. Somehow this still implies that these artifacts could not have been appreciated where they originated, which was in our humble adobe homes and churches. On the other hand, perhaps in our enthusiasm to modernize our homes we unknowingly gave away or sold cheaply what we now look back on and wish we still owned as part of our cultural heritage.

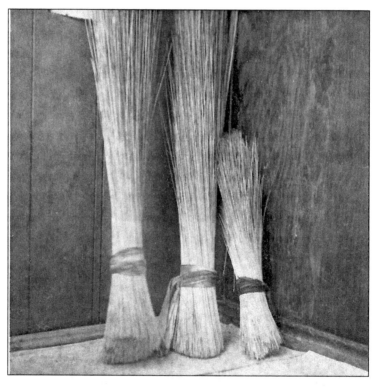

Escobas de Popote (grass stalk brooms).

Cuba Catholic Cemetery hand crafted grave marker.

Small altar with pedestals for *santos* and small tabernacle. Cuba *Penitente Oratorio.*

Large hand-crafted altar piece with crosses, Cuba *Penitente Oratorio.*

Antes, Comíanos con Provecho y Salud
Foods for our Benefit and our Health

There are several reasons why, prior to the mid-twentieth century, the people here in Cuba and rural northern New Mexico had the kind of diet that is currently being advocated by nutrition experts as being good for us. *Antes*, the primary reason that we ate as we did was because people here were fully engaged in subsistence agriculture for their survival and had no other alternatives for feeding themselves and their families. Ironically, this kind of farming involved many of the same factors, such as growing our own organic food for ourselves and for our animals, which experts now tell us produce a safe and healthful cuisine.

Antes, Cuba was a community that could feed itself, something that I doubt very much we could do today. Every household had its own animals. These usually consisted of a few happy chickens that wandered around the yard. There were chicken droppings in the yard but we also had eggs with bright orange yokes and hard shells. There was also at least one pig or maybe two for larger families. These pigs were fed some grain but mostly they ate what many people today dump down their garbage disposals or call leftovers. However smelly these pigs might have been, by late fall or early winter they were invaluable. When butchered at that time, if they were well fattened, they would provide a year's supply of lard, as well as a considerable amount of meat. In those days tortillas were made with lard and they were made every single day, so lard was one of the basic staples in every household. The family pig would also have been the source of the meat for the approaching holidays when traditional foods would include *carne adobada*, (pork meat marinated in hot chili and herbs), *chicharrones* (the crisp meaty residue left from hot fat when rendering the pure lard) as well as the meat for the household's favorite holiday special, *empanaditas* (small turnovers filled with spiced meat, raisins and piñon). There would also be *cueritos* (strips of pigskin after the fat was removed). These would be hung up to dry in the *dispensa* (the cool store room or storehouse) to put into the beans long after all the other meat was gone. Most people here did not make hams but they did make *chorizo* (pork sausage) and *morcilla* (blood sausage), which would also be hung up to dry for later use.

Although these pork products are high in fat, they were only eaten in the winter when we needed the calories, or were special holiday foods. The rest of the year we ate other meats such as beef, mutton, goat and game of various kinds. These meats were cooked and served in small amounts, mixed with potatoes, chili and many other kinds of vegetables, such as *calabacitas* (summer squash), insuring that everyone at the table had some meat at least once a day. People here rarely ate chicken. Chickens provided eggs and did so well into old age. Turkey was not available to us.

On days when any butchering was done, the family's menu was pretty well set. It would be *tripitas* (tripe) with a big stack of fresh tortillas for dinner and then *menudo* (tripe and stomach-lining stew, with or without *pozole*) for lunch the next day. Despite the fact that there was no refrigeration, no part of an animal was wasted. The internal organs were all cleaned and processed for eating, with the exception of pig's liver. That liver was never eaten. The rest of the organs were cleaned and prepared according to traditional recipes and everyone partook, including all of the children.

Families also had at least one milk cow or several goats to provide dairy products. From these cows or goats a family had milk, which we drank fresh, right after milking, or frequently made into *cuajada* (curd and whey). *Cuajada* was eaten by young and old as a snack or as dessert. On a good day, when there was enough *cuajada* left over, the women would make *queso blanco* (fresh white cheese) which was also eaten fresh and did not last long at anyone's table. No household was ever without *cuajo* (rennet), the agent that is essential for curdling cheese. This *cuajo* was usually a piece of sheep or cow's stomach that had been cleaned and put into a sealed container with whey and stored in a cool place for future use. On special occasions, *natillas* (custard pudding) would be made in large quantities because everyone liked freshly made *natillas;* they were considered a special treat.

Early in the spring, the men and boys would begin preparing the fields for planting. In Cuba it does not freeze in July. At every other time there is a possibility of crops freezing. Therefore, a maximum growing season of about 90 days meant that people survived on what they could grow and harvest within that short period of time. A crop planted too early or too late could be lost in one night. Yet, there were fields of peas (planted in April), beans, lentils, corn and wheat. As well, there were summer squash, pumpkins and various root vegetables, including onions and garlic. Experience had taught people when it was appropriate to plant each of these crops. People also ate native plants such a *quelites* (wild spinach) and *verdolagas* (purslane), as well as a large variety of native herbs such as the essential *yerba buena* (mint), oregano, *manzanilla* (chamomile), *polello* (peppermint) and many others, used for medicinal teas and other remedies.

Since there was no refrigeration, people ate what was in season and food preservation and processing were essential parts of every household's duties. In season, many foods, such as apples, plums, chili and other fruits and vegetables were picked or gathered at the peak of ripeness for sun drying then stored in cool places for use during the long winter months. Even yellow pumpkin was cut into strips and dried in the sun for *tasajos*.

The grain harvest, which was an indispensable part of survival for both people and animals, was carried out with tremendous care, making sure not a grain of wheat was lost in the process or an ear of corn missed in the final pick. The wheat was cut by hand with sickles, done communally or at least by neighborhoods. Older people who grew up here have related stories about how neighbors would gather very early in the morning at one end of a field and cut and stack wheat until noon when coffee and a snack would be taken to the fields for the workers. The workers would take a short break then and return to work until 2 o'clock. At that time, they would come to the *ramadas* (arbors covered with fresh cottonwood branches used for shade) at the house near where they were working. The main meal of the day was served, the workers would rest until around 4:00 p.m. when the day started to cool down and then return to work until dusk. This was the routine until all the wheat in the neighborhood was cut and stacked. After the stacking, each family would complete the threshing process as they were able. After the wheat had been winnowed, it would be taken either to a local flour mill or transported by horse-drawn wagons to Bernalillo, where a flour mill was still operating well into the 1950s. The wheat crop would provide families with white flour, *harina cemita* (whole wheat flour), and the bran called *salvado*. This *salvado* was roasted and used to make a mush cereal like modern, commercial Wheatena.

Of all the crops harvested here and in the surrounding areas, corn was the most labor-intensive. With the exception of *chicos* (specially prepared dehydrated corn used for flavoring beans, pork and other dishes), people here only ate green sweet corn, either roasted or boiled on the cob. Once the corn ripened, it was left on the stalk to mature completely for winter fodder for the cattle, sheep and horses. The cutting, husking and threshing of corn fields was all done by hand. Because the corn stalks were already hard, dry and sharp, this was extremely rough on people's hands and arms, and very time consuming. These may be some of the reasons that the highly valued blue corn meal used for *atole* (blue cornmeal, mush or gruel) and for *chaquegue* (a mush or thick porridge) was either traded for or bought from Pueblo people and then stored with great care for these specialties.

Given Cuba's climate, altitude and lack of dependable sources of water, the repertoire of wholesome foods eaten *antes con provecho* by the local people is amazing. Furthermore, it is a testament to their intense labor, imagination and determination to provide quality foods for their families and to enjoy the fruits of their labor.

I have only mentioned the most obvious foods, omitting such specialties as the Lenten dishes, the different breads, soups and foods for people with special needs, such as new mothers. These are yet more stories to be looked into later to help us recall how delicious freshly cooked beans with *cueritos* used to be, *antes*. For now, I am proud to have been a part of a people who, despite their lack of resources, have never been so poor that another plate could not be added to the already set table or room found to squeeze one more person onto the *tarima* (bench) to share a meal *con provecho y amistad* (with benefit and friendship).

Nuestras Curas y Remedios
Our Cures and Remedies

Antes, our cures and remedies for whatever ailment people might be suffering were carried out by family members or by the local folk practitioners. Professional medical care was simply not available. Such medical services as existed were slow in coming to our remote villages until well into the middle of the twentieth century. Furthermore, most people here had neither the money nor the means to get to a doctor or to a hospital. During very severe cases and during child birth, families could call upon the expertise of local *médicas* or *curanderas* (female folk practitioners) to help alleviate a crisis. Otherwise, they depended on family members to use their knowledge of traditional remedies along with common sense to restore the sick person's health.

These cures and remedies were derived from an accumulation of bicultural practices and knowledge that had worked over a long period of time. One part of this came with the early Spanish settlers who undoubtedly brought their traditional remedies with them, such as *Ruda* (Rue), an ancient medicinal herb, and *Rosa de Castilla* (Rose from Castile), both still used here by some people. The other part of this medicinal treasure trove came from the Pueblo peoples who had over a thousand years of practical experience with local plants such as *Ocha* (wild celery) and *yerba del oso* (cow parsnip) along with hundreds of others.

People in these remote areas of northern New Mexico had no practical options but to resort to their own devices to treat their sick. Given the lack of roads, as well as the great distances between settlements, a patient could die while being transported to a distant place such as Albuquerque. There are several reported instances of sick or injured people dying on the five-day wagon trip to Albuquerque. While being treated at home, the sick person would have available all of the resources of his or her family as well as those of the entire community. Incidentally, rural medicine here was rather similar to what was practiced in much of the rest of rural America into the early twentieth century.

Among the situations that were feared most were injuries due to accidents. These frequently resulted in deep flesh wounds prone to infection, broken bones or, worst of all, head injuries. There was little the local people could do for a person with a severe head injury and those people very likely died after several hours or a few days of intensive care at home.

As for fractured limbs, there were people who had experience at setting bones. These people would craft splints out of thin, rigid strips of wood set along the broken bone to keep the pieces in place or to keep a part of the body in a fixed position long enough for the bones to heal. Homemade slings for supporting fractured arms were also widely used. The risk of infection following a fracture brought into play the use of the herbs that people knew were good for the prevention of infection, such as *ocha*. This herb was also used to promote healing.

Given that there were several people here in Cuba who were amputees and who lived well into adulthood, one can surmise that even some amputations were performed locally and with success. It is supposed that these people's survival can be attributed to the local remedies and care the person received during the crisis or otherwise they were simply such tough, rugged individuals that they were able to withstand the trauma of such an injury, operation and healing.

Antes, every family had their own store of medicinal herbs, roots, homemade salves and even tinctures. What they lacked were really effective antiseptics. However, being the resourceful people that our *abuelitas* (grandmothers) were, they eventually learned to utilize things such as lye soap for medicinal purposes. Take the following incident as an ingenious way of using lye soap as an antiseptic.

A child in the household had a badly smashed thumb which had become infected, causing the child a great deal of pain. The grandmother, recognizing that the infection was deep and the loss of the thumbnail was inevitable, began to collect what she needed for the treatment. She took *trementina* (piñon sap) and warmed it up until it was soft and gummy. She then took a thin slice of lye soap and mixed it with the piñon pitch while she soaked the child's hand in warm water until it was nice and clean.

Grandma then covered the thumb with the warm mixture of pitch and lye soap and thickly wrapped the thumb with a clean strip of cloth many times over. Following that part, she bandaged the thumb to the child's next two fingers to protect it and instructed the child not to wet or remove the bandage. Three or four days later, the grandmother removed the dressing, along with the sloughed-off, infected tissue and the thumb nail. She soaked the child's hand again and repeated the bandaging procedure, this time without the soap or pitch to keep the injury clean and give it time to heal. Eventually the thumb nail grew back and looked and behaved perfectly normally. What is important in describing this procedure in detail is that this was a common practice among people who had to be pragmatic and knowledgeable about the healing properties of those things they had available.

Mothers used 3-in-1 oil as a remedy for earaches. What is 3-in-1 oil, the modern reader might ask? On the label it is described as high quality oil that can be used anywhere a light lubricant is needed. It is a petroleum product not much different from mineral oil which many people use today to clean wax out of their ears with the recommendation of their modern doctors. So if a child is crying in the night from an earache and the household doesn't have anything other than 3-in-1 oil, that was the remedy of choice, used with loving care.

The next example of local remedies is going to cause some readers to believe that people here practiced such things as blood-letting well into the twentieth century. Well, we didn't, but people did what they could to heal their wounds. Admittedly, some of these practices were unorthodox but most of the time they worked. In this example, one of the children in a household had a nasty-looking, seeping sore on the face that would not go away. One day, the *madrecita* (great-grandmother) took a look at the oozing sore and asked for a small bowl of cream that had been set aside to make butter. She took the cream and smeared it heavily on the child's face. While still holding the child on her lap, she asked that the faithful family dog (named *Hueso*, or "Bone") be let into the house and brought to her. She put the child down on the floor where *Hueso* could smell the cream on the baby's face and the dog started to lick the cream off, much to the baby's delight. *Madrecita* put more cream on the child's face and continued to let the dog lick the cream off the sore. She repeated the process for several days until the dog had cleaned the sore. The seeping soon stopped and eventually the sore healed on its own.

In this case, the dog was very healthy and instead of contaminating the sore or making it worse, it promoted healing. What *Madrecita* knew was that dogs continue to lick their wounds repeatedly until they are healed. Given that very basic principle, she applied it as a remedy for one of her own great-grandchildren and, in that case, it worked. One has to assume that neither the cream nor the dog's saliva was contaminated in any way beyond what was normal for the household. What is important for readers to understand is that, while some of these cures or remedies might appear to be primitive, they were in fact instances of people acting out of past experience and observation, using treatments that worked more times than not.

Beside the amputees mentioned earlier, there were also other kinds of crippled people who lived here and who survived well into old age without much medical intervention. For instance, there was a man called *Don* Salomon who could not stand or walk at all. He sat cross-legged, usually on the floor, where he used to repair and mend shoes. What the cause of this man's crippled condition was no one alive today seems to know. What the older people recall is that *Don* Salomon must have been born that way. It is difficult to believe that *Don* Salomon could have made a meaningful living repairing worn out shoes; but in those days, people did try to mend old shoes rather than replacing them as quickly as we do today. What is significant in this story is that *Don* Salomon had a purpose in life and he had a role in this community. Perhaps that purpose and that contact with people was all the *remedio* (remedy) that he needed. In thinking about such people who not only survived but lived productive lives without today's safety nets we might wonder how *Don* Salomon would fare in today's world.

Beside injury and disease, people here also had other very special remedies and practices for pregnant women, for postnatal care and care for new-born babies. This category of care seemed to involve all the women in the family as well as *Doña* Gregorita Sanchez during her many years of practice as a *partera* (mid-wife). During a woman's pregnancy, delivery and postnatal care, the voice of authority came from the *abuelitas* (grandmothers) and the *madrecitas* (great-grandmothers). There were special foods prepared for a pregnant woman, especially if this was her first pregnancy. Many men ended up having two or three wives because so many women died in child birth. Therefore, the women in the family did their very best to have the young females survive their child-bearing years.

Once the baby was delivered and mother and child were well, the new mother had to remain in bed for ten days. While in bed, the available female members from both the husband's family and her own family waited on the new mother hand and foot. And woe be unto her if any of these women even thought of breaking that rule.

After ten days, the new mother was able to get up and do light housekeeping and help take care of the baby. However, for forty days following the birth of the baby, the mother *estaba en dieta* (was keeping her post-partum regime). This was a period in which the mother observed traditional ways of caring for her well-being. This included special food and drink, sponge baths and little if any public exposure. Needless to say, the *abuelitas* were serious about the survival of their women and their newborns. It could not be confirmed that the forty-day period of the *dieta* had religious connotations related to the Virgin Mary's *dieta* following the birth of Jesus. Whether or not the regime was religious in origin, no young mother would break the rule.

As difficult as it might be to believe, there were many premature babies here that survived well into adulthood. Again, the experience and the well-tried methods of keeping a premature baby alive and well are amazing. The *setemesino(a)*, (the name applied to a premature baby) was delivered and put into a bag of warm cornmeal and kept warm near the stove. The cornmeal would be changed as needed and the baby was fed and cleaned while in the constant warmth of his or her cornmeal incubator. As the baby became stronger and gained weight it would be taken out for longer and longer periods of time until it was big enough and strong enough to live outside the cornmeal bag. Given a premature birth in a household, the *madrecitas* were on duty day and night until they felt confident that the baby was ready to be taken care of by the mother alone.

The *curas* and *remedios* described in this article may lack much of the sophistication of modern medical practice. However, these traditional practices did not lack the effectiveness or the loving commitment of family members and communities to help one of their own survive the ravages of our isolated rural life. This life style has sustained and shaped so many of us that, even though we know there are better ways of getting rid of sores than having *Hueso* lick them off, we remain proud of the way our people have survived and what can still be learned from them. In fact, some of the traditional *remedios* are still used by some of the members of our community. Others, such as *trementina,* are still referred to fondly but probably not often used. In time, other medical practices were introduced to our community by people who moved here from elsewhere and slowly replaced our ancient practices. But that is another story!

Los Bailes, Las Canciones y Los Musicos
Dances, Songs and Musicians

Los bailes y las canciones de antes were derived from a conglomeration of sources that are both amazing and at times amusing. Local musicians learned and played this music for all manner of occasions. Whatever the sources of these pastimes, the people of Cuba have been active and willing participants in singing, dancing and playing the few musical instruments available to us. Whether the occasions were religious and somber, such as a funeral, or happy, such as a wedding or feast day dance, people were there to provide music. The singing might be an *alabado* (a religious hymn of praise) or a popular *corrido* (originally a popular ballad patterned after the Spanish romances of the eighteenth century). Instrumental melodies spanned a wide range and there was also a wide range of dance styles.

People around here have had a long tradition of being religiously faithful, *cantadores con alegria* (happy in their singing) and from early on we have been known to be a people, both young and old, who dance with *gusto sincero* (sincere joy).

Antes, mucho mas antes (a long, long time ago), the older people would reminisce happily about the dances they had enjoyed in their youth. They used to talk about dancing *la jota*. This must have been an ancient dance that came here from Spain. It survived as a favorite into the early twentieth century. The origin of this dance is attributed to the ancient province of Aragon, in Spain. It was also popular in the neighboring provinces of Valencia and Navarra. A further clue to indicate that this is an ancient dance is its name. *Jota* is the Spanish word for the letter *j*. In a somewhat complicated fashion, this word can be traced back through the ancient language of the area of Aragon to a Latin word that means to hop or to jump.

The dance was made more challenging by the fact that those who were dancing also recited *coplas* (couplets or poetic verses) as they hopped or jumped past their partners in time with the music. Only very specific *coplas* would be appropriate and a person with a wide range of *coplas* would have been a very popular dance partner. For those who think modern dances are complicated, they should try to imagine moving arms, legs and bodies in time with the music while also singing *coplas*.

There was another favorite dance the *abuelitos* (grandfathers) talked about and remembered laughingly called *el chatis*. It turns out to have a German name, *schottische*, which refers to a dance of partners involving a complicated pattern of steps and hops. The dance seems to have originated in Bohemia and then passed through the rest of Europe before coming here. The dance is a form of round dance in 2/4 time, similar to a polka but with a slower tempo. This must have been a very popular dance back in olden times. One might wonder, however, how such a dance ever got to such a remote place as Cuba.

Yet another dance is particularly interesting because it survived here in Cuba well into the middle 1950s. Traditionally it was the third to the last piece of music the band would play before the end of the dance. (This was the first signal to the celebrants that the party was about to come to an end.) Here in Cuba, the dance was called *la varseliana*. In standard Spanish, the proper name for this dance was *varsoviana*, which comes from *varsovia* and refers to the city of Warsaw in Poland. This was a kind of ballroom dance known in New Mexico and southern Colorado as *Put Your Little Foot Forward,* That this dance survived so long is no doubt because it was enjoyed very much, it had a traditional place in the structure of dances and it was simply passed on from one generation to another.

Following *la varseliana,* the next-to-last piece the musicians would play was called *la raspa.* The verb *raspar* in Spanish means to scrape. This act of scraping is exactly what the dancers did when they danced *la raspa.* This is a folk dance of Mexican origin in which the dancers scrape or shuffle their feet back and forth in time with the music.

In my youth, by the time *la raspa* was starting to play, our long-time County Sheriff, *Don* Sambrano would have stepped quietly into the back of the dance hall and just stood there talking to people with his big hat on and his big pistol at his side. Everyone knew it was time for the tired *musicos* (musicians) to start playing *Home, Sweet Home.* When that number ended, the dance was officially over.

After the dance ended, the women and children who had been occupying the rough benches along the walls of the hall would prepare for the trip home. The mothers would pick up the bundled-up babies from under the benches as fathers signaled the teenage girls in the family to join the rest of the brood. As for the young men, *Don* Sambrano was already outside making sure that all disagreements were settled peacefully between the local young men and those from places such as Gallina who had been at the dance.

Typically, the *Gallineños* (young men from Gallina) would have arrived at the dance rather late and entered the dance hall together, checking out all the young women in the audience before asking anyone to dance. Different from the local boys and young men, the fellows from Gallina wore their pants tucked inside their cowboy boots. This immediately identified them as being from Gallina. Naturally, the local young men felt compelled to protect their territory. These were the kinds of disagreements *Don* Sambrano was an expert at settling without too much injured pride to either side.

Among the many other dances people enjoyed before the jitterbug and other more modern dances came along were *las valses* (waltzes), the polka and *las cuadrillas* (quadrilles). This last one was a type of square dance of French origin that older people also remember fondly.

The dances were paid for by charging the male dancers ten cents per dance, which was collected half way through each song. The band would stop playing just long enough to give the people collecting the money time to collect from each male dancer. An alternative method of payment was to buy a ticket for one or two dollars and dance all evening. Those young men who chose this method would get a little strip of ribbon pinned to their collar to signal the collectors to go on to other couples. Wedding dances were free since the musicians were part of the wedding expenses. Also free of charge were the impromptu dances that occurred in people's patios or in their homes.

Unplanned dances came about in a couple of ways. An individual would go out of his house in the evening to play his guitar or violin and a neighbor or two might come over to join him. Otherwise, several *musicos* might have gathered at someone's home to practice together. In either case, the other people who were attracted to these gatherings sang as the musicians practiced. *Antes*, everybody sang. From a very early age, children were taught the words and the tunes of old children's songs and lullabies. Many of these songs had religious connotations and associations to the Blessed Mother, angels or saints. These included the traditional birthday song or a child's saint-day song, called *El Día de tú Santo* (The Day of your Saint). Another children's song, which contains words suggesting it is very old, is titled *Naranja Dulce* (Sweet Orange). As well as oranges, this short song also refers to lemons. Considering the scarcity of any citrus fruit in this area, this little song was likely imported from some place, such as Mexico or Spain, where sweet oranges and lemons are more common.

By the early twentieth century, people of all ages were singing popular songs from Mexico. This was especially true during and following the Mexican Revolution of 1910. From this period of time we got such songs as *Adelita*, which had been the call to arms for the women of Mexico to join the Revolution and fight alongside their men. Interestingly, in the 1970s, *Adelita* again served as the call to mobilize the Chicanos of the American Southwest toward political activism.

There was another popular song that very likely came from this same period titled *Soy Soledado de Levita* (I am a soldier in uniform). As popular as *Adelita* and this song were, they could not compare with *Allá en el Rancho Grande* (There at the big ranch) or *La Cucaracha* (the cockroach.) This last song was so popular that by the time a gregarious child was four years old, he or she could already sing two or three verses plus the chorus of this song. Verses had been made up to fit local situations. These verses used the names of well known people and described situations that were ironic or simply amusing. Very young children could also belt out *Allá en el Ranch Grande* while the adults urged them on and might even have given the kid a few pennies for singing it well. According to reliable folklore sources, Pancho Villa's revolutionaries called Villa's rather unpredictable jalopy *la cucaracha*. To this day, one hundred years later, a jalopy or a car in poor running condition is still referred to here as a *cucaracha*.

By the early 1920s there were song books being brought into Cuba through the schools, the Protestant Churches and the local merchants. These song books were inexpensive and contained popular songs, spirituals, mountain ballads and cowboy songs. It was probably from such a songbook that local musicians learned a song called *Oh, Dem Golden Slippers*. This song, originally an African-American spiritual, became the music used for wedding marches at the beginning of wedding dances. Why this song came to such a use is unclear. Probably people simply liked the song and it fit the occasion rather well.

Corridos (ballads) were also among the songs people enjoyed very much. These are songs with simple melodies and countless verses, describing some adventure, love triangle or tragedy. Among the local cowboys, one of the favorite *corridos* is titled *Kiansis* (Kansas). This *corrido* tells the story of a cattle drive to Kansas that was difficult and filled with danger and adventure. It was endlessly romanticized through a dozen or more verses and at least two written versions. This became the *corrido* that a real *vaquero Mejicano* (Hispanic cowboy) could identify with.

The story of the *musicos* and their instruments is as interesting as the songs themselves. The guitar was the first instrument to get to northern New Mexico. Guitars very likely came with our earliest forefathers and mothers. Music has been in important source of entertainment since earliest colonial times. How else would we all have become such good dancers and singers? Ask any local person over the age of sixty, either male or female, to sing a couple of verses of *la cucaracha* and without doubt you will hear a passionate version of Cuba's most popular song from *antes*.

According to Lena Gallegos Cordova (pers. comm.), early in the twentieth century her grandfather, *Don* Juan Bautista Gallegos, played what she called a bull fiddle (a string bass). He also bought a violin for his son, *Don* Elizardo, Lena's father. The family folklore says that *Don* Elizardo would sit under a tree and scratch or pick at the violin until he learned to play the instrument. These two musicians, together with *Don* Meliton Lovato on guitar or violin, played with *Don* Meliton's brother *Don* Arturo, who played the banjo. They formed a band that included *Don* José Peña on violin and guitar, and *Don* José Maria Lovato on guitar. This is how the local musical groups were formed. These so-called bands were simply groups of friends and relatives who enjoyed making music together.

There were other musicians, such the young Tomas Aragon and Frank Trujillo who played accordion and guitar, that were not associated with a band, but could be counted upon to fill in if some members of a group were away at the sheep camps when a band was needed.

Mr. Frank Duran, one of our surviving musicians, reported that he could play guitar, violin, accordion and trumpet and played in groups for many years (pers. comm). The expert accordion player in that group was *Don* Bernardo Valdez. *Don* Bernardo's brother Rosenaldo is still a gifted guitarist was in that group along with two Lucero brothers, Esequiel and Dick.

There are two things related by Mr. Duran that are relevant to how towns developed musical groups. For the most part, musicians learned how to play their instruments from each other. They also taught each other any new tunes or songs that they heard. When asked where they would hear a new tune, Mr. Duran quickly responded, *"en las cantinas"* (in the bars). By then, even here in Cuba, the bars generally had a Victrola (a very early record player) and a few records. Later all the bars had a Nickelodeon, an early version of the jukebox that was operated by inserting a nickel. These local musicians could take their guitars, violins, accordions and other instruments to the bar and listen to a tune over and over again until they learned it and could teach it to the rest of the group.

Mr. Duran also said that, with the exception of his trumpet, there was not much variety in the type of instruments our local musicians played. Since few types of instruments were in use, these were the only ones local people learned how to play.

Before the Victrolas and Nickelodeons, much of the music likely came to this area with the *fleteros* (freighters). These individuals traveled regularly to Albuquerque or Santa Fé and occasionally as far south as Chihuahua or Durango, Mexico. They likely took their guitars or violins with them for their own entertainment. Along the way, they probably picked up new songs and perhaps even new dances in the places they went to buy the goods needed by the people of this area. In fact, after some time, local people might have come to expect a new song or dance step from each returning *fletero*. Other songs and perhaps some dances came here with new residents or passers-by, such as those who fled the 1910 Revolution in Mexico.

Unfortunately today there are few places to dance and few musicians to play a good polka or even *la varseliana*.

4

– Community and Commerce –

Las Tiendas de Antes
The Early Stores

*A*ntes, people in the Cuba area survived by working their subsistence farms and ranches and through bartering with their neighbors and with Native peoples. In those days, this was not a money economy; there was very little money held by families or individuals and there were very few means by which to earn money. The local economy was dependent on the family farms and herds of sheep, cattle and horses. People could only make money by working somewhere away from Cuba, herding sheep for someone else or mining or doing something else for which they could earn cash.

Still, people needed products that could only be bought from a store for cash. Early stores were established at *La Posta* (Cabezon) where one of the stage coach stations was located and to which mail was delivered. This was a place that people came to or passed through when merchandise and services were needed. One of the first merchants at *La Posta* was a Mr. Ricardo Heller. He was apparently very successful for a very long time because he related well to his clients who included Hispanics from the neighboring hamlets as well as the *Diné* (Navaho people) and other people going through on the stage.

There was also a store in La Ventana, an area thought to have potential. Coal had been discovered there and some believed the mines held great promise. There was enough interest in this coal that a railroad line was extended to that area to haul the coal to commercial centers. The store at La Ventana was owned by a Mr. Mathias. The coal supply did not meet the expectations of the speculators of the time; however, the store survived well into the 1950s under several different operators. Mr. Joe Marchetti owned and ran La Ventana Store for many years. After Mr. Marchetti closed the store, the building was used for many other purposes and is still standing today.

Closer to home, there were many stores and businesses in Copar (Copper City), where there are still remnants of a copper mine just east of Cuba. Early on there was much more activity and there were more people in Copar than in what is now Cuba. This did not last very long beyond 1900.

When these boom towns exhausted their resources, the merchants (and some of the population) saw a completely different and more sustainable way to gain wealth. What these enterprising people saw was that the people in the Cuba area had assets in the form of livestock and land.

Las tiendas de antes in Cuba were established slowly but the *tienderos* (merchants) that migrated here did so because they perceived that there was a market. As we all know, where there is a market, there is money to be made. It was this potential that motivated the early entrepreneurs such as Mr. J. H. Matthews, *Don* V. S. Miera and Mr. Aron Eichwald to come to this area in the late nineteenth century.

These merchants had observed the local people's tremendous need for modern, more efficient tools, better clothing and more durable goods. Unlike today, those early merchants didn't even have to advertise their goods; people were already longing for the advantages these merchants could deliver. Granted, many people didn't have money to purchase commercially made goods, but that would change. These new merchants, knowing the local people didn't have much money, simply accommodated their customers by giving them credit. This was especially true in instances where the merchants knew that eventually any debt could be paid with wool, hides, livestock or ultimately with land.

By 1880 the railroad had expanded into New Mexico on the

northern frontier as well as into the central and southern parts of the territory, including Albuquerque. This made general merchandise available to more people in more places, including places as remote and isolated as our own hamlet. It also provided a much larger market for local products such as wool, hides and livestock. Merchandise sold in local stores was still transported up the hill from the Albuquerque area and local goods were transported out by wagon until the early 1920s when trucks replaced them. During this time large herds of livestock were driven to sell in what is now the town of Corrales (the corrals).

Las tiendas de antes in and around Cuba were, by today's standards, relatively small structures but held large and varied inventories. The general merchandise in these *tiendas* would probably have seemed simple and unexciting by modern standards, but it could have provided for virtually all the needs of the community of Cuba or any similar community. These *tiendas* would maintain inventories of every available kind of hardware, for which there was a real market. This would have included items such as steel-bladed knives, axes, saws, hammers and factory-made nails. The dry goods inventories were equally large and were real money-makers. Dry goods were much lighter in weight than tools and were thus much easier for the *fleteros* (freighters) to transport up from Albuquerque in their wagons. This stock would include ready-made clothing for men, women and children as well as shoes and boots for the whole family. There were also big bolts of cloth, such as muslin, to make the *mantas* (spreads) that covered the undersides of mud-filled ceilings inside local houses. There were also large bolts of ticking used for making casings for the wonderful wool-filled pillows and mattresses used here until very recent times.

In the household goods departments these merchants provided everything, including cast iron stoves, metal pots and pans, scissors, clocks, highly valued steel needles and a wide variety of other metal cooking and eating utensils, all of which were in great demand. These *tiendas* either had or could provide furniture such as commercially-made chairs and dressers with mirrors.

One could also find name-brand medicines such as the all-purpose *aceite Mexicano* (Mexican oil), iodine, mercurochrome, liniments, salves, ointments and aspirin. Among other sundries, there were the all-important bars of commercially-made soap as well as a few cosmetic items for ladies. Now women could stop powdering their faces with traditional finely-ground corn meal and use modern face powder instead. All of these items were welcomed commodities in a society that had been entirely dependent on herbs and other home remedies.

The groceries in these establishments included a variety of canned foods, wooden boxes of dried fruits and sacks of flour, salt, sugar and coffee beans. There were also cured meats as well as barrels of molasses and syrup.

In the corrals, barns and outbuildings sale items included animals, stored grain and perhaps the bigger, bulkier farm tools, such as wagon wheels and other parts for wagons and buggies. There would also be saddles, harnesses and other kinds of tack for horses along with carefully stored building supplies, including the indispensible metal roofing, factory-made doors and windows (at least those that survived the trip from the railroad yards in Albuquerque over the infamous road system to Cuba).

By 1889 Mr. Eichwald was well established in his general merchandise business in Cuba. Mr. J. H. Matthews was still maintaining his general store at that time, but had also become a partner with a Mr. Hye in another general store and liquor establishment. Mr. Matthews was also a partner with a Mr. Smith in a grist mill.

Prior to Mr. Eichwald coming to Cuba to establish his store, he had bought the general merchandise store in La Ventana from Mr. Mathias. There had been much speculating as to the wealth that the coal mines in La Ventana could bring and Mr. Eichwald was willing to test the waters there, at least for a time. As it turned out, the coal mines were not as lucrative as it was initially thought they would be. La Ventana never realized the boom town status that Copar enjoyed.

However, before Mr. Eichwald sold his store in La Ventana, he came to Cuba and started a store. According to Eichwald family sources (pers.comm.), when he opened his Cuba store he began buying livestock, pelts, wool, angora skins, and Mexican goat skins from the ranchers. He also bought all kinds of pelts from local trappers. Mr. Eichwald was successful enough that by 1908 the only competition he had here in Cuba was the local businessman, *Don* Juan José Salazar, who had also opened a general merchandise store.

A few miles southeast of Cuba, a large, active general merchandise store owned by *Don* José Maria Cebada was located in San Pablo and was in operation from early in the twentieth century to the late 1930s. According to family members (pers. comm.), *Don* José Maria's store was also part of the *estafeta* system between La Posta (Cabezon), Copar and Nacimiento, back when these settlements were towns. *Don* José Maria Cebada's store served a population that was scattered between La Ventana and Señorito as did the other stores described above.

By 1919 there were six general merchandise stores operating in Cuba, including one owned by Mr. Frank Bond and and operated by Mr. H. L. Wiese. This store opened here around 1917 when Mr. Wiese came from Wagon Mound as a representative of the Bond enterprises to speculate in the wool market.

At this time, there was also a flour mill, two saw mills and a variety store owned by a Mr. J. L. Scott. The John F. Young family enterprises, which were very diverse, became prominent in the 1920s, as did the J. M. Mahboub General Store and Mr. Limen B. Putney's branch of the Albuquerque Grocers. Members of his family say that Mr. Putney never owned the store that he managed, but rented the store from *Don* Juan José Salazar and sons. These and other businesses sprang up more or less along a road that connected the Post Office and the Catholic church. As time went by, this became the Main Street of Cuba. The earlier settlement of Nacimiento was located a few miles east of what is now downtown Cuba.

There were several local merchants who had opened general merchandise stores which for various reasons did not survive the Great Depression of the 1930s. Among these merchants were *Don* Epimenio A. Miera and his brother *Don* Venceslao, *Don* Manuel Martinez and *Don* Bartolo Sandoval.

By the 1940s, a new generation of merchants took over business in our community. These included *Don* Pedro Cebada, *Don* Isidore Gurulé and Mr. Rodolfo (Rudy) Velarde. Mr. Velarde had actually started out as a wool and sheep dealer before going into the general merchandise business. Of the old timers, only H. L. Wiese was still in operation for a short time into the 1940s. Mr. Eric Freelove, in nearby La Jara, successfully continued his general merchandise store and later rented Cuba Supply Company from the Bartolo Sandoval family.

During this same period, a couple named Mr. and Mrs. Joe Glenen came here and opened a large general merchandise store that survived through the end of World War II. In that era, Glenen's was the biggest store in Cuba. Among other attempts at meeting the needs of the local market, we had *Doña* Eumelia and *Don* Porfirio Casaus with two small stores and Mr. José La Luz Montaño with a small sundries or variety type store. These merchants carried a limited inventory but served the local people well in their small establishments.

By the time this new generation of merchants had established themselves, the glory days of the big general merchandise stores were over. Furthermore, the large herds of sheep were gone and there was no wool to sell as a cash product. The local cattle herds had been reduced to a few head which could be pastured on limited National Forest permits in the summer months only. People had a few horses left, but no one had herds of horses as they had *antes*. Many families had lost large portions of their land to their creditors and, while Cuba families still needed merchandise, they had few resources by which they could generate income.

It was during this period that individuals or whole families began to leave this area to work in industries in other states. Some came back regularly after a season working for money elsewhere in order to provide for their families. Many never came back. A few have returned more recently and still recall *las tiendas de antes* and at which *tienda* their first pair of cowboy boots had been bought and when Levis only cost two dollars. And yes, we can recall when salt and sugar came in cloth sacks and you could buy *cuatro reales* (fifty cents) worth of potatoes which would feed the whole family for a week.

Many other changes occurred in Cuba area stores between the period of *antes* and today but again, that is another story!

Un Último Testamento
A Last Will and Testament

What could we have possibly inherited when there was so little material wealth to distribute or to pass down? Inheritances don't necessarily have to be tangible, material goods. Elsewhere I have written about our history being our legacy. I also wrote about the honor in our tradition of inheriting names that were passed down unchanged for generations. There were farming and ranching families where, upon the death of the head of their family; each offspring would inherit an equal number of cattle or sheep or the family brand that had been used to identify their stock.

According to local custom, land was generally passed down in families and frequently divided into smaller and smaller plots until the last heirs are unable to do much farming or grazing on their inheritance but would at least have a place to build a house and still live among their relatives if they chose to do so.

Our language is also among the most precious gifts of our history. There is the language that allows us to communicate with other Spanish speakers as well as the language we use with other English speakers. Then there is the language of a period of time or a specific place. Our Spanish, for instance, is more like the Spanish spoken in the sixteenth century than it is like modern Spanish. This is a unique inheritance for us, the inhabitants of northern New Mexico. This inheritance of language has given me the capability to decipher and translate a one hundred year old "last will and testament," handwritten in Spanish, which had been passed down to me. Over the years, I have valued this document for its symbolic and historical importance to me and to that part of my mother's family to whom it pertains.

This last will and testament was carefully dictated by *Don* Francisco Vigil and very formally written, signed and witnessed on March 16, 1901. After deciphering and evaluating the formality of the will itself and the companion document that required the formal disposition of inheritance to the heirs on June 1, 1901, I had to ask myself why the will was written. Why did *Don* Francisco go to such immense effort to have this document drawn up as formally as he did? Seen from today's perspective, it seems there was so little to leave to his wife, *Doña* Eugenia, and his eight surviving children.

After reflecting on this question and doing further research, I realized that there was probably much more to *Don* Francisco's efforts in preparing this will than meets the eye. Given that the will was written in March and the distribution of property occurred in June of the same year, *Don* Francisco may have been sick and may have actually died between those dates. I have no evidence that shows when he died. However, I do have evidence from the old Cuba cemetery that shows that his wife, *Doña* Eugenia, was only fifty-two years old in 1901 and did not die until 1921, at the age of 72. Furthermore, his youngest daughter, Lázara, was only fourteen years old in 1901 and twenty-one years younger than Petra, the oldest of the children. *Don* Francisco only had two sons among his eight children and there is evidence that the oldest son, Rumaldo, was thirty years old in 1901 and unmarried. Yet, *Don* Francisco did not leave the family's possessions in Rumaldo's name with the hope or understanding that Rumaldo would be responsible for the care of his mother and unmarried sister.

I believe that *Don* Francisco was trying very hard to make sure there were no loopholes in this will that might later deprive his wife or his young daughter of a means to a livelihood. So precise are the details dictated to the scribe that concern, if not desperation, come through to the reader.

The will begins by stating the location as being "in the territory of New Mexico, Bernalillo County, precinct 20." (Sandoval County was not established until 1903.) *Don* Francisco then dictates that, being of sound mind, he is determined at this time to divide among his family "that which his last effort and human will have produced." And then he states, "I declare and say that I have been married legitimately to my wife, Maria Eugenia Montoya de Vigil, and between us with consent have had 8 children, 2 sons and 6 daughters." The will then lists the children from oldest to youngest by first and last name. Following the names of Rumaldo and Domingo, the scribe wrote "son" in parentheses.

Another question that arises is why, in listing his daughters' names, does he not mention their married names? Instead, he lists all the children as Vigil, when evidence shows that at least the four older women were married. Petra would have been thirty-five years old in 1901 and the mother of several children by then.

Don Francisco then reaffirms that he is of sound mind and that this testimony as presented here is his last wish and that the two witnesses agree with him and will show this agreement with their signatures.

Now the inheritance is presented and Don Francisco dictates with such tenderness, "These are my possessions I wish to leave with pleasure to my wife, Maria Eugenia Montoya de Vigil. I leave the furniture and the household effects and the animals, horses, cattle, mares and the house and the properties around the house, the house and all properties as explained above for her use and her good favor." How much property? How many horses? How many head of cattle? However many animals or acres of property Doña Eugenia was left with, we don't know from this document. What we do know is that Don Francisco left this to his wife "with pleasure" and "for her use and good favor."

This paragraph tells the reader something about Don Francisco and Doña Eugenia's relationship as being one of much devotion and allegiance. This might help explain why son Rumaldo is not left as administrator as one might have expected at that time in history.

When I first read this document, I found the following section amazing and even now have difficulty putting it into perspective. It reads, "Furthermore, I wish to declare that I leave my daughter, Petra Vigil, $1.00 in money (un peso de dinero), for my daughter, Anizeta Vigil, $1.00 in money (un peso de dinero)," and so on down the list of his eight children in exactly the same way. Here we see Don Francisco following the tradition of giving an equal share to each of his children.

In the next and last section of the will, Don Francisco says, "Having here recognized my intentions as I have explained as best I could and with what I could afford in their behalf, I will sign the present, on this date in front of said witnesses." The witnesses appear to have signed the document themselves, while Don Francisco signed with an X and his name was signed by the scribe.

The second document is dated June 1, 1901 and it states that each of the eight children received from their mother one dollar in money from the estate of *Don* Francisco. Furthermore, the heirs claim to be satisfied with what they have received and will make no further claim against the estate. Again, the location is formally given as being Cuba, Bernalillo County, Territory of New Mexico.

Each of the eight children signed. The two oldest daughters signed with an *X* and their names are written in. The others appear to have signed their own names. To the side of each name appears a blackened star or seal which indicates they are in agreement. The scribe signs as a witness to the agreement and as being the scribe.

These are interesting details but not as puzzling as when originally looked at. Given the properties, the animals, the house and the furniture, this family possessed, I have concluded that "one dollar in money" was merely symbolic and followed the tradition of equal shares to each of the children. One dollar, even in 1901 could not have been very much for anyone to consider as a total inheritance. Furthermore, what could one buy with one dollar in Cuba in 1901? I also concluded that great-great grandfather Francisco acted in a rather progressive and modern way by not being bound by tradition in his obvious effort to provide for his young wife and youngest daughter's long-term care. Given the language of the will as it refers to what *Doña* Eugenia was to inherit, this man apparently had a great deal of confidence in his wife's competence and would let her decide what to do with these possessions when the time came to pass them on to the children.

Finally, in reading this document many times over, I came away thinking that it has the ring of a modern community property agreement where each spouse leaves all their property to the surviving partner in the marriage and the exceptions are then stated as they were in *Don* Francisco Vigil's will: *un peso de dinero* to each of his children. The fact that the family seems to have agreed to *Don* Francisco's terms is in itself amazing, given the size of the family. *Sean como fueran, estas son nuestras herencias de antes* (be they as they are, these are our inheritances from the past), and they continue to enrich our lives as long as we keep the memory and the language alive.

La Primera Guerra Mundial
World War I and *Antes*

World War I began in 1914 in a place called Serbia, in Europe. At that time, few Americans had any idea where Serbia was or why events there could precipitate such a war. In fact, centuries of political instability and generations of ethnic and religious hostility made this just the sort of place a war could start. At this time, Serbia was a part of the Austro-Hungarian Empire and was being visited by Archduke Ferdinand of Austria. The Archduke and his wife were assassinated by a Serbian Nationalist in the city of Sarajevo on June 28, 1914. Since most European nations were locked into alliances with each other at that time, the war escalated very quickly. By the end of the war millions of people had been killed and much of the continent was in ruins.

Even though the United States did not declare war on Germany until 1917, well over four hundred thousand Americans served in the short time until the war's end. There were more than one hundred twenty thousand American casualties. The war ended with an armistice at eleven o'clock on the morning of the eleventh day of the eleventh month (November) of 1918. This day, used to be celebrated as "Armistice Day" in honor of the end of the war. Later, veterans and victims of other wars were also remembered on that day and it came to be called "Veterans' Day."

On the surface it would appear that World War I had little impact on the lives of the people of Cuba. If we look a little closer we can see that, at least for these individuals and their families, there were life-long changes. The most immediate change for the participants was that they got to travel far beyond the boundaries of their familiar environment. It is said that at least a few of these men actually got to Europe. Without doubt, it also provided them with experiences beyond the sheep camps or mines which had been their only opportunity for employment in this area.

Among the men who served in the war were thirty-two from this area. Fortunately, none of those who served from the Cuba or La Jara area was killed during their service. However, there were a few men who returned from the war with permanent injuries or disabilities.

According to the late *Don* Lucario Herrera of La Jara (pers. comm.), his father, *Don* José Leon Herrera was shot in the knee and always walked with a stiff leg. Another veteran who returned disabled was *Don* Daniel Montoya. Family members report that *Don* Daniel had suffered gas poisoning and did not live long after he returned. Gas poisoning was one of the major causes of death and disability during what was later proclaimed to be "the war to end all wars." *Don* Abel Lobato's family relate that he went into service on June 1, 1918 and returned from the war "sickly" and that by July, 1924, he had died. Even though he was not likely diagnosed as disabled, he seems to have been a latent casualty of the war.

However there were also benefits for the families of some of these men. As a result of military service, there were some veterans who were paid government pensions. Meager as these pensions may seem today, these monies must have had a tremendous economic impact on the lives of the families who received them. This would be especially true for the people who continued to collect these pensions through the Great Depression of the 1930s. For instance, one of *Don* Elizardo Gallegos' sons reported that following his father's death in 1945, his mother, *Doña* Genoveva Gallegos was paid a small monthly widow's stipend until her death in 1990. Similarly, the elderly mother of one of the other veterans who died young received a small pension which allowed her to live in her own home, rather independent of the rest of her family, until her death.

Along with veterans' benefits, these men probably also had death benefits. Again, these benefits may not seem very much to us now, but, the white marble headstones that we see in our local cemeteries were provided by the government and to my knowledge, without cost to the families who wanted them.

One of the facts that make our local roster of thirty-two veterans interesting is that there were five families who had more than one individual volunteer for the war. The Read family, who used to live at the Bar-R Ranch on Trail Creek near San Miguel, had three members serving in the war. A nephew, John Read (pers. comm.), who now lives in Texas, reported that Howard Read was in the Navy, probably on a battleship,

Kenneth Read served with the Army Engineers, mapping trenches, and Leslie Read served in the US Cavalry in France. Mr. Read also says that he has numerous papers and artifacts related to his uncles' service.

There were also Frank Gutierrez and his brother Jesús, the Lovato brothers, Candido and Francisco, as well as brothers Carmel and Ambrosio Segura. From La Jara, brothers Celestino and Genovevo Jacques also served. A woman who grew up here recalls that when she was quite young she accompanied her mother to *Don* Ambrosio Segura's *velorio* (a wake or vigil for the dead) in the Nacimiento area. Being a small child, the thing that impressed her most at that time was that *Don* Ambrosio's coffin was draped with the American flag. This story would suggest that military honors were part of his funeral and part of the benefits awarded to these veterans.

The following two photographs associated with our World War I veterans document the pride these young country boys and those around them seem to have felt about their service. The photographs also raise some questions as to what it meant to these men to have been a part of such an enormous world event and then return to an unchanged and slow-moving village like Cuba.

In this first photograph we see Jesús Gutierrez standing to the left of his brother Frank, both in full uniform. Next to them in the front row is Guadalupe Montoya. Behind these three men, on the left, are Eduvigen Gurulé and his brother, Abenicio. These five men were all from La Jara. A question that arises is whether the three men in civilian clothes were saying farewell to their Gutierrez friends or welcoming them back after their service. A further question one might ask is why it was important to have their picture taken with the two soldiers. This is a question that will arise again later in this article.

This photograph also holds local historical importance because it is the only evidence we have that Jesús Gutierrez was among the local men who served their country in World War I. Were this photograph not carefully labeled and preserved, he would likely not have been included in our roster of World War I veterans. Keep in mind that many of these young men were likely monolingual Spanish speakers and probably were not highly literate. Was the motivation to volunteer purely economic? Was this an opportunity to move beyond the sheep camps, as mentioned earlier, or could these young men have been among the most adventurous of our recent ancestors? Did the fact that they were going off to faraway places with strange-sounding names give these men status beyond anything they could have gotten here? Is this why those left behind wanted to have their pictures taken with these proud, sharp-looking young men?

This last question leads us right into looking at the other photograph, which offers us yet another wonderful story related to Cuba's World War I veterans. This photograph is not what you are probably thinking it is at first glance. This is not a photograph of a bride and her handsome groom. In fact, it is a picture of a bride, Delfina Lucero Montoya, on her wedding day, with her cousin, World War I veteran Fidencio Olivas Sr.

According to Olivas family sources (pers. comm.), *Don* Fidencio had just returned from the military when *Doña* Delfina's wedding to *Don* Miguel Montoya occurred. Being family and being single, *Don* Fidencio went to the wedding. While at the wedding feast, the bride, *Doña* Delfina, insisted on having her picture taken with her dashing, newly returned veteran cousin, *Don* Fidencio.

This photograph, which documents this seemingly casual incident, could well imply how favorably the returning veterans were looked upon by other members of the community. It suggests that these veterans may very well have enjoyed a great deal of prestige and status for having served in the United States Army, short as their service must have been. The United States did not enter World War I until 1917 and the war ended in November of 1918. This limited involvement made service for Cuba's volunteer soldiers somewhat short, but daring enough to give these men status among friends and family far beyond what they might have had before. Furthermore, having served in the war, these men probably had more money than they could ever have earned herding sheep or staying at home.

We know from Herrera family members that *Don* José Leon Herrera came home from the war with a motorcycle, even though he also had an injured knee. In those days following the end of the war, a motorcycle would have been quite a novelty in La Jara. Having such a vehicle would have been quite unlikely except that *Don* José Leon had served in the army where motorcycles were in common use. Imagine also the status that the motorcycle must have given this young man!

In honor and in memory of these courageous volunteer soldiers who enriched our lives with the tales of their adventures, here are their names. May we always remember them with pride and a smile for what they contributed to the history of our beloved Cuba.

Complete list:

Raphael Archibeque

Frank Archuleta

Elias Casaus*

Manuel Casaus*

Frank Chavez

Romolo Chavez

Jacobo de Herrera

Requel de Herrera

Holly Dobbs

Elizardo Gallegos

Manuel Gallegos

Frank Gutierrez

Jesús Gutierrez

José Leon Herrera

Celestino Jacquez

Genovevo Jacquez

Abel Lobato

Candido Lovato

Francisco Lovato

Toribio Martinez

Hijinio McCoy

Alfredo Montoya

Daniel Montoya

Fidencio Olivas Sr.

Esequiel Padilla, Sr.

Jack Parsons

Howard Read

Kenneth Read

Leslie Read

Amado Romero

Ambrosio Segura

Carmel Segura

*According to *Don* Elias Casados' son (pers. comm.), both his name and his cousin Manuel's is shown as "Casados" on their military records. The name is now spelled Casaus.

Los Jareños. Jesús and Frank Gutierrez in uniform with their friends Guadalupe Montoya and Eduvigen and Abenicio Gurulé. Courtesy of Frances Chavez Santillanes.

Don **Fidencio Olivas, Sr., pictured with his cousin Delfina Lucero Montoya
on her wedding day.**

Registros de Dos Caballeros
Histories of Two Gentlemen

Nuestra Gente de Antes worked, lived and died on this land, as we do today. Yet, in most cases, they have done so leaving little, if any, evidence of their contributions to our community.

A few families have, among their photographs, and other memorabilia, recorded dates of births and deaths of those who came before us. In rare exceptions to this brief documentation of life as it was in the past, there have been a few journals or notebooks containing more detailed accounts of what seemed important to some individuals.

Part of a copy of a journal written by *Don* Manuel Reyes Lucero has been made available to me.(Lucero, 1914) Given its small size of three by five inches and its plain black cover, this meticulously written source could easily have been lost forever. This would have been a real tragedy, given that it contains a lot of information relevant to the history of this man's family, as well as to the history of Cuba.

This thin, tiny ledger-ruled book was copied from *Don* Manuel Reyes Lucero's journal by one of his six daughters. This daughter did so on the eve of her departure to a Catholic convent in Wisconsin on April 13, 1914, in order to take it with her. The *Registro de Manuel Reyes Lucero* had been started January 23, 1909. Written in Spanish, the gentleman states that the purpose of this *Registro* (account) is to inform his family and lineage, if they ever cared to know his genealogy and who he was as a person, they would have this from him.

Early on in the account, *Don* Manuel Reyes states that he had taken every opportunity open to him to get an education which, given his professional record, must have paid off very well. In 1884, he became *maestro de escuelas en el distrito numero 6* (Director of schools in district number 6), which included Cuba. He established a school here in Cuba and was a teacher for eleven years. He has a list of pupils whom he apparently boarded during the school term at no expense to the students' families. The list of students consists of four boys and two girls. This does not seem like many children to be responsible for except that he and his wife had six female children of their own and three adopted boys. One of these boys was his wife's nephew, Eudoro Montoya, who came to live with them in 1903, after Eudoro's mother died.

Shortly before 1900, *Don* Manuel became aware that the United States government was going to conduct a census of the territory so he applied for a job, passed the exam and was certified at third level to help with the census. He rather proudly states that, having been certified, he went to work for the U.S. government at the rate of $5.00 per day.

In addition to being a teacher, *Don* Manuel Reyes lists his public service separately and states that he had served as a *deputado* (deputy officer). He also served as *Alguacil Mayor* (Constable) in Bernalillo County before Sandoval County was separated from Bernalillo County and for two more years in Rio Arriba County. For another four years, he was *Juez de Paz* (Justice of the Peace). In addition to all this, after Sandoval County had been defined in 1903, *Señor* Lucero ran for the office of *Juez de Pruebas* (a judge delegated to conduct judicial proceedings on behalf of a superior), was unopposed and was elected by all who voted in Sandoval County.

Without a doubt, *Don* Manuel Reyes Lucero was a remarkable man in what he calls his public service but as well in his generosity to the youth in his community. He was also a very religious man and states that, by the age of thirteen, he had become a member of *La Santa Cofradía de Nuestro Padre Jesús* (a branch of the order of *Penitentes*) and states that this was his life-long avocation. Yet, people in Cuba today have little knowledge of this man as a public servant, as a teacher or as a member of a large, extended family.

The little copy of *Don* Manuel's journal stops suddenly where the pages were cut out for reasons unknown. There is only one further piece of written evidence that shows he was still alive in 1918, when he would have been only fifty-six years old. This evidence is in the form of a small, single piece of paper which he wrote to document the death of his oldest daughter, Leonor. With the same careful order the journal reflects, he writes that day's date, the place, his daughter's full name, the date of her birth and the exact hour of her death.

Today, all that is left of the legacy of this seemingly bright, ambitious, sincere and hard-working man is a small remnant of the ruin of the house he built for the large family he had been responsible for. Was the house big? Was there more than one building? What happened to the part that is now missing? It appears that everyone there had taken for granted everything that *Don* Manuel had built for all of them. Except for him, no one else seems to have made any notes anywhere related to a house or land where so much occurred because of one man's energy and dedication.

In addition to the Lucero journal just described, there is a fifty-page monograph about Mr. Aron "Augustin" Eichwald, titled *Don Augustin*. (Eichwald, no date) This small book was written by his son, Alex H. Eichwald and was published in the early 1990s. This family history contains many details about Cuba and the people here during Mr. Eichwald's active life as a merchant, rancher and influential political figure.

For instance, this Eichwald account contains the names of the major sheep and cattle ranchers from this area. As well, it describes the sheep and cattle herds as containing up to thousands of animals. This alone reinforces the stories of the wealth that existed here in livestock prior to the 1920s. Conversely, it also illustrates the people's dependence on this particular source of livelihood. There is information about the Eichwalds' General Store and the many local people who were employed by Mr. Eichwald in his various business ventures. In addition, this book contains information about other business families in Cuba such as Mr. John F. Young, Mr. H. L. Weise, and *Don* J. J. Salazar and Sons. These accounts extend from one of the earliest merchants, *Don* Epimenio Miera, to one of the later entrants, Mr. Eric Freelove. As well, there are many interesting photographs in this book. A couple of these are of particular interest in that they show Main Street in Cuba in the early 1900s.

Again, as with *Don* Manuel Reyes Lucero, *Don* Aron (Augustin) Eichwald was a remarkable man who contributed greatly to his community. Yet, both of these accounts provide only a bird's eye view of the history of the community as it relates to these two families and their associates. The Lucero account was written in 1914 and the Eichwald monograph was written in the 1990s and there seems to be little else in the way of written history available about our community.

It seems to me that the history of Cuba is on the brink of being lost unless, together, we start an urgent campaign toward systematically documenting and saving what still remains in the scattered written notes, legal documents and letters still stored in the shoe boxes and grandmothers' trunks. Otherwise, our history will remain in its current oral history form or worse, someone else will fall out of the sky on a moonless night and write our history for us. This is especially likely because there are now so few of us left who recall some of the people and the contributions they have made to our community.

Señor **Manuel Reyes Lucero. The boy on the horse next to** *Señor* **Lucero is believed to be Eudoro Montoya. The other boys are more than likely some of** *Señor* **Lucero's students.**

La Estafeta de Antes
The Early Post Office

La Estafeta de antes is locally significant for several reasons. In 1887, when the United States Post Office was established in our settlement, its Spanish name, *San Joaquin del Nacimiento* was changed to the present-day name of Cuba. Originally, *San Joaquin del Nacimiento* was the name of the land grant from the king of Spain in 1769 extending from modern-day Regina to La Ventana.

This grant included the area that became Cuba. Cuba means "cask" or "barrel" if it is closed. It also means a "vat" or a "tub" if it is open. A *cubeta* is a bucket. It can also be a "trough." It has been said by our elders that back when we used to have heavy runoff during the spring thaw the water would accumulate in the low areas between what is now Cubita and the higher ground to the east. This *cuba*, or trough, and the wetlands that surrounded the trough, were probably what some unknown official decided would be an appropriate name for our settlement. Thus, *San Joaquin del Nacimiento* became Cuba. Although the name was officially changed in 1887 and we did get a post office then, for many years following the change, people here continued to refer to this place as Nacimiento.

La estafeta de antes is of further significance because the word itself is one of the archaic Spanish words that people here have hung onto tenaciously to this day. A Spanish-speaker using the word *estafeta* instead of *oficina de correos* (post office) is surely someone from this area or some other part of northern New Mexico. Other people in the Spanish-speaking world simply don't use this word any longer.

The definition of the word *estafeta,* as it has been used here traditionally, is actually quite accurate, meaning "branch or rural post office." Originally, it also referred to a place to which ordinary mail was delivered by a rider on horseback. Apparently the local population never got beyond "the rider on horseback." Interestingly, there are good reasons for this that give credence to the term's true meaning and which will be noted later in this article.

According to material provided from the Post Office files, (U.S. Post Office, no date) the Post Office was established on March 9, 1887. In accordance with the law, a Mr. James Price had been selected as the first postmaster of Cuba. We know nothing about Mr. Price, except that he must have been able to read and write in order to fulfill the responsibilities of the job. Mr. Price served in this capacity until May 12, 1888, when he was replaced by a Mr. James R. Smith, who served for exactly a year. Following Mr. Smith, Mr. Aron Eichwald became postmaster and also served for just one year. Mr. Eichwald left the post office in May of 1889 but his family continues to live in Cuba today. A complete list of postmasters is included at the end of this article.

During these early years of having a post office, the mail that came to Cuba and surrounding areas was picked up at Cabezon. In those days, Cabezon was also known as La Posta. In Spanish, *la posta* refers to a place where the next team of horses was kept and made ready for wagons or riders going along the next stretch of road to deliver the mail. Thus, Cabezon was where the exchange of horses took place before proceeding to Cuba. In this time, the term *estafeta,* meaning mail delivered by a rider on horseback, was really quite appropriate.

The first team of horses carrying the mail would have started out in Corrales, where the mail was brought across the river from the stage coach station in Albuquerque. Since this was before any bridge was built across the Rio Grande, there would be no mail delivery during the spring runoff when the river was too high to ford near Corrales.

Having reached La Posta on good days, the mail would then be put on a small buggy with very high wheels so as to maneuver through the rough, muddy terrain. Such a buggy was also necessary in winter to drive through deep snow drifts. This buggy was also part of the stage service provided to the infrequent travelers to Cuba and neighboring settlements. From La Posta the mail did not come directly to Cuba. The mail buggy first went to San Luis. From San Luis it went across La Vega de la China east to San Pablo, Copar and Señorito. For a time mail was also left at the *estafeta* in Señorito for people who worked, lived and wintered in the mountains. That mail then went to an *estafeta* at Rio de las Vacas. From

Señorito, the mail would finally come down to Cuba, arriving late in the day, weather permitting, or late at night if the road conditions and weather were particularly bad. According to postal records, by 1910 the Cuba route was changed to originate in Bernalillo. By then, automobiles were used on the routes when road conditions permitted.

As you look back at the list of postmasters that follows and their dates of appointment, you will notice that, with few exceptions, these earliest people served for only a year or perhaps even less. However, between 1896 and 1902, *Don* Manuel Martinez served as postmaster for a period of six years. *Don* Manuel was a member of a long-time Cuba family and many of his descendants still live here. Following *Don* Manuel's term, three other people served as postmaster before the end of 1902. This seems interesting since there must have been some status related to this position as well as a steady paycheck from the government.

In 1915, Bessie L. Young became postmistress and served in this position until 1934. She and her husband John also founded Young's Hotel and started what became the Hernandez sawmill in Cubita. It was also in 1915 that the mail to Cuba was brought directly from Albuquerque. In 1935, Robert F. (Pete) Fisher became postmaster and he and his wife, Esther (Betty) Fisher ran *la estafeta de Cuba* for thirty-eight years. Their names became synonymous with *la estafeta*. They ran the Cuba *estafeta* with the consistency and dependability of the British railroad system and with much kindness. Apparently these people never took a vacation or closed the post office, except on Sundays, Christmas and Thanksgiving. The Fishers held letters and packages for people for months, helped address envelopes, helped children learn the combinations for the family mail boxes and made sure the baby chicks people had ordered by mail didn't die before the farmers arrived to pick them up. Looking back on Mr. and Mrs. Fishers' thirty-eight years of association with the community, they must have known people from childhood into adulthood or from adulthood into old age for at least two generations. Imagine the stories they could have told about all of us who grew up in the *antes* period with Pete Fisher at the helm of the Cuba Post Office.

In 1960, the very young Fabiola Atkinson went to work for Mr.

and Mrs. Fisher until Mr. Fisher retired. At that time, Mrs. Atkinson was appointed acting postmistress on July 3, 1968. She served over two years in that position and was then appointed postmistress on November 28, 1970. As is sometimes said, "The rest is history." Fabiola retired in 1998 after serving this community and surrounding areas with extraordinary dedication and friendship for nearly thirty years. Along with the rest of her staff, she always had a cheerful smile, no matter how much mail needed to be moved.

After Mrs. Atkinson's retirement, the postmaster's position went to another local person, Bernie Martinez. Bernie and his staff have served the community with dedication and a great sense of humor. As of this writing, Mr. Martinez has recently retired after ten years of service. During Mr. Martinez' tenure as postmaster, one of the most important services our local *estafeta* has come to provide for us is passport application and processing. Try to imagine anyone here back in 1887 even dreaming of having a passport! Today, anyone in Cuba or surrounding areas needing or wanting a passport can apply right here in our very own *estafeta*.

Following is a list of all the postmasters in Cuba and their appointment dates from 1887 to the present:

POSTMASTER	APPOINTMENT DATE
James Price	March 9, 1887
James R. Smith	May 12, 1888
Aron Eichwald	May 29, 1889
James B. Frans	April 3, 1893
James H. Matthews	September 1, 1893
Juan Jose Salazar	February 14, 1895
Paulin Montoya	October 15, 1895
Manuel Martinez	June 1, 1896
Oliver P. Hovey	May 5, 1902
Marino Cordova	August 15, 1902
Trinidad Vigil	November 5, 1902
Florencio Sandoval	March 22, 1904
Trinidad J. de Miera	October 12, 1907

Bernard Dannenbaum	February 7, 1908
Celso Sandoval	September 8, 1908
Telesfor Sandoval	October 19, 1910
Leonor Montoya	January 14, 1911
Franc M. Buin	August 20, 1912
Leonor Montoya	February 11, 1914
Bessie L. Young	March 16, 1915
Fernando Vigil (acting)	July 5, 1934
Robert F. Fisher	May 23, 1935
Fabiola Atkinson	July 3, 1968
Bernie Martinez	January 18, 1998 to March 31, 2009

**Postmaster Mr. Robert (Pete) Fisher standing in front of an early Cuba Post Office.
Courtesy of Larry Fisher and Flora Lopez.**

No Teníanos Electricidad
Life Before Electricity

Antes, we did not have electricity in Cuba. It might be appropriate to remind people of how we lived without this service that is now taken for granted. There were no street lights along our roads and byways and our homes were dimly illuminated by kerosene lamps. Prior to the lamps, our homes were lighted only by tallow candles or the warm, soft flames of wood burning in an adobe fireplace in the corner of a room. This was a time when there were no night-lights glowing to keep a person from bumping into the furniture or the door frames should one have to make his or her way to the outhouse in the middle of the night, tend a crying child or simply find out what the dog was barking about.

Electricity is one of the post-World-War II modern conveniences that came to us rather slowly in the mid-twentieth century. As essential as electricity has become for lighting homes and ranch buildings, lighting seems minor as compared to some of the other hardships people here endured without electricity. For instance, consider doing the family laundry in a tub half filled with hot water, a washboard and a bar of home-made lye soap. This job alone in a big family with babies in cloth diapers was an arduous and continuous chore, a chore done primarily by women and young girls. These same women also did all the other household chores women were expected to do, *antes.*

Around here, water was always in short supply. The water for the laundry would have to be hauled by hand from the river, a well or a cistern. It was then heated, usually outdoors, and while still hot was used for the first wash. Following the soap wash, there was at least one rinsing. Compared to the scrubbing on the washboard, rinsing and wringing clothes was considered the easier part of the job. Wringing clothes out by hand is a truly difficult task requiring strength in the hands, wrists, arms and back, especially since many of the wet pieces being wrung out would have been large and/or heavy. Today, this back-breaking task is easily accomplished during the rinse and spin cycles in our automatic (electric) washing machines. Now, all this formerly unpleasant effort goes unnoticed by almost everyone.

Prior to having electric washing machine there were, in the early to mid-twentieth century, gasoline powered washers which some people here used. These washers were noisy, they were not automatic and they still had to be filled by hand. Whatever their disadvantages, these machines were a great improvement over the washboard and the tub. These washers had two roller wringers to squeeze the water out of each piece of laundry as it was fed through the wringers. As convenient as these washers were at the time, people were frequently injured by getting their hands, hair or other body parts caught in the rollers.

A modern reader, likely never having washed clothes by hand, may not fully appreciate the importance of an automatic electric washing machine, or having electric outlets throughout the house, inside and out. Let us return to *antes*, that time when there were perhaps no more than two kerosene lamps per household here in Cuba. It is the middle of winter, late in the day and very cold. By now every man, woman and child would have done all their outdoor chores. At any moment now, the sun would drop down behind Cuba Mesa like an anchor and it would be dark.

One of the family's kerosene lamps would have been lit in the kitchen to allow dinner to be prepared. This was also where the family usually gathered around the table to eat and to stay warm. Following dinner, the family would remain in the warm kitchen to converse and relate their day's activities while the children played. This would also be the place where, under the dim light of the kerosene lamp, any reading, letter-writing or homework would be done. In winter, when there was *piñon* available, it would be roasted in the oven and there would be stories told, or adult family members and children might take part in a guessing game called, *Pares, o nones* (Odd or even numbers), using the piñon as the prize for the person who guessed correctly. At the end of the game, the person with the most piñon would be considered the winner.

No other part of the house would have light. The food, if any was left over, would have been put away. Recall, there was no refrigeration other than the fast-falling temperature outdoors. The dishes would have been washed and preparations for the next day's breakfast would have been taken care of. Grandmother would then begin her summons for everyone to pray at the family altar. A candle would be lit at the altar and the lamp moved into the room where the altar was located. The family would pray, on their knees, and following the prayers, the fire would be stoked up, the lamp blown out and everyone would go to bed.

Houses here were not large. A big house would have been difficult to heat. There were few windows and those would very likely be covered up to keep the house warm. Several children would likely sleep on the floor where, as the fire died down, it would become colder. There were no electric thermostats or central heating to keep houses warm during the night. In homes where there was a pot-bellied stove in the sleeping area, an effort was made to keep the fire burning through the night. This meant an adult would have to get up in the dark to add fuel to the fire. Where fires were not kept up, it was not unusual for families to get up in the morning to find the water in the kitchen buckets frozen. Early morning temperatures in Cuba frequently drop well below zero in the winter. Building a fire as early as possible in the morning would be essential to starting the day with a hot cup of coffee and some warm food.

Before electricity was brought to Cuba, keeping lamps lit and fires going presented tremendous financial as well as physical challenges. Although kerosene may not seem expensive to us now, it was a considerable burden then. Even at prices between ten and fifteen cents per gallon, this expense was a hardship for most families. They had to purchase kerosene year round, but especially between October and May. Every family had either a two-gallon or one-gallon *aceitera* (kerosene oil can with a spout on it) from which the lamps were filled every day. This was one of those chores that could not be neglected or taken lightly. The lamp was filled, the wick trimmed and the fragile chimney was washed, dried and made ready for the evening: y *no lo permita Dios* (and Heaven forbid) that the chimney be broken, especially due to carelessness. Even though a lamp chimney might only cost fifteen cents, this was fifteen cents people here did not have: they would have to do without something else in order to replace the broken chimney.

Gathering, cutting and splitting firewood to keep the stoves and fireplaces going year-round was a major undertaking. All the wood was cut by hand, either with a two-man saw or an axe. The wood was then hauled on a horse-drawn wagon and split with an axe. The kitchen stove had to be kept going summer and winter in order to have cooked food. There was also the matter of heating water for laundry and other household chores and for bathing.

Bringing electricity into rural homes across America has been one of the most significant improvements ever in the day-to-day lives of millions of people. The impact of electricity was far more significant than just being able to turn lights on and off. Electricity in a home actually liberated individuals and allowed them to do other things. For example, with electricity, the family member who had formerly stayed home all day to tend the wood-burning stove to cook meals could now do other things. The individuals responsible for the continuous wood-cutting and splitting were now available to perform other chores. With an electric iron, the person who ironed the clothes with heavy irons (heated on top of the wood stove) could now do the ironing in another room where it might be more comfortable, and ironing itself was made easier. For the women doing the laundry, the electric washing machine not only liberated them from the heavy labor but probably helped extend their lives and keep them healthier.

As liberating as electricity was in the areas of labor-saving appliances, it was in the area of refrigeration that the greatest benefits occurred. With electric home refrigerators, food storage for the average family was revolutionized. Milk and meat products could be stored safely and used more efficiently over longer periods of time. People could now grow and store more fruits and vegetables, resulting in more variety and overall healthier diets. With a home freezer, meat could be stored safely for long periods of time and ice could be made for the sheer pleasure of having a cold drink.

Yet the electrification of rural America is only about eighty years old. The March 2008 issue of *Enchantment* magazine marked the 75th anniversary of the New Deal Program of 1933 under President Franklin

D. Roosevelt. The Rural Electrification Act of 1936 is what really benefitted New Mexico. This piece of legislation provided the funding for electrical distribution systems in rural areas. This then paved the way for the sixteen rural electric cooperatives that now serve New Mexico, including our very own Jemez Mountain Electric Cooperative.

Although the rural electrification project started before World War II, electricity was slow in coming to Cuba. After the World War II, there were a few people in the Jemez Valley area, such as Mr. Fred Abousleman, his brother and *Don* J. Antonio Montoya, who pursued their dream of bringing electric power into their homes. What these men wanted to accomplish was what they had seen all over Europe, especially in Germany, when they were serving in the American military. They saw that where there were fast-moving streams, such as the Jemez River, electricity could be generated. That plan worked for a while but bigger and better methods soon became available. Finally, in 1948, people from Jemez Valley, San Ysidro and Cuba incorporated our electric cooperative. People from Cuba were able to sign up for membership in the Cooperative for $5.00 per household. Following all of the usual red tape, and legalities, work on the power lines into Cuba finally began and the dream came into fruition.

The first representatives from the Cuba area on the eleven-member board of directors of the Jemez Mountain Electric Cooperative were Mr. Eric Freelove, Mr. Walter Hernandez, Mr. Rudy Velarde and Don Epifanio Gutierrez.

This evening, as you walk into your nice warm house and turn your light switch on, knowing your kitchen lights will go on (not just one bare bulb, as was the case originally), and perhaps you unplug the slow cooker full of your freshly cooked dinner, you might just want to say, "thank you." Thanks to those who came before us and who participated in this cooperative effort without pay and on their own time, so we can now live a far brighter and more comfortable life than they ever dreamed possible during their *antes:* a time when our kerosene lamps barely illuminated the area around our tiny kitchen tables during cold winter nights.

No Había Buenos Caminos
There weren't any Good Roads

We know that *antes*, there were many *veredas* (foot paths) and later donkey paths and horse trails. We also know there were old, narrow wagon roads. These first roads had followed the earlier *veredas* and successfully brought the ancient *carretas* (two-wheeled carts or wagons made almost entirely of wood and leather, drawn by two oxen) into northern New Mexico. These crude *carretas* had been loaded with the essential tools and supplies for settlement during *Don* Juan de Oñate's expedition in 1598. Again, nearly a century later in 1692, *Don* Diego de Vargas, using the same corridors his predecessors had used along the Rio Grande, arrived in Santa Fé. This expedition contained so many horses, cattle, sheep, *carretas* and people that it left a permanent mark on the landscape. Yet, the roads were no better than they had been before.

Despite the lack of good roads, by the mid-1700s, outposts and small settlements had been established as far north as Abiquiu. By the 1770s, settlers had also moved westward along the Rio Puerco and into the Mount Taylor area.

Miraculously, these settlers, *nuestra gente* (our people), had carved out these narrow, rutted, bumpy and frequently muddy paths through mountain passes at the feet of the mesas and around the deepest arroyos to find water and a place to live. What this meant though, was that once settled in these places, most people didn't go anywhere. When they did travel, with few exceptions, they didn't go very far away from home because there were so few roads.

As American influence increased during the nineteenth century, better wagons were brought over the Santa Fé Trail. Although the wagons were better, the wagon roads were not. During the territorial period in New Mexico an effort was made to connect the remote and isolated Hispanic settlements with the mining camps which had sprung up around mineral resources. There were also homestead villages, cow towns and later railroad towns that people wanted to get to. However, there were still very few roads. As old and narrow as these few roads were, an elaborate system of buckboard and overland stagecoach companies evolved to move people, goods and mail into these communities. One of these regional systems had a line that went from San Ysidro, New Mexico to Durango, Colorado with a stage stop in Cuba. This line essentially followed the same route that became our current highways.

There was a network in northern New Mexico of what were called main wagon roads. People here could use one of these main wagon roads to get to Bernalillo. This wagon road would have taken them to Guadalupe, in the Cabezon area, across to San Ysidro and then down into Bernalillo and Albuquerque. This was also one of the routes the local *fleteros* (freight haulers) took to bring trade goods up to Cuba and to take locally produced wool and grain down to Bernalillo and Albuquerque to process and sell. As essential as these roads were and even though they were recognized by the authorities, there had been no further improvements done on them since they were established. The ruts had become clearer and deeper and the roads were virtually impassable during rainy weather.

By 1940, State Highway 44 was actually black-topped from Bernalillo to Cuba. However, this improvement ended at Cuba and from here northward the road was still only graveled or just dirt. Yet this narrow, undivided and unmarked road was the best thoroughfare for miles and miles around Cuba.

Here in town people simply walked, rode a horse or donkey or transported goods on heavy horse-drawn wagons. These wagons were used when they could get up and down the so-called roads. For instance, getting from Cuba to Los Pinos, only about five miles away, was a real challenge. According to WPA (Works Progress Administration) records(Meltzer, no date), the road from Cuba to Los Pinos was not built until August of 1938 and was not paved until the 1980s.

A woman who used to live in the Los Pinos area related that in the late 1930s she, her mother and her little sister had walked to church on First Holy Communion Sunday in mud so thick and deep that they could barely keep their overshoes on. However, the devout mother was determined to get the little sister to church on time so she could make her First Holy

Communion. In the really muddy parts of this journey, the mother and the older sister would carry the first communicant in order to keep her white dress and shoes from getting totally ruined.

Since First Holy Communion is usually in the spring of the year, the irrigation ditches would have been running high and spilling over and the spring thaw might have been at its peak. Since most of the side roads in Cuba were along ditches, the situation this informant related would not have been unusual on any of the roads around town.

Antes, fences in Cuba were not quite as formidable as they are today and people felt comfortable taking the shortest route possible to get from one place to another. Walking across other people's fields was not considered trespassing and, since everyone knew each other, the owners also knew why their neighbors were *iban por aqui derecho* (taking the most direct path). Otherwise, the neighbor would have had to take the long way around the field just to get home.

A family that lived off of *el camino de la sierra* (the road to the mountains east of Cuba) had relatives in Las Lagunitas, located west of what is now Cuba and on the other side of the river. who they liked to visit. This family, with all the children in tow, would get up early in the morning and walk westward along the Rito de Leche irrigation ditch all the way to what is now the highway. There the ditch veered slightly southward but the family would stay along the ditch and, at the Rio Puerco, walk on the *canoas* (flues or troughs) that carried the irrigation water over the river and into fields on the other side. By then, the travelers would be on their relatives' land. They would then walk across those fields until they got to the houses that were up against the mesa and arrive just about lunch time, when the happy reunion would begin.

Beside the *canoas,* there were also planks and logs up and down the river where people could cross from one side to the other without having to go to the bridge. Up until the early 1930s, the only bridge crossing the Rio Puerco in Cuba was at the extreme north end of town. This used to be a part of the main road to Farmington. Sometime in the late 1930s the bridge and the road were moved to their present location. Later, probably in the late 1950s, the old bridge was replaced with the current structure. Shortly after

World War II, in about 1946, Highway 44 was paved and widened slightly but none of the side roads were paved until much later.

There is no doubt that the lack of passable roads in and around Cuba affected life in the entire area. First of all, there was the isolation. People were simply not able to get from one place to another. Secondly, in such isolation, there developed a limited world view. Since travel was so restricted, there was no opportunity to meet different kinds of people, experience different types of foods or have an exchange of ideas with people of differing points of view.

Education also was restricted and frequently narrow in perspective. Many one-room schools became necessary in this area because the roads were so poor that children could not be transported to and from a centrally located school safely. Instead, the teachers, who worked for a county school system, were assigned to the schools in Vallecito de Los Pinos, Nacimiento, Vallecito de los Martinez, Las Lagunitas and even as far away as La Jara, Guadalupe or San Luis. The teachers were then expected to travel to their assigned schools or to board with a family living in one of these settlements. Students now travel as much as eighty miles each morning and afternoon to reach the public schools in Cuba.

Mrs. Angelita Olivas (pers. comm.), a teacher who taught in this area for over forty years related that early in her career she had been assigned to teach in Vallecito de Los Pinos. (This old school is still standing but not in use.) Mrs. Olivas liked the assignment, except she lived in La Jara and there was no road between La Jara and Los Pinos, a distance of about six miles. In good weather, she was able to ride a horse over the hill from La Jara to Los Pinos each day. Luckily for her, her uncle Frank Gutierrez lived in Los Pinos. During the winter, when the snow was deep, the uncle would wait for her at the top of the hill on horseback. By then, he would have cleared a path through the snow for her horse so she could get down to the school house. They would ride to the school house together and then he would take her horse to his house until school was out. In truly inclement weather, Mrs. Olivas would simply stay with her Uncle Frank and Aunt Lydia until she could ride back over the hill to La Jara. Today, there is still no road between these two settlements without coming into Cuba.

Eventually there were three major occurrences that helped end the isolation and open windows onto the world beyond Cuba. One was the establishment of the U.S. Post Office in 1887. (This is also the time at which the name of the community was changed from Nacimiento to Cuba.) One of the justifications for the regional overland stagecoaches was to deliver the mail to isolated and remote settlements such as Cuba. The many advantages that regular mail service brought to the people of the area are yet another story.

The second thing that widened the world view of the local citizens was the mail-order catalogs. The impact Montgomery Ward's and Sears Roebuck Companies had on our communities, *sin buenos caminos*, is legendary and again another tale to tell.

Finally, the coming of regular bus service to Cuba in 1936 gave people the opportunity to travel, conduct business out of town or simply go visit relatives. The bus also brought the mail and packages from far away and, very importantly, it brought newspapers regularly. Young's Hotel faithfully served as bus depot and lunch stop for passengers. All the while dear Harriet Young Hernandez, who ran the depot for over sixty years, would try to answer as many questions as she could for those of us who were prospective travelers but were unaccustomed to travelling anywhere beyond La Ventana, much less travelling on a bus. A further advantage was that the people who rode these buses and happened to stop here in Cuba also provided the opportunity for our community to become acquainted with people different from ourselves.

Until our two-lane State Highway 44 became our modern four-lane Highway 550, *no había buenos caminos* but "Old 44" did bring a slightly wider view of the world into our otherwise remote homes, as it does even today.

5

~ Children Growing up in Cuba ~

Había Respeto, Caridad y Hermandad
Respect, Charity and Brotherhood

In the middle to late nineteenth century and through the early part of the twentieth century when writers, artists and other outsiders started filtering into our isolated Spanish-speaking communities, many of these strangers found our community bonding and caring so extraordinary they started referring to us northern New Mexicans as *los manitos*. This comes from a diminutive of the word *hermano/a* as *hermanito/a*, among children evolving into *'manito*.

It appears that the name arose from these newcomers continuously seeing a slightly older child affectionately caring for a younger child or several children. The strangers would ask, "And who is this little one?" The answer was always the same, *"Es mi 'manito/a."* (This is my little brother or my little sister.) And thus the name for northern New Mexicans came to be *los manitos*, a name that says a great deal about how, *antes*, we obviously and openly cared for each other as one would care for a little brother or sister. What the immigrants had witnessed was our *hermandad* at its most basic, grassroots level.

Antes, children growing up in Cuba were taught from infancy who our relatives were, what their names were and what their relationship to each of us was. We were never allowed to call a *Tío* (uncle) a *Primo* (cousin) and in most families we knew "unto the seventh generation" what our elders' names were and whether they belonged in our father's linage or our mother's. Also, because our communities have been so stable and interrelated, second and third cousins were recognized with the same affection as brothers and sisters and first cousins.

Name recognition and relationship of all the members of our large extended families were, in modern terms, hard wired into us from early childhood. Our very survival might well depend on knowing who we were and where each of us belonged in these families. The following example shows that there can be good reasons for children knowing this information.

When my father, Ruben Cordova, was only eight years old, his mother died in the influenza epidemic of 1918. From then on, my father and his two younger sisters lived among relatives who would or could take them in, both here in Cuba and in Gallina. My father lived in this manner until the age of 12 when he was sent away to Menaul School in Albuquerque, then a boarding school for boys. His younger sisters, on the other hand, remained with various relatives until they became adults. However sad this might seem, their situation was not unique. Following the influenza epidemic of 1918, there were dozens of children who were left with only one parent or were orphaned and were raised by members of their extended families, in most cases with genuine affection and love. This was *hermandad y caridad.*

In addition to the strong bonding required of children within our families, we were also taught that any adult, whether related or not, was to be treated with respect at all times. A child was never allowed to address an adult by the informal *tú* form of the address for "you," but always by the formal form of *usted.* All adult males, when referred to were *Don,* and all adult females were referred to as *Doña.* These are Spanish titles used before Christian names, such as *Doña Maria* or *Don Manuel.* This matter of respect for our elders was another survival mechanism built into our society and was taken very seriously by all members of our community. After all, who would want to take in a child who was either disrespectful to their elders or was disobedient. No one could afford to tolerate such behavior. A disrespectful child was said to be *mal criado,* badly or poorly raised or ill bred. Such behavior was not only bad for the child but reflected badly on the entire family.

Antes, there were many local customs and practices which demonstrated both respect for our elders and taught discipline to the children as well. In turn, the children were rewarded with mutual respect and abundant affection.

Our godparents too, whether they were related to us or not, were always referred to as our *padrinos* (godfathers) and our *madrinas* (godmothers). These people were chosen with great care and consideration since, in our parents' absence due to death or crisis, they were the most likely to assume the role of our parents and look after their godchildren. In reality, this was yet another layer in our safety net in what was then a harsh and unforgiving environment.

Antes, in many families, given names and *nombres de pila* (baptismal names) were handed down for generations as a way to honor and respect those who had come before us. Along with many of these names being passed down, so was the mythology related to the name and the question of who or how new members of the family would inherit the honored names.

Several years ago, while attending a family gathering, I became aware that some of my city cousins did not recognize the guest of honor, our aunt, by her proper given name, Eloida Dolores Cordova. These cousins had only known our aunt by her modern Anglicized name of Lois.

If my city relatives had known our family history as it was taught in earlier times, they would have known that our aunt was named after an older half-sister who had died in childhood and after our great-grandmother, *Doña* Dolores Jaquez Cordova, the wife of *Don* Pasqual Cordova. The names Eloida, Dolores and Pasqual show up again and again both before and after the naming of my aunt. This pattern also exists in many other families throughout Northern New Mexico. Without the history and mythology, our ancestral names become as meaningless as they were to my cousins and *el respeto* is lost. In all fairness to my city relatives, they did not grow up in Cuba as I did and they simply did not have the opportunities that I had to learn who we are as an extended family.

Why is knowing about our family histories of interest and importance? I believe our history is our birthright and inheritance. If we squander this inheritance we will never appreciate the social and spiritual treasures we once possessed. Furthermore, our tightly-knit hamlets, *neustras placitas,* with all their safety nets, will no longer exist. These places where we all once knew each other and were all interrelated are our past. If we don't make an effort now to salvage what we still have of this history, soon there will be few people alive who can provide confirmation to who we are or give credence to the historical wealth we have inherited as a community. Furthermore, it is our history that allows us to develop pride in who we are and what will become our children's legacy.

As beautiful as the tales of *los manitos* are, eventually *los manitos* all grew up and many went charging out into the wider world, taking with them *el respeto, la caridad y la hermandad.* Unfortunately, with very few exceptions, these cherished values are not being passed down to subsequent generations.

Nuestros Nombres de Antes
What we were Called in the Past

Our names from *antes* are as archaic as some of the other aspects of the culture of Northern New Mexico and Southern Colorado. Over the last three centuries, these ancient names have so frequently been misspelled, misunderstood or mangled while being transcribed, that it is amazing they have survived at all into recent times. These were, and in some cases still are, the names that were passed down with pride from one generation to the next. This occurred not only here in Cuba but throughout the northern New Mexico's Spanish-speaking populations.

Antes, y mucho mas antes (Earlier, and going back a very long time), we had *nombres de pila* (baptismal names), as well as names given at the time of birth. We also had *sobre nombres* (nick names), abbreviated names and, among the most interesting, names of castigation or rebuke. As well, there are the beloved names of endearment which were so generously bestowed upon us all from infancy and into young adulthood.

So what is in a name, some may ask, indifferent toward this matter. Actually, there is a great deal to consider. The name at birth is the name a child is given by parents according to generally universal custom. In many countries it is a legal requirement, including the filing of a form or certificate of birth or the entry of the name in the baptismal record of the church in which the child was baptized. Even today, there are people who come back to Cuba to search old church records for what is referred as *la fecha de bautizo* (the date of baptism.) For some, this might be the only record that would prove their date and location of birth and their legal name. This was especially true for people born before statehood in 1912 or born in remote areas that ceased to exist as settlements or had their names changed before and during the territorial period in New Mexico.

In those places where births are officially registered, a name is entered onto a birth certificate and becomes a legal name. Given this legality, it is assumed that the name or names from birth, along with the family name, will persist into adulthood. In the normal course of events, this given name becomes a matter of public record.

The exceptions to this so-called normal course of events can at times become complicated. There is, for instance, a person's use of a middle name instead of the first name as written on the birth certificate. Another exception is the use of diminutive forms of a name or a nickname which can become confusing and complicated. There is also the matter of a person's choice of surname if the parents divorce or were not married at the time of the child's birth. In addition, there is the exception of adoption. If the adoption is legal and handled through the courts, lawyers take care of such matters and a new birth certificate is issued. In whatever way these given names come about, in most cultures they are what differentiate each and every one of us from the other members of our families and identify us at a personal level within our communities.

Scholars who have studied New Mexico's *nombres de pila* (baptismal names) acknowledge that many of these names were also commonly used in the rest of the Spanish-speaking world. (Sisneros and Torres 1982, prologue) However, the archaic names have fallen into disuse elsewhere while remaining in common use here. A majority of these names seem to have been taken from Greek or Roman mythology or from the Bible. The *Santoral* (the ecclesiastical calendar of saint's days) also became a traditional source of names. What is important about this information is that these given names were apparently brought to New Mexico during the early colonial period and were handed down over the next three hundred years. Given that the population here was not highly literate, some of the names survived with variations in spelling and pronunciation and very likely with very little understanding of the source or the meaning of the name.

For example, the following were names given to children here in the 1930s: Nimpha or Ninfa for a girl or Apolo for a boy. There are at least four different variations for the name Apolo. A related name, Apolonia, was used as a girl's name. Today, we know that these names were derived from Greek mythology, as are Narciso, Adonias and Nestor. Nestor was used for a girl's name as Nestora or Nestorita. Among the most popular of girl's names was some form of Elena, itself a variation of Helen, the mythical queen of Troy.

There is also a group of names taken from Roman historical figures. Probably foremost here is Augustin, from (Caesar) Augustus, also used as Augustina for girls. Because some Augustinas were little, we also had Augustinitas. Interestingly, the name César (Caesar) was not popular here but Cesárea was a common girls' name. We also had various forms of Claudio for boys but Claudia was not a common name for girls. From the Roman heritage, we had boys named Romolo, Justiniano and Lepido. To this day, Julia and Juliana have been passed down in every possible form. We also have had many Pablos and Pablitas, possibly from the Latin name Paulus but more likely from the Biblical St. Paul.

Biblical names used here for both male and female children are still easily recognized. There have been many boys named Arón, Moisés, Abran, Salomon, Adan or Benjamin. Pascual is not exactly a biblical name as such but comes from the Latin word *Pascha* (*Pascua* in Spanish), meaning Easter. Again, this is a name of ancient origin.

Today many of the biblical names have been anglicized and are spelled differently but are still the same name. A Jacob today possibly had a grandfather or great-grandfather named Jacobo. A young Joshua today comes from a Josué. Elí did not change in spelling but is pronounced differently today. An odd local variation has the biblical name Gabriel pronounced as Grabiél.

Basically the same thing has happened to biblical names for girls. While there have been changes in spelling, we still have Requel, Sara, Ester, Eva, Lea, Isabél, Salomé and Rebeca. The name Maria, which was the most popular biblical name and saint's name among the early New Mexicans, was considered too holy for secular use until the twelfth century. However, following that time the name Maria was commonly used in combination with every other possible name. It might be used as a first name, as in Maria Teresa or as a middle name, as in Teresa Maria. Thus we still have names such as Maria Natividad, Maria de la Encarnación, Maria Ána and Ána Maria. There are literally hundreds of other combinations associated with the name of the Virgin Mary, the mother of Jesus. Interestingly, the name Maria was also used for males in combinations like José Maria or Jesús Maria. Mariano is another name related to Maria. All of these names continue to be popular today.

Back in the 1930s, when people were trying to anglicize their traditional names into more acceptable English names, there was a young boy whose name was José Maria. One day he came out to go to school and announced to his friends that from then on he wished to be called "Joe Mary" and he was known by that name from then on. This change was astonishing to the Anglo kids because they had never heard of a boy called Mary. Most of the other José Marias and Jesús Marias simply became "J. M."

In many cultures the name Jesús was considered holy and therefore it would have been sacrilegious to use it as a given name. In the Spanish-speaking world, the name *Jesús* is used as a baptismal name, sometimes in combinations such as *Jesús Maria* or *Juan de Jesús* for boys or as *Jesusita* (little girl Jesus) for girls.

Traditional male names were often modified to become names for girls. Among the most common feminine variations of male names used locally were, and still are, names like Carlota, Estefanita, Victoria, Felipita, Josefina, Pablita, Antonia, Fidela and Filomena. On the other hand, feminine names were also used for boys. There have been boys named Margarito,

Merced, Aurelio, Erineo, Carmen, Genovevo, Isabél, Ursulo and Requel.

Nicknames and shortened forms of names can often complicate people's lives. It is wise to keep children aware of the source of their abbreviated names. For instance, if a child is called Dora, is she really Dorotea, Isidora or Teodora? Is someone called Fina really Josefina, Delfina or Serafina? How about the ever popular Tinas? Off hand, I can think of at least fourteen possibilities from which Tina could be derived. Among these are Albertina, Florentina, Cristina and Valentina.

Among the more common abbreviated names for both boys and girls is Lupe, a shortened version of *Guadalupe*, the name of the patron saint of Mexico. There are literally hundreds of old names that have been abbreviated, mainly for the convenience of the world beyond Cuba who have to cope with names such as Encarnación or Bernardita. What about a name such as *Plajeres*? Or is it *Prajedes* or maybe *Praxeres*? What did non-Spanish speakers hear when presented with such a name? More importantly, what did they write down, because this often became the official version of that person's name for the rest of their lives?

Along a totally different line, there is a whole category of names of castigation and rebuke used locally. These names were used to let a child or adult know they had stepped outside the limits of acceptable behavior. In practice, use of these names avoided a lot of scolding or punishment. These names simply described levels of misconduct by their nuances. *Soroche* is a name given to a grouchy, ill-tempered person who does not play well with others. This is an old word whose use in this area is unique and has no relationship to the meaning of the word as given in a standard Spanish dictionary. On the other hand, if you refer to someone as *carajo*, you are referring to a mischievous, perhaps impish individual who is also destructive. "*Este carajo* got drunk at the dance last night and couldn't go to work today."

A *vaquetón* is a slightly brazen rascal who is also shameless but not destructive; a sort of daring but good natured person. *Estos vaquetónes se comieron toda la sandía.* (These rascals ate all of the watermelon.) The name *garifo* has a sharp edge to it. This is a pompous, showy person who is skinny and assumed to be physically weak. He would be a know-it-all and probably in some position of authority, such as a teacher, a health provider or even a lawyer. *¿Que sabe ese garifo?* (What does that show-off know?)

A *gachupín* is held in low esteem. This is a Hispanic person who speaks Spanish with a twang or pretends not to speak Spanish at all. In Spanish, a *chancla* is an old, worn out shoe. *Chanclón* (a large, worn shoe) is a name reserved for all sorts of government agents or any uppity law enforcement officer.

The name *mala cacha* is given to members of the family who are cantankerous and a general nuisance within the family. The elders would simply tell other members of the family to leave him or her alone. *"Ese mas mala cacha,* she won't play with you anyway."

Finally, there are the names of endearment, such as *hito* or *hita* (from *hijito (a)*, little son or little daughter). This word is usually preceded by *mi* (my). What is actually said should be *mi hijito/hijita* (my little son/daughter) but actually sounds like *mihito/a* or *mi'ito/a* because the words are fused together. Whatever the case, all children respond to this name and seem to recognize its significance as being very positive.

Antes, mucho mas antes an *abuelito* (grandfather) would come into a house and the children would rush up to greet him and he would gently pinch a child's little nose and say, *"chata narata, narizes de gata"*. *Chata*, meaning flat or pug-nosed, was a playful name of endearment, especially as *mi chata* (my pug-nosed child, with a nose like a cat).

Ancient as our New Mexico *nombres de pila*, names of rebuke and terms of endearment are, there still remain such wonderful stories and history behind each one. Just as an example, we might look at a name like Flavio which actually means yellow hair (blonde). We then have to realize that over the centuries the meaning of the name has become lost. Otherwise, why would parents choose to give a dark-haired child such a name? The answer to this is likely that someone else of high esteem in a previous generation also had that name.

And so, to answer an earlier question, what is in a name? Hopefully, there is a meaning and a history that will enhance the life of the person to whom the name is given.

¿Que Comían Nuestros Niños?
What did our Children Eat?

Antes, children here were constantly reminded to be polite and to mind their manners at all times. Among the most important and earliest lessons learned was that children ate whatever was offered to them or what was served to them. Unlike today, a child's likes and dislikes were not an issue. *Antes,* life here in Cuba was about survival. Therefore, pampering a child or indulging a child's food preferences was looked down upon and considered an injustice to the child. The *viejos,* the *abuelitos* (the old ones, grandparents) did not believe children here had the luxury or the privilege to refuse any kind of well-prepared food, presented with care and kindness, and in many cases, with considerable sacrifice. The result was that children from a very early age ate everything without complaint. Again, this was a community that in those days could still feed itself.

Babies were, in most instances, breast fed while slowly being introduced to table foods. There were no baby foods back then, *ni dinero para comprarla* (nor money with which to buy it). *Atole* (blue corn mush), mashed beans, *papitas* (fried potatoes with a little meat) or bean juice were among the first foods a baby would start eating. When teething time came, babies were given pieces of tortilla to suck on while being watched so that they wouldn't choke on the tasty morsels. When the *raciones* (soup bones) were put into the beans or *chicos* (dehydrated corn) to cook, the *tútano* (bone marrow) was carefully taken out and customarily given to the younger children unless there was a toothless elderly person at the table. People appreciated the fact that the bone marrow was the richest part of the soup bone and contained nutrients necessary for a small child's growth and development.

Previously, I described some of the ways milk products were prepared to everyone's pleasure and wholesome nutrition. Milk and milk products were essential staples and people drank whole milk well into early adulthood. However, children of all ages were especially encouraged to drink as much milk as was available to them. Keep in mind that, other than water, children did not have the unlimited beverage choices young people have today. Much to our probable benefit, we drank as much milk as we liked.

Antes, large amounts of sugar in our children's diets was simply not an issue. First of all, there weren't large amounts of sugar readily available to children, as there are today. Secondly, because sugar was one of the basic commodities that had to be bought with money, it was almost always in short supply. The sugar that a household could afford to buy was put into the hands of the *dueña de casa* (head of the household) for safe-keeping. In certain households the big *trastero* (cupboard) at grandmother's house was always locked. On the few occasions when children were allowed to look into this vault, they saw that the sugar was stored there, along with the wooden boxes that raisins and dried prunes came in. I expect that coffee would have been kept in there also, since coffee was another item that had to be paid for with money.

Sugar was mostly used for baking and for cooking foods for special occasions. Adults did use sugar to sweeten their coffee and children were allowed to drink sweetened coffee, but not on a regular basis.

Desserts and candies such as children are surrounded with today, just didn't exist for most children here. Again, the lack of money simply eliminated these things from our diet. People did not feel deprived by the lack of extremely rich or sweet foods. After all, no one else we knew had these luxuries either. Furthermore, as with our milk drinking, the lack of sugar ultimately worked to the advantage of the local children.

We already know our *antes* diet was not perfect. Despite the fact that it contained some highly nutritious foods, it lacked variety. For instance, especially in winter, the children didn't have any source of Vitamin C. The previous summer's fruits and vegetables were long gone, except for what had been dried. As well, the autumn apples and other fruits that remained were also dried. The nutritional value was still good, but the Vitamin C contained in these foods was probably minimal. This would also have been true of the potatoes. Although potatoes were generally plentiful in the diet, by late winter they would have contained very little Vitamin C and citrus fruits in any form were simply not available.

As well, the *antes* diet was heavy on red meats and fat, but adequate for highly active children who played and worked outdoors year round, especially given the harsh winters and lack of modern home heating. Obviously, this would not be appropriate for today's sedentary population. Furthermore, our *antes* diet had very little white meats or fish. The only source of fish that people had here was canned sardines, mackerel and salmon. Although good for us, they were not a common part of children's diets. Again, because they had to be bought with money, the sardines were used almost exclusively to pack in men's lunches when they were laboring away from home or even as day laborers. The salmon and mackerel were mostly reserved for Lenten dishes and again not a part of the regular diet.

Today, we know that part of the problem with the diet of modern children is the snack foods. *Antes,* children also snacked, but not in the extreme manner of children today. Furthermore, their snacking was limited to piñon, jerky or roasted pumpkin seeds and was controlled by three factors. First was the matter of supply, which was not endless, as seems to be the case today. Second was time, which was also limited. Snacking was usually a time of sharing but was short, more like a special break from what ever else was going on. In our *antes*, children did not snack alone, or constantly. The third controlling factor was adult supervision, which the adults took seriously. One of my close friends recalled that when he was young and arrived home from school each day, his mother generally had a small snack for him to eat while they talked about his day at school. After the snack and the conversation were finished, my friend and his mother worked in the fields until she had to go in the house to prepare dinner. Whatever the snack had been, it had been worked off well before the day's chores were done.

In looking back at what children ate, *antes,* we recognize that the diet could have been supplemented with such things as white meat and more fruits and vegetables. Yet, overall, this was a hardy diet that had controls and limits and generally worked well for the children who lived and worked here in our *antes*. It was also this diet, with its restrictions, that met the goals of our ancestors for the survival of their children and allowed us to grow relatively strong, healthy and, for the most part, content with what our families could provide.

Currently, much is being said about the foods of tomorrow but we don't know what they will be. Whatever these foods turn out to be, we should be asking whether or not we will use them wisely. The alternative is to continue to indulge our children until they keel over. This would not be because they didn't have enough, as our *abuelitas* feared would be the case for us but rather because they have had too much and under so little guidance.

Los Juegos de los Niños
The Games Children Played

The games, amusements and pastimes of the children of *antes* bear little resemblance to the way children spend their time today. *Antes, mucho mas antes* (a long, long time ago) the games children and young adults played were the relics of ancient games from colonial days. Many of these games were very likely brought from Spain through Mexico with little change from the way they had been played in Spain.

Evidence for this shows up in a painting in the Museo Del Prado in Madrid, Spain, by the Spanish painter Francisco Goya, who lived between 1746 and 1828(Andrade 1975, plates II, III). Goya is known for having painted scenes of the everyday life of common people. This particular painting is titled *La Gallina Ciega* (The Blind Hen). It depicts well-dressed young adults playing a game called *La Gallina Ciega* outdoors along a river bank or lake shore. Here in northern New Mexico and specifically in the Cuba area, the game became *La Gallinita Ciega* (The Little Blind Hen). It was a children's game. One can suppose that since the players were little, the hen ought to be little as well. Nevertheless, it was the same game and it was played here in Cuba well into the late 1940s. Basically this game is a version of "Blind man's Bluff" and was a game that could be played indoors as well as outdoors. Furthermore, the only things needed to play the game were a few children and a blindfold.

Another very popular pastime from among these ancient games

was one called *Iglesias* (The Churches). This game required a bat or sturdy stick used to hit a soft ball. The ball was homemade, of course. *Iglesias* was a team game, played in a field. The number of players on each side could vary; it didn't seem to matter how many people played. A space, either square or round, was marked off at one end of a field. This was called "The Big Church." Every member of the team at bat was required to stand in that enclosure. Farther down one side of the field was another enclosure which had been marked off and was called "The Little Church." This smaller enclosure roughly corresponded to first base in baseball. The team at bat was the "inside team" and each member got to bat in rotation.

A member of the "outside team" pitched the ball to the batter in the Big Church. If the batter chose to try to hit the ball and missed, he or she was out. If the ball was hit, the batter tried to run to the Little Church without getting tagged or hit by the ball. If the batter was hit by a thrown ball, he might try to tag or hit a member of the other team before he or she could get to one of the churches. Whenever a player was hit or tagged, the inside team became the outside team and the outside team became the inside team. These roles could change several times within a matter of a very few minutes. The basic concept involved in this game dates back to the Middle Ages when churches were viewed as sanctuaries for anyone on the run. Admittedly, there are some similarities to modern baseball but the object of the game was to remain the "inside team" as long as possible rather than to score the greatest number of hits or runs.

Like *La Gallinita Ciega*, *Iglesias* was played here well into the 1930s. However, by then, modern baseball had been introduced into the community, primarily by the staff at the convent school and by students returning from boarding schools such as Menaul School in Albuquerque.

There are many more of these ancient games and children's songs that few people alive today even remember hearing about. For instance, it is said that there used to be a very popular checker-like game played among shepherds. Lacking checkers and a checker board, the players scratched out a checkerboard pattern on the ground, with one player using beans for checkers and the other player using pebbles.

In the 1970s, educators tried to reintroduce the old games and songs into the bilingual curriculum in the hope that some aspects of our ancient culture could be preserved, along with our ancient Spanish language. However, by then it was probably too late. The children were already more inclined to watch television than to amuse themselves as their ancestors did.

To current families, surrounded by yards full of wheeled toys for both young and old and rooms filled with stuffed animals perhaps as big as a live bear, it must be difficult to imagine a time when people here did not have toys. Yet that was the reality of this place until very recent history. It must also be difficult to believe that children did not die as a result of not getting the latest Barbie Doll or the latest video game or CD.

So what did children in olden times do? Children worked, sang, danced and memorized prayers, riddles and *dichos* (adages, or sayings). They also played in incredibly imaginative ways. They did so by constantly making things out of the few resources available to them. The toys children had were all handmade. Some were seasonal. For instance, once it started snowing, it was time to craft a new sled. Over the summer, the old sled had probably been taken apart to make something else out of its few boards. Possibly, one might have come across a much better board to make a lighter and faster sled than the one from last year. The common practice was in winter one played in the snow, found a higher hill or river bank to sled on or simply used the frozen river as the sleekest slide anyone could possibly have.

By spring, the snow was getting slushy, the river and ditches were starting to thaw and it was time to look for your best *trompo* (wooden top) and a high quality piece of heavy cord for spinning what you hoped would be your champion *trompo* for that season. *Trompos* was highly competitive and required great skill at spinning a well-made top. Here in Cuba, a girl had to be very good at the game before the boys would even let her compete. Players would throw their *trompos* into a ring marked out on the ground a few feet in diameter while pulling back very quickly on the cord that had been wound around the *trompo*. This action would set the *trompo* spinning very rapidly on its sharpened bottom point. The object was to knock another player's *trompo* out of the ring and not get knocked out yourself. Even worse than having your *trompo* knocked out of the ring was to have it hit so hard that it broke. If this were to happen, it would probably take someone with skill several days to carve another one in order to get back into the game. Another disaster might have to do with a girl being so good at *trompos* that a boy would end up having to give her his very best *trompo* because she knocked it out of the ring!

Next in the general order of spring games came the little Bull Durham tobacco sacks where the *bolitas* (marbles) had been put away until the first warm, sunny days of spring. Like *trompos,* marble shooting was highly competitive. Again, the object was to knock opponents' marbles out of a ring. If you weren't a very good shot, you could end up losing all your marbles. (No pun intended here.) Incidentally, the word used locally for marbles is *bolitas* (little balls) while in other Spanish-speaking places they are called *canicas.* This word has never been used here to describe marbles.

While the boys tried to augment their collections of marbles from the limited local supply, the girls would generally be jumping rope. Ropes were such an essential part of our agrarian life style that whatever short piece of rope could be spared to play with had to be shared and was highly prized. The long pieces of rope which two people turned from the ends and one or several people jumped in unison in the middle was something that was only done at school. No family here would give up a useful length of rope just so children could play with it.

As the days got longer in late spring children would play outdoors after dinner. Among the favorite games were "kick the can" and "hide and seek." However, at the first hint of dark, the children would automatically start heading home without anyone having to call them. The rule was to be home by dark. By then all the chores had been done and it was time to be home.

By the late spring, children everywhere were longing for summer. Summer was the season when children had many more chores to do but it was also the season for real creativity. The days were longer and there were so many new places to explore and new things to make.

Among the first things everyone had to have by the time that school was out was a pair of *zancos* (stilts). The word used here for stilts was actually *ancos,* a corruption of the proper term that comes about by dropping the *z* from the beginning of the word. Incidentally, another of the paintings by Francisco Goya in the Museo Del Prado (*Goya Reproducciones* [1975], plate 801) shows men playing on stilts. Again, this painting seems to imply that the people of northern New Mexico had a long tradition of making stilts, a tradition that was handed down for generations and was enjoyed into the late 1940s.

The *zancos* were essential for children in the spring and summer because one of the favorite pastimes was to attempt to cross the river during the spring runoff without getting knocked off the stilts. A child could get knocked off the stilts by the high, fast-moving water or could get stuck in the soft sand of the river bottom and fall off. This was, of course, an "I dare you" sort of game that provided great entertainment for both the participants as well as the less daring by-standers. Although many children got wet and a few stilts were left in the river for a while, no one was ever seriously hurt or drowned in this game.

Another item that had to be ready for use before summer was a *jonda* (slingshot). A *jonda* required finding some highly specialized materials. The first thing was to go out among the budding trees looking for just the right fork on a branch: not too big but straight and sturdy. This branch would be cut to just the right length, carefully peeled and notched at the two top ends. The next thing to search for was an old inner tube. Two strips of inner tube were used for the bands on the sling shot. Inner tubes were not that common an item since there were so few cars. Once the inner tube was found, the bands were cut and tightly tied into the notched ends of the Y-shaped branch. Following this procedure, the crafter went out to the nearest family dump and looked for an old leather shoe. The leather tongue was carefully removed to make the pouch that would hold the stones for shooting the slingshot. As can be seen through this abbreviated description of slingshot making, the process took time, exploration and much creativity. Furthermore, when the project was complete, the child had the satisfaction of having made something that worked and that could be enjoyed.

The slingshot was one of those creations that were saved until school was out. This was primarily because slingshots were not allowed at school and the worst thing that could happen after all the work involved in making it was to have it discovered by the sisters at school and have it taken away.

Summer was the time of year when children indulged in a lot of make-believe games. The days seemed endless, even after all the chores had been done. Suddenly someone in the play group would decide that it was a great day to play "Mass." An altar would be set up and a priest and servers designated. The appropriate costumes would be improvised and the "congregation" would proceed with the prayers.

Having had enough of prayers, someone might suggest that since the altar was set up, why not have a wedding, or even better still, a funeral. Once it was decided whether it would be a wedding or a funeral, everyone would run around looking for the appropriate props for the event. For the funeral, one of the very small children would have to be convinced to lie very still in a wagon all through the procession while the rest tried to sing *alabados* (very old traditional hymns of praise), imitated as the children heard them at real funerals and wakes.

During the really hot days of summer, the entire neighborhood group would play in the river, creeks and ditches. This was a time when the children would work for days trying to build a dam. The hope was that once the river or the main ditch was dammed, enough water would collect for a wonderful swimming hole. No one really knew how to swim but having a swimming hole was a real dream. In those instances when the children succeeded in damming the main ditch or creek, some irate neighbor would generally walk up to find out what had happened to the water that was supposed to be used for irrigation. Once discovered, the dam would have to be removed so the water could be used for farming again. In the meantime, the children had spent several days outdoors, in and out of the water, enjoying their really cool swimming hole. Taking the dam apart could turn out to be as much fun as building it. Think of all the mud-slinging that would go on before having to go home and attend to the chores and the animals.

As with other aspects of our life in Cuba, World War II had the greatest impact in how children played and in how their time was spent. By the 1940s, children were exposed to radio, movies and music different from what had been available before the war. Most importantly, children began to ride bicycles instead of horses. Commercially manufactured toys such as dolls and metal toy trucks and airplanes were becoming more common and hardly anyone wanted to play "funeral" anymore. Eventually, there were more ropes to play with, but nobody wanted to play rodeo; everyone wanted to be Hopalong Cassidy.

By the time television became part of nearly every home in Cuba, everyone had forgotten the rules for playing a good *trompo* game or how to make a pair of *zancos* on which they could cross the river without falling off. No one cared about playing *La Gallinita Ciega* or *Iglesias* when you could be watching Uncle Milty on television. Nonetheless, for the generations of children who experienced the ancient games and songs, their lives were enriched in ways that modern children cannot understand. Nor would modern children seeing the Goya paintings described in this article understand the connections between those paintings and life in Cuba in olden times, in our *antes.*

6

− Religious Rituals and Artifacts −

¿Y Nuestros Pastores de Antes?
Preparation for Christmas

*A*ntes, mid-December was a time of preparation for Christmas, much as it is now, except more so. In the mid-twentieth century and before, preparations for the religious pageantry related to Christmas took place at the parochial school. In those days, this was also the public school. For non-Catholics the selection of roles and the many practices leading up to the Christmas Eve program took place at the other churches in town.

In accordance with the tradition of that period, the prescribed roles involved in the reenactment of the birth of Christ were rather limited. There were the roles of the three kings, which were normally assigned to the older boys, dressed in long and colorful bathrobes and carrying something shiny to represent rich gifts. These fellows simply marched in looking devout, during the hymn *We Three Kings Of Orient Are.* Then there was the manger scene with Mary wrapped in a blue shawl, with Joseph at her side. Mary was usually the girl in the group with the lightest hair and lightest skin. Joseph was sort of nondescript, but important. He was wrapped in a brown robe and holding a stick to represent a staff.

In this scene there were also angels and a band of shepherds. The role of the angels was usually given to the very young children, generally those with light skin and light hair. I wanted very much to be an angel. The angels got to wear white choir robes, halos and wings trimmed with silver tinsel. The angels just stood around, except for the one who told the shepherds not to be afraid of the bright star.

The shepherds, on the other hand, included all the rest of us. Every year, I was a shepherd. I was too dark and had a massive head of dark brown hair that no ribbon, barrette or curler could have tamed to make me look like an angel. So, until I decided I would rather sing in the choir, I was a rustic looking shepherd.

The Christmas pageant was not always like this. *Antes,* before the local traditions were changed, there was a different way of preparing for Christmas. *Antes, mucho mas antes* (a very long time ago), and into the early twentieth century, there was *Los Pastores* (The Shepherds). In the traditional *Pastores* version of the reenactment of the birth of Christ, the roles of the participants were very different and were scripted. The written script for speaking parts was passed down between people who had some skill in reading. The script was likely also memorized by individuals who coached their fellow villagers. This script had been handed down since colonial time and presented by the people of the villages, including both children and adults. Neighboring villages would take turns staging and performing *Los Pastores.* According to legend, these reenactments were a very important part of the Christmas celebration and were performed each year on Christmas day.

I first learned about *Los Pastores* being performed here from my mother, Eursinia DeLaO Cordova, and from her family. The family used to talk about certain characters that were a part of *Los Pastores.* In addition to these recollections, Eursinia also took great pleasure in telling the story of how her grandfather, *Don* Facundo C de Baca, who was a blacksmith, never called her Eursinia. Instead, he always called my mother *Gila* (pronounced HEE-la).

When I would ask why my great-grandfather would call her *Gila,* Mom would play innocent and say, "*No se* (I don't know), but when grandpa needed me to work the bellows at his blacksmith forge, he would yell, '¡*Gila!*' and I would run as fast as I could from where my brother Frank, my cousin Tomas and I were herding the goats, and I would go pump the bellows for him."

Years later, while reading an excerpt of the script of *Los Pastores*, as traditionally performed across northern New Mexico and southern Colorado, I came across information about the role of one of the main characters in *Los Pastores* whose name was *Gila*. At least for me, the mystery of why great-grandfather called mother *Gila* was finally solved.

In *Los Pastores*, *Gila* is a spunky young woman who pretty well manages and feeds the shepherds but keeps them in line as well. For instance, there is good-natured humor in the parts where Gila is constantly quarreling with Bartolo, the lazy shepherd, for not doing his share of the work. She threatens not to feed him if he does not do his work. In *Los Pastores* there are many more characters, such as one for a hermit and even one for Lucifer.

According to family accounts, *Don* Facundo C de Baca was a devout Catholic, an ardent and faithful *Penitente*, and keeper of the faith. It is very likely that this man would have known the entire *Pastores* script. He would have been familiar with the parts, either from having been in performances as a youngster, or assisting during a time when his village was in charge of putting on the pageant. I find it interesting that he selected the name of the spirited, competent female from *Los Pastores* as a nickname for his oldest granddaughter, Eursinia. He very likely saw her in that role in real life and not just as an acting role.

Given information people have shared on the topic of *Los Pastores*, it is very likely that the last time *Los Pastores* was performed in Cuba was in the early- to mid-1930s. According to local mythology, a woman from here had been in *Los Pastores* in her youth. I was able to confirm this. Given her age and her estimate of when she performed in the play, the last time *Los Pastores* was performed must have been in the 1930s. She also told me that because her father knew the script and had parts of the written script, he had helped direct the performance she had been in.

Knowing that preparations for the celebration of Christmas were different, *mucho mas antes,* leads me to believe that perhaps I could have been an angel in *Los Pastores*. Better still, perhaps I could have played *Gila*.

Las Fiestas de Santiago y Santa Ána
The Feasts of Saint James and Saint Anne

Antes, in Cuba and surrounding communities, we celebrated *el día de Santiago* (Saint James' Day) on the twenty-fifth of July and *el día de Santa Ána* (Saint Anne's Day) on the twenty-sixth. These were traditional religious feast days as well as established social events.

Santiago is the patron saint of Spain and it is possible that many of the activities related to his feast day have their roots in Spain in the Middle Ages when chivalry was a noble practice. Saint James is not the patron saint of Cuba and neither is Saint Anne, yet these two days were among the feast days people looked forward to every summer in communities throughout northern New Mexico and southern Colorado.

Interestingly, these two days of celebration were specifically segregated for the participants. The twenty-fifth included activities for men only, while the activities on the twenty-sixth were just for women. There was no question in anyone's mind that the most important and popular of the two celebrations was the feast of Saint James on the twenty-fifth.

El día de Santiago was a time for the men of our communities to show off their horses as well as to demonstrate their horsemanship. These were days of *Caballería* (horsemanship and long-lost memories of chivalry). *El día de Santa Ána* was a time for women to show off their equestrian talents and to show off any family horses that had not been shown the day before by the male members of the family.

Antes, most families had several, or perhaps many saddle horses. This was especially true in families that also had young and unmarried males who rode horses on a daily basis for work as well as their only means of transportation. These young men had a great deal of experience with horses and, hopefully, some knowledge of their own abilities on a horse.

By the beginning of July, families would begin to discuss who would ride which horse on the twenty-fifth. The grooming of the favorite horses would begin along with the preparation of saddles and tack. Naturally, there was also a discussion among the young men about the appropriate attire for the occasion, most especially the hats that would be worn on this special day.

El día de Santiago would begin with the entire family attending mass. The men would arrive at church on their beautifully groomed horses and looking *como verdaderas caballeros* (dapper and gentlemanly). The women in town would walk to church while those living farther out would ride in horse-drawn wagons so all the children as well as grandma could be in town for the festivities. By mid-morning (after mass), all of the posturing and showing off of horses would be over. By then, the betting on who was going to do best in the races and contests would take place. The bets were down and it was time for the activities to begin.

Unlike today, there were no arenas in any community to accommodate the races and other forms of horsemanship, so contests took place on the main street or in some nearby field where the whole community could watch. Among the highlights of the day's activities were the horse races. Most of the money put down as bets had to do with these races. Since there were few if any cars around in those days, it was relatively easy to clear the main road of all the dogs and any children who might have been left unattended. The number of races would depend on the number of participants. The final race consisted of the winners of the previous races and the winners of this race were proclaimed the fastest horse and the best rider for that *fiesta* and for the next year.

But there was more to the day than racing. Among the most challenging of the games was one called *las corridas de gallo* (the rooster races). In this game, a rooster would be buried in the ground leaving only its head exposed. One by one, the horsemen would race past the rooster at full speed, attempting to lean over and grab the poor rooster's head. Eventually, one of the horsemen would succeed in unearthing the animal. (By now, the rooster was likely already dead.) This horseman would then swing the rooster over his head, shouting triumphantly while the other horsemen would chase after him and try to take the rooster away. The rooster might change hands several times amidst a great deal of shouting and swinging the remains of the poor bird until it was finally completely torn apart. This crowd-pleasing game would be repeated until the riders and the horses were completely exhausted or until there were no more roosters available to be torn apart.

By late afternoon, families would start heading home with their very tired children and their slightly or totally drunken young horsemen. It was time to get home to do the day's chores, to have dinner and to tend to the horses that had worked so hard during the day's exciting activities. Furthermore, it was time to get ready for that night's dance. As usual, the dance was the real highlight of the day's activities. By the time the dance started, the *caballeros* (horsemen) would have recovered and would be ready to dance the night away. The women who had been spectators cheering their men along would have freshened themselves up and they too would be ready to dance the night away, having had another memorable *día de Santiago*.

The very next day was *el día de Santa Ána* (Saint Anne's feast day). This was the day designated for women in the community to publicly show off their riding skills, unattended and unescorted. Sources indicate that this celebration might have been when women dressed in their finest riding habits, rode side-saddle and simply showed themselves off rather than their horses or their equestrian talents. There are also sources that indicate that some of the women participated in the *corridas de gallo* (rooster races). This activity must have taken place after side-saddles were no longer in use and women riders were using standard western saddles. Women found the game so distasteful that it soon fell out of favor. The women finally decided just to cook the rooster rather than tear it apart in a game.

El día de Santa Ána simply didn't generate the same kind of excitement that *el día de Santiago* did. Apparently there were women who would participate in some horse races and there were certainly women around who rode well enough to compete in such activities. In any case, the women riders attracted more attention simply by being seen and by enjoying riding around with their friends.

As on the day before, the feast day of the twenty-sixth began with a mass attended by the whole family. Those who were going to participate in the races and games would have to go home after church and change clothes before they could go out and join in the festivities. In those days, church attire for women was strictly dictated. Following the costume change, the women would mount their horses and join their friends on the main street.

The women would parade up and down the road for a while, then go to someone's home to eat and talk about what they were going to wear to the dance that night. Following this period of rest and conversation, they would get back on their horses and parade around town again until it was time to go home and prepare for the dance.

In actuality, *el día de Santa Ána* was really more fun for the sub-teen group of girls than for the older single females. In most families, the younger girls had to ride two to a horse, as can be seen in the accompanying photograph. By having two girls on a horse, the older girl would be able to take care of the younger child while also managing the horse. This arrangement would allow even some of the youngest girls in the family to ride and to participate in the festivities.

Among the reasons that Saint Anne's day didn't arouse as much excitement as the activities of the day before was the quality of the horses. The horses used by the women and the younger children were the mares, the old family nags and other mild-mannered horses considered safe enough for the children to ride unattended. Unlike the older single females who stopped frequently to make sure they looked good for the young men who were observing them, the younger girls were less inhibited and rode all day having a good time.

A group of riders can be seen in the photograph gathered around the Sandoval Grocery Store, probably to spend the small amount of money they each had been given to buy some small treat while riding on this special holiday. It seems remarkable that as conservative as families here were related to the supervision of their single young females that there would be this special day set aside especially for women to ride without male interference. However, this was the holy day that honored Saint Anne, the mother of the Blessed Virgin Mary and it was supposed that in her honor and respect families believed their daughters would be safe on this special day.

Among our many cultural losses attributed to World War II, we can also count the loss of the celebration of these two holidays. During the war, there were few if any young men in town available to race or participate in *corridas de gallo*. Furthermore, with so many of our young men away fighting the war, there was little incentive to celebrate. By the time the war ended, our lives had changed so dramatically that there was very little interest in celebrating such archaic customs as those related to *El Día de Santiago* or *El día de Santa Ána*.

Everyone was looking towards the future and toward the day they could have a new pickup truck instead of a horse. Parades of horses gave way to showing off cars and pickups and *corridas de gallo* ultimately gave way to mud-bogging.

Photograph of girls on horseback gathered around the Sandoval Store. This photograph was probably taken in the late 1930s on *el día de Santa Ana* which would have been the only time so many girls would have been riding around in pairs and gathered in one place at the same time. The house next to the store appears to be the house of Don Barolo Sandoval and is still standing today. Courtesy of the Center for Southwest Research, University Libraries, the University of New Mexico, collection number #994-014. The original photograph was taken by Sotero Casaus.

Los Primeros Protestantes
The First Protestants

Los Protestantes de Antes were the Presbyterians. *Protestante* was the word used here to describe only Presbyterians and not members of other protestant denominations. These *protestantes* were the few local families who were members of a small Presbyterian congregation that celebrated its 120th anniversary in October, 2010. Perhaps a reason for the close association of the word *protestante* with Presbyterians is that local Presbyterians were predominantly of Hispanic origin and were Spanish speakers.

One may ask who these people were who have survived since colonial times in what was essentially Catholic territory. The first generation of protestants would have been converts from Catholicism, including Jews and perhaps Arabs who had converted to Catholicism during the earliest Spanish Inquisitions. These people would have converted to Catholicism in order to avoid punishment from some of the later Spanish Inquisitions of the eighteenth century. Another group of people who joined this and other small Presbyterian groups would have been easterners moving westward, following the end of the Civil War in 1865.

After the American conquest of what became the southwestern United States in 1848, and when New Mexico became a territory in 1850, religion became closely linked to the United States' colonization efforts of this area. Churches were reorganized or established wherever there were enough people to support them. Furthermore, as if to add to the political and linguistic changes the local people were trying to cope with, an American version of the Roman Catholic Church was imposed on a Spanish Catholic tradition which had existed for three hundred years. Under the American Catholic system many local Hispanic priests were removed from service in the New Mexico communities, primarily by the newly appointed, French-born American Bishop Jean Baptiste Lamy, who arrived in Santa Fé in 1851. Two years after the arrival of Bishop Lamy, New Mexico's Catholic Church was removed from the Mexican diocese of Durango and made a part of the diocese of Cincinnati, Ohio. Bishop Lamy's actions caused a great deal of dissention in the Catholic community in northern New Mexico. Some families may have converted to the Protestantism in protest against the changes in the Catholic church.

In the meantime, the other non-Catholic churches were getting their start in New Mexico. Baptist missionaries and ministers began arriving as early as 1849. By 1854 the Baptists had built a church in Santa Fé. By 1850, both Methodists and Presbyterian missionaries had also arrived in New Mexico. Protestant clergy had also accompanied the army, worked as Indian agents and organized churches in many towns and villages. These new American religious leaders recognized the need for schools but in addition also determined that formal education could achieve more than one goal. Among other things, their schools could evangelize and consolidate a new religious tradition among a diverse student population that included both boys and girls. They could also Americanize both Native American and Hispanic students. In addition, medical missionaries came from the east to address the acute need for medical services all over the territory of New Mexico.

The Presbyterian congregation that has existed in this area during the past 120 years is part of the Americanization of religion and derives its history from several sources. According to local church documents (Session of the Capulín Spanish Presbyterian Church [1940], 13.), the original members of this church came from two particular places in 1889. One was a Presbyterian Church in Jemez. A possible reason for this is that, as early as 1878, the Home Board of the Presbyterian Church had sent the Reverend Doctor J. M. Shields and his family to Jemez as missionaries, where he established a church.

Others came from the Capulín Spanish Presbyterian Church which was organized in 1887. Capulín was a small community located near what is now Gallina. Church records indicate that the church in Capulín was also organized by the Reverend Doctor Shields, with fourteen members "all by letter [of transfer] from [the] Jemez Church, with nine more expected to unite as soon as they had opportunity."(Session of the Capulín Spanish Presbyterian Church [1940], 3.)

The fourteen members listed on the church register are basically all members of one extended family and their in-laws. These founding members of the Capulín Presbyterian Church are, for the most part, the ancestors of many of the life-long members of today's Presbyterian congregation here in Cuba.

However, some time following the organization of the Capulín Church in 1887, a group from the Jemez and Capulín churches moved to Nacimiento (Cuba) and organized a church in 1889. Unfortunately, the records from the original Nacimiento Church are not available because that church burned down some time in 1924 or 1925. Informants reported that the 1889 church was located near the current Presbyterian cemetery overlooking the settlement of Nacimiento and the area that was starting to become Cuba. (pers. comm.)

Again, according to the Capulín Church record in 1890, *Don* Pasqual Cordova, his wife *Doña* Maria Doloritas Jaquez Cordova and their four sons, Lugardo, Francisco, Julian and Marino, along with their daughter Josefa, all transferred their membership to the Nacimiento church. This left *Don* Pasqual's brother, *Don* José Antonio Cordova and his branch of the family, in charge of the Capulín church. Incidentally, *Don* José Antonio served as elder of the Capulín church from the time it was organized in 1887 until his death in 1926.

In 1927, the National Board of Missions assigned the very young Reverend Uvaldo Martinez to Cuba. He was just out of McCormick Seminary in Chicago and Cuba was his first mission. The supervisor of ministries in New Mexico instructed the young Reverend Martinez that his first duty was to build a new church. Instead of building the new church at the old site, the parishioners wanted a new location. Ultimately Reverend Martinez and his building committee: *Don* Lugardo Cordova, *Don* Julian Cordova, *Doña* Lydia Gutierrez and *Don* Francisco Chavez, were able to acquire a new site. That site, the location of the present Presbyterian Church, was donated by *Don* Aron (Augustin) Eichwald. The new site is closer to the center of the developing community of Cuba and somewhat removed from the location of the original church.

According to Mrs. Uvaldo Martinez (Emma Eichwald), who later wrote about the construction of this church, "the people of Cuba, many of them Catholic, donated labor and materials for the new church," thus making it possible to have the adobe walls completed by the end of the summer of 1927. Mrs. Martinez also says that in the fall of 1927 Reverend Martinez' supervisor came to Cuba to see for himself how the construction of the new church was going. "When he saw the building, he scratched his head, was silent for a while and then asked, 'Who gave you the plans for the church?'" Reverend Martinez replied by telling his supervisor that no one had given him plans, he had drawn them himself. They consisted of a rectangle with a basement under the sanctuary. "The supervisor then said, 'It looks terrible, but I suppose we'll give you money to put a roof on those walls.'" (Vasquez & Atkins,1999, pp 38-39.)

The money for the roof was apparently slow in coming; the church was not finished until the summer of 1928. By the time the building committee and its crew were ready to install the roof, the walls had been exposed and not plastered through the winter and had started to bow outward. No one wanted to put the roof on the church because of the condition of the walls. It is said that finally, *Don* Francisco Chavez devised a means by which the walls could be brought back into alignment so the roof could be constructed. The solution was to place two threaded metal rods across the tops of the walls and gradually tightened the rods to pull the walls back into alignment. Those rods are still visible in the interior of the sanctuary and have done their job for the last eighty-two years.

In the last fifty years, the Cuba Presbyterian Church has gone through several major renovations. Among these has been complete remodeling of the basement, modernization of the whole church with electricity, natural gas, running water and bathrooms. There was also the construction of a greenhouse Trombe wall as an alternative source of heat. On numerous occasions the sanctuary has been plastered and painted and had a large stained-glass window installed. In its eighty-two years, it has also required new doors, new windows and, not too long ago, a new roof. These renovations have not only made the "terrible-looking" church more attractive but have also made it more comfortable and more useful to its members.

In our current high-tech age, there is another feature in this little church that adds to its unique character. This is the only church in our community that still has a real bell that is rung by pulling a rope to call members of the community to worship.

Establishing and building new churches was not the only goal in the Americanization of religion. Education was also one of the means by which religious groups sought to Americanize native New Mexicans. *Los protestantes de Cuba* were not among the congregations such as those in Chimayó, Truchas, Dixon and other northern New Mexico villages that had Presbyterian day schools established shortly after the arrival of the missionaries. Therefore the children of the local *protestantes* usually attended the local Catholic school until they were old enough to be sent away to a Presbyterian boarding school. Not until a Supreme Court decision ended this practice in 1949, did a pubic school system appear in Cuba that was separate from the convent school that children attended up to that time. Early in the twentieth century, the girls were sent to the Allison-James School in Santa Fe. Given how difficult it was to get to Santa Fé in those days, many of these girls were sent to Harwood Girls' School, a Methodist school, in Albuquerque.

The boys, with very few exceptions, were sent to Menaul Boys' School. In the 1930s, both the Allison-James and Menaul became co-educational. The Allison-James became the Junior High School (seventh grade through ninth grade) and Menaul became the High School. This provided a much greater opportunity for both boys and girls to attend the University of New Mexico upon graduation from Menaul. Again, with few exceptions, the children of the founding families of the Presbyterian church throughout northern New Mexico went to school at the Allison-James and/ or Harwood and then on to Menaul. Ultimately, these schools became the source of generations of Hispanic teachers, ordained ministers and other professional people, including many in the medical professions.

The third goal of protestant missionaries in Americanizing New Mexicans was to provide badly needed health services. That story involves everything from establishing well baby, eye and dental clinics and the building of hospitals and other clinics, including the original Presbyterian Hospitals in Albuquerque and Embudo.

As seen from the point of view of *los protestantes de antes*, their successes in the evangelization of local people and the educational and health services provided over the last century and a half are testimony to their mission. As for the little Presbyterian Church of Cuba, its small congregation can take pride in having kept the doors of their church open to the community for one hundred twenty years, while maintaining a voice in the overall structure and activities of the Presbyterian Church, USA.

Historia en Registros Olvidados
Stories in Forgotten Documents

Our *antes*, our history, has been preserved in a variety of documents that are obscure and frequently forgotten. Probably they were put away in a safe place to keep the records from damage or from being lost. The result of that, however, has been that some of our history has not been accessible to people who might want to know about it.

So much of what tells us about ourselves as a community has been secured in places such as old, but official church registers. There is also the Convent School Archive, old *acequia* (irrigation ditch) association records, water rights maps, as well as timeworn and faded survey plat maps and property title abstracts.

The focus of this article is on information gleaned from one of the Cuba Spanish Presbyterian Church registers (Session of the Cuba Spanish Presbyterian Church [1977], 3-23.), describing the building of the first manse on church property. The manse was the residence of the Presbyterian minister and his family who served the local congregations. The ministers who occupied this manse not only ministered to the people of Cuba but also served the communities of San José (Regina), Gallina, Lindrith and a church in Tapiecitos, which was located ten miles north of Lindrith.

The old manse still stands on Church Lane only a few yards from the Presbyterian Church. It is a relatively small house without any distinguishing features except for its size. It actually measures only 43 feet by 24 feet on the outside.

This story is important to the history of our community because it illustrates and reiterates three important points about how slowly Cuba evolved into mainstream society. The first of these points is that even though this whole project took place between March, 1941, and the end of July, 1942, the actual construction of the house was done in the old, traditional ways.

Secondly, even as late as the early 1940s, the people of Cuba were still almost totally without money. The sums of money recorded throughout the building of this tiny house are pathetic and heart-breaking. Yet the little manse still stands and bears witness to the dedication of the few members who donated the small amounts of money they could, along with their time and labor, in order to accomplish their goal.

The third point involves the isolation of Cuba from the rest of the world. Even though the United States became involved in World War II during the building of the manse and young men were leaving Cuba to join in the war effort, there is virtually no mention of the war in the church records during this time. There is no mention that this or that person had been drafted, had joined the military or had gone off to work in a defense plant, as many had actually done. It is as if nothing else was happening in the world except the building of this little house. In April, 1944, a record of the church session (officers) indicated that Mr. Francis Valdez was absent from the meeting because he was serving with the armed forces of our country. By then, Mr. Valdez and many of the other young men associated with the Presbyterian Church and all the rest of the community had been gone for as long as two and a half years.

Granted, the war was not the business of the session of the Presbyterian Church, but it seems that some reference would have been made as to how the drain on the population was having an effect on the building of the manse. The Session of the Cuba Presbyterian Church did not necessarily reflect the attitudes or the priorities of the entire community. There were people in town who were very much aware of what was going on in the rest of the world. There were people here who followed the war closely, through the newspaper as well as their battery-operated radios. Nevertheless, between the end of March, 1941 and the end of July, 1942, when the manse was completed, Cuba was still very much in the world of *antes* and would remain so until after the end of World War II.

But let us return to the neatly written records of how the manse came to be part of Cuba. At the congregational meeting of March 3, 1941, when it was decided to build the manse, the congregation also voted to apply for financial aid from the Presbyterian Board of National Missions. The congregation was well aware that it did not have enough money to build the manse on its own. In fact, it appears that the congregation had started to remodel the church basement some time before and had not been able to complete that project for lack of money. The congregation also voted to ask the Board of National Missions for a $200 loan in order to complete the basement project

What was always described as the Cuba Spanish Presbyterian Church was a mission church. In those days, the Presbyterian Church had a Board of National Missions and a Board of Foreign Missions. It was through these organizations within the church that hundreds of mission schools and churches were supported all over the world including schools such as Menaul and the Allison James schools and Presbyterian hospitals in Albuquerque and Embudo.

At a meeting of the congregation held on April 20, 1941, the Reverend Moicelio Cruz reported that the Presbytery had acted favorably on Cuba's request for a grant of $843.00 for the construction of the manse and the request for the $200 loan for completing the basement. Ultimately, the church never got the $843 as had been expected. Sometime following this announcement the Board of National Missions decided to allocate only $725 towards the building of the manse.

With the promise of money to help carry out these two projects, the members of the session had several decisions to make. At that time the session was composed of the minister, Reverend Cruz, and three elders from the community. These elders were *Don* Lugardo Cordova, *Don* Julian Cordova, Sr. and *Don* Francis Valdez. Among the decisions this governing body had to make was what sort of contribution would be asked from members of the congregation towards the completion of the manse. After several meetings between April, 1941, and February, 1942, the session decided it would recommend to the congregation that (1) the head of each family would be responsible for providing 225 adobes, (2) each family would be responsible for two horse-drawn wagon loads of rock and two wagon loads of sand, and (3) each would be willing to donate labor as asked of them until the completion of the building. (In those times, foundations were made of rock and sand packed tightly into trenches under all of the walls. It is assumed that the rock and sand were for that purpose.)

It was also decided that Mr. Ruben Cordova and Mr. Henry Archuleta be given the responsibility of transporting all materials needed for construction from Albuquerque. No mention was made as to whether either of these members was consulted before being given this responsibility. What is recorded is that at next congregational meeting, both men accepted the responsibility for hauling the materials from Albuquerque. The date set for actually starting construction was June 1, 1942. (By then, Mr. Cordova was already away serving in the Navy.)

Cuba was still in the world of *antes*. We are talking here of families having to make 225 adobes and providing two horse-drawn wagon loads of sand and another two of rock. In February of 1942, following the sinking of much of the Pacific fleet at Pearl Harbor the previous December and declaration of war against both Germany and Japan, the congregation of the Presbyterian Church was looking at starting this building. In 1942, Cuba was still isolated from the rest of the world and this allowed some of the people to go on as they had done for generations before.

At the May meeting of the session it was agreed that the quota for each male member of the congregation for the building should be changed. They decided to continue the call for two wagon loads of stone, but reduced the sand to one wagon load. Members were still responsible for 225 adobes or $3.00 in cash, along with labor as needed. Money was so scarce in most households that providing three dollars instead of 225 adobes would have been a real challenge. However, making 225 adobes in the spring time would also have been very difficult. Money would remain scarce until the military allotment checks started coming in on a regular basis and until the defense plant jobs opened up and people left Cuba to work in those faraway plants. This would have left only the older men, the women and some very young boys to participate in the labor-intensive job of making the required number of adobes.

In May, 1942, just two weeks before the starting date for construction, Mr. Henry Archuleta was hired as the contractor for the building of the manse. The church was $118 over budget before they started the project because the church had only received $725 of the requested $843, but payment to Mr. Archuleta would be $150.00, which would be set aside for such a purpose. Labor would be furnished to him by the building committee composed of elder *Don* Julian Cordova (Mr. Archuleta's uncle), elder *Don* Lugardo Cordova (another uncle) and church member Mr. Daniel Archuleta (Mr. Henry Archuleta's younger brother. By 1942, neither of the Cordova brothers was young. In fact, they were well past middle age and *Don* Julian Cordova's three oldest sons were of military age and would serve in the military in World War II.

At the July 26, 1942 meeting of the session, the pastor made a formal report on their progress. He reported that the manse had been completed as of July 25, except for the plastering and other minor details that would be taken care of by the pastor. Curiously, he does not explain how he would take care of the plastering (another labor-intensive job) or what the other minor details consisted of. He also commended the building committee for their untiring effort, their faithful behavior and for working double or more to make up for those who had failed in their commitment to the project. The pastor then proceeded to name the church members who did not help with anything in the building of the manse, which seems unusual for a pastor to do and record.

The work on the manse had been started on June 4, 1942, as had originally planned and completed on July 26, 1942. According to the records, a year later on May 16, 1943, the session held a part of its meeting in the new manse. Reverend Moicelio Cruz served as pastor of the Cuba Presbyterian Church until March 1, 1945. At his last meeting of the session on February 25, 1945, the elders voted a grant of $16.66 to Reverend Cruz as a present. Again, note the scarcity of money available for an appropriate gift of appreciation for the minister's many years of services.

There are other examples of the lack of money within this church and in the community at large. At a congregational meeting in 1941, a committee of three members was appointed to collect fifty cents from each member to pay the church's dues to the Board of Pensions which each church was required to pay. In another instance, in November, 1941, the congregation voted to increase Reverend Cruz' salary by $40.00. This made the total salary paid by the church $140.00 per year. Early in 1942, the congregation failed to approve a recommendation to increase the pastor's salary by another $60.00. They felt that the raise of $40.00 given November 2, 1941, was all that they could pledge for that year. The records do not show how much Reverend Cruz received from the Board of National Missions, but given that he had a wife and a child, it was apparently not enough. Nor is it recorded where the pastor lived prior to the building of the manse. In February, 1945, the congregation voted to increase Reverend Cruz' salary to $250.00, beginning in April, 1945. By that time, however, Reverend Cruz had announced that he had accepted a new position in Antonito, Colorado.

The next minister and family to occupy the manse were Reverend Ubaldo Martinez and his wife Emma Eichwald Martinez. This would be Reverend Martinez' second time as pastor of Cuba Presbyterian Church. He had come to Cuba is 1927 right out of seminary. It was Reverend Martinez who designed the church and under whose leadership the Presbyterian Church was built. It was also during that first assignment that he met his bride-to-be, Emma Eichwald. They were the first couple to be married in the new church. During his second tenure in Cuba, Reverend Martinez was very proactive in the community, helping to bring in the post-World War II amenities. Reverend Martinez was especially active and involved in bringing health care to Cuba, serving on the committee responsible for the building of the Cuba Health Center. However, prior to the building of the Health Center, Reverend Martinez had arranged for Ms. Ruth Herron, the registered nurse assigned to the Lindrith Parish Health Center to come to Cuba and conduct clinics at the Presbyterian manse. It was in the little manse that many of us had our first physical, dental and eye exams. In the living room of the tiny manse, where Mrs. Martinez' enormous upright piano took up half of the room, many babies got their first immunizations. That living room was also where Mrs. Martinez tirelessly taught many of us the appropriate music for each season's holiday celebration. Church members and friends were always made welcome at the tiny manse whether from Regina, Gallina, Tapiecitos, and Lindrith or from right here in Cuba.

Late in 1946 the manse and church, like much of the rest of Cuba, had been supplied with electricity and running water. By 1951, natural gas was the main source of heating for both the church and the manse.

The little adobe manse was occupied by the resident ministers of the church until the late 1970s. At that time, the minister's residence was moved to a modern double-wide trailer situated elsewhere in Cuba. The little adobe manse has gone through several restorations and used as a rental on several occasions over the years. Currently the little building is used for extra storage and is again in dire need of restoration to protect it from the harsh sun and cold winters. Only four large lilac bushes, probably planted at the time the manse was first built, decorate the yard. But if walls could talk, the tiny manse on Church Lane would have many a story to tell. Perhaps, this is why even in its present silence it still evokes countless fond memories of all of the good things that occurred within its small but thick adobe walls.

Presbyterian Church manse as it appears today, built in June and July, 1942.

Las Tres Campanas
The Three Bells

Antes, there were three bells by which people in the community punctuated their day, planned their activities and, in some instances, modified their behavior. *Antes* these bells pealed loud and clear throughout the community and echoed off Cuba Mesa to resound as far away as Nacimiento and Vallecito. In those days there were so few motorized vehicles, equipment or appliances that could interfere with the function of the three bells, that everyone could hear their conveyed message and act accordingly.

The most prominent of these bells was the bell at the old Immaculate Conception Catholic Church, built in 1915. The second bell was at the convent school next to that church and the third is the existing bell at the Cuba Presbyterian Church. Each of these bells had a different sound and conveyed a different message to particular segments of the population.

The bell at the Catholic church first rang at 6:00 a.m. to signal the call to worship for the six o'clock mass. Shocking as this may seem today, *Antes* many people here attended daily mass at that hour of the day. These were mostly women who would walk to church before beginning their endless and arduous daily chores.

The second time the bell above the Catholic church rang was at 7:50 a.m. This was called *el primero* (the first bell or warning bell). This was also a call to worship. The next bell, called *el segundo* (second bell), rang at 8:00 a.m. and marked the beginning of the eight o'clock mass. This mass was for those who had not attended the six o'clock mass and for the students attending the convent school. Again, as unbelievable as this might sound to a modern student, *antes*, all Catholic students were expected to attend daily mass before going to school.

At 12:00 sharp the bell would signal *medio día* (mid-day) at which time people working outdoors would pause for a moment of silence before continuing their tasks. In the case of a man wearing a hat, which was usual, he would remove his hat during that pause and bow his head. This was a sign of respect and reverence before returning to work.

In the evening, at exactly 6:00 p.m. the bell would ring *los angeles* (the angelus). Originally the bell rang at this time to announce a prayer of the same name. Here, *los angelus* told the inhabitants that the day was done.

On Sundays, the bell schedule included a 10:00 o'clock mass in addition to those and six o'clock and eight o'clock. *Antes*, there were no masses in the evenings.

As soon as the priest was informed of a death this bell would toll slowly, with regular, repeated strokes, to announce the death of a member of our community. This tolling was referred to as *doblar*. In many instances, the priest, upon returning from having administered last rites to the person who had died, would toll the bell himself, regardless of the time of day or night.

Antes, as can be seen in the accompanying photograph below the Catholic church had a steeple in which the bell was housed and the heavy rope used to ring the bell came down into *el campanario* (the church foyer) at the front of the church. When the bell was not being rung, the heavy rope was pulled to one side of the double-door entrance and rested on a hook. To my knowledge, only the priests or the head of the *mayordomos* was ever allowed to touch that rope. That is how seriously people here considered the bell's importance.

The church bell also rang during feast day processions and following wedding masses. It is my understanding that, in the unfortunate event of a big fire in the community, the bell would also sound as an alarm to get people's attention to come and help put out the fire. I also know that, on the day the Second World War ended, that conveyor of many messages rang loudly and endlessly. It was the middle of the afternoon when news of the War's end reached Cuba. It was summer and, as usual, children were outdoors playing or doing chores, as were many adults. Suddenly the bell began to ring. Soon after that the convent school bell began to ring as well. They kept on ringing and ringing. People ran into the roads to see what was happening. Not seeing any smoke anywhere, they knew it was not a fire. Soon after that, the joyous news got out and everyone started to cheer.

Some people were weeping and laughing at the same time and everyone was telling their neighbors that the war was over. The few people who had cars or trucks were blowing their horns, wanting everyone to know that the war had finally ended.

The bell at the convent school had a completely different sound than its neighbor next door. The school bell first rang at 9:00 a.m. There was no warning bell or "first bell." At the sound of the nine o'clock bell, all the students would line up at their entrance on the assigned side of the ten or twelve steps that led up to the porches on the north and west sides of the school building. With every student in line among his or her classmates the sisters, each on her own cue, would signal their classes to march up the stairs into the hallways and classrooms.

Although there were recess periods both in the morning and in the afternoon, the big bell would not sound again until 1:00 p.m. when the lunch break had ended. Given that many children walked home for lunch, when the one o'clock bell rang, the same drill of lining up would be repeated in the same ritualistic manner for the afternoon session. At four o'clock sharp, the bell would ring to mark the end of the school day.

The convent school bell was housed in a belfry at the very top of the building, as can be seen in the following photograph. Like the church bell next door, this bell rang only when the rope was pulled. The hefty rope that rang this bell came down three stories into the main hallway, right outside the door to the sisters' living quarters and hung down next to the big pendulum clock. To my knowledge, similar to the church bell rope, no one ever touched this rope except the Sister Superior. Apparently only she had the authority to ring the bell that dictated the movements of every student in the only school in Cuba at that time.

Our third bell was the bell at Cuba Presbyterian Church. This is the only one of our three bells from *antes* that is still in place and still in service. Furthermore, this is the only bell left in town that rings only when its old, hefty rope is pulled. Currently, the bell at Immaculate Conception Church is electronic and rings automatically when set to ring (and when we have electricity). Originally the bell at the Presbyterian church had a belfry. This bell is now housed in the lower part of the attic on the southeast end of the church, over the foyer. The rope that rings this bell simply hangs down over the main entrance, high enough that it doesn't hit anyone on the head upon entering the church.

This bell normally rings at eleven o'clock on Sunday morning as a call to worship. Unlike the other two bells, there is little formality or ritual associated with who rings the bell. *Antes,* it may have been the duty of one of the elders to ring the bell. Today, it is not uncommon for one or several of the children present, with the help of an adult, to participate in the ringing of the bell and the call to worship. This bell is heavy enough that it requires an adult to reach the rope and to hang onto the child who continues the ringing, lest the child be lifted up higher than expected.

In addition to the Sunday morning call to worship, this bell is also happily rung after wedding services and traditionally during summer Bible School. To my knowledge, this bell does not toll following the death of one of the members of the congregation. Today, the small congregation of the Cuba Presbyterian Church still takes great pride in calling their members to worship by manually ringing their historic old bell.

The local *Iglesia Pentecostal* (Assembly of God Church) goes back in Cuba's history to the early twentieth century. Although its location has always been the same, that church apparently has never had a bell. However, upon looking at early photographs of the local *Penitente Oratorio* (*Penitente* Chapel) which used to be located west of the Catholic cemetery, one can see that a belfry was originally built onto that building. So perhaps, *Antes, mucho mas antes* (a very long time ago), there may have been a fourth bell that rang through our village to call that special segment of our community to worship.

Today it is difficult even to hear the electronic bell, with its four speakers pointed in all directions, unless one is in or directly around the Catholic church area. Such is the din of highway traffic, motorized tools, appliances, radios and televisions that surround us all twenty-four hours of the day. Today we each rely on our own devices to mark the time and the passing of the day instead of relying on sources that informed the entire community.

Immaculate Conception Church with the convent school to the right, circa late 1940s.

Franciscan Sisters Convent School, 1939.

Cuba *Penitente Oratorio,* 1972.

Había Respeto para la Muerte
Death was Deeply Respected

Antes, mucho mas antes (a long time ago), a death in the family was an event of somber respect and deep bereavement, as well as a tremendous amount of work. The rituals related to death were not dismissed or forgotten in time for everyone to return to life as usual on the following Monday morning as sometimes appears to be the case today. A death in the family literally involved every member of the family. Each person was expected to participate, including the children. For the immediate family, the observance of this rite of passage lasted a minimum of six months. In most families here in Cuba, the formalities lasted for an entire year.

Slow death normally occurred at home, either due to old age and its complications or as the result of a serious accident or long illness. It was rare for people to die in a hospital or in the care of someone other than family members. The only exception was those who died in the state mental institution and there weren't many of those. Generally, people died at home, surrounded by family and the familiar sounds and smells of their lives. People passed away in much the same way they were born, among their family and in a most familiar setting.

Sudden and unexpected death either due to accident or stroke or heart attack frequently happened away from home. However, the body of the deceased was transported home as quickly as possible.

In either case, once the extended family was notified of the death, the traditional preparations would begin immediately. Traditionally, the family would gather and duties would be assigned. Whatever resources, such as money, materials or food, that were available would be brought forward. The rituals associated with death would now swing into motion.

The first order of business was to notify the priest, if he wasn't already present. It was essential in the case of those near death to receive *los santos olios* (last rites, which included anointing the body with holy oils) and perhaps to have their last confession heard by the priest. For those who died before the priest arrived, they would also receive *los santos olios* and the priest's blessing.

By this time all of the women and older girls in the family would have covered their heads in black shawls or simple black scarves. The next of kin would also have changed into black or other dark-colored clothing. The priest would bless the body as well as the family and prayers would begin. Candles would be lit and the priest would leave to toll the church bell. This tolling of the bell was the signal for the rest of the community to begin its preparations on behalf of the family now officially in mourning.

With the help of neighbors and friends, men would begin the butchering necessary to provide meat for at least two wakes and a funeral meal. The women of the family, also along with neighbors and friends, would begin removing all the furniture from the room where the body was to lie in state. *Los Hermanos Penitentes* (a lay religious organization described elsewhere), traditionally in charge of building the casket, would have to be notified. It would be the goal of those building the casket to have it ready by sundown in time for the first *velorio* (wake, or vigil), which would last all night.

In those times, caskets were made out of the best lumber available. Some of these coffins might end up being made out of rather rough lumber if nothing better was available. The coffins were simple wooden boxes with a lid that would be nailed in place at the time of the funeral mass. Before the mass the pall, or mantel, was put on to cover the wooden box during the mass and the trip to the *campo santo* (cemetery). The inside of the coffin was lined with satin or taffeta bought locally from one of the merchants. Bolts of satin and taffeta in various colors were standard merchandise in the local stores, as was muslin. Muslin was sometimes used to line the coffin and the more expensive taffeta or satin was only used more decoratively next to the body itself.

By the time the casket arrived, the women would have cleaned the body and dressed it in appropriate apparel to be presented with dignity and respect for viewing and for the *velorio*. By sundown, the room where the body would lie in state was completely clean and all the *santos* (carved wooden statues of saints) owned by the family were placed by the coffin.

There would also have been huge amounts of wood chopped to keep the cooking stoves and outdoor ovens well stocked for several days. This wood was also needed for outdoor bonfires which were kept burning throughout the two nights while wakes were in session. These bonfires served two purposes. First, they provided light around the exterior of the house in a time before electric lights or street lights. They also informed members of the community where services were taking place.

The wake itself consisted primarily of *Los Hermanos Penitentes* praying the rosary and singing the *alabados* (hymns of praise) designated for the occasion. The guests from the community would join the family in these prayers and hymns in the room where the body was laid out. There would be several rounds of these prayers and hymns, with one group leading and participating in the prayers and hymns and another taking a break. The body would be accompanied throughout the night as these groups alternated with their offerings until sunrise. While some of the people prayed, others ate or walked around outdoors among those tending the fires or visited with relatives and friends.

Traditionally, there was also a lot of quiet socializing during these gatherings. There were people coming and going all the time, bringing food, helping with the cooking or doing whatever they could to be supportive while paying their respects to the family. Outside the house, men visited quietly, perhaps sharing a few sips of *mula* (moonshine, or something equally potent). The children were required to kneel throughout the first rosary their family attended. Following that, the children would go outdoors and run around the bonfires, play tag and try to scare each other with a good ghost story. Some would also sneak up behind another and surprise them, just to scare them. Occasionally, one or another adult might have to reprimand some children for being too noisy and not showing enough respect. Only a single reprimand was generally enough to bring the kids back into order for a while. The more timid children either remained indoors or stayed very close to the house. Being out in the night without any lighting except the bonfires could be a very scary thing for a child.

At midnight, there was a final rosary prayed by the *Hermanos Penitentes,* and everyone came in for that except a few men left to tend the fires. Following that rosary, the children would be gathered up, the babies bundled and the guests and *Hermanos* would leave. The immediate family, along with members of the extended family and a few *compadres* and *comadres* (godfathers and godmothers of family members) would be left to continue praying until daybreak. Some members of the family would rest while others began the preparation of more food for the next day and the second wake.

As well as honoring the deceased person, there were some very practical reasons why the burial was not until the morning of the third day. It took time for such essential things as digging the grave. *Antes,* graves were dug with picks and shovels. Imagine digging a grave during a rainless, hot June day or trying to dig a grave in the middle of winter. This was a horrendous task. First, in winter, the snow would have to be shoveled off the grave site, then a fire built and kept going for some time to thaw the ground enough for the picks and long iron bars to break up the frozen ground before the shovels could be used. Think also of the men doing this work in a typical cold, windy winter day in Cuba.

Other tasks that required time during a death in a family included preparing the huge amounts of food needed to feed the people who would gather for such an event. Keep in mind, travelling was very difficult in these times. It could take an entire day to journey to Cuba from Gallina. If they heard about the death in time, people might travel from such places as La Jara or even Gallina and some might very well stay and eat with members of the family living here in Cuba. Also keep in mind that there was no refrigeration (except in winter), no electricity and no running water. All the water for such a gathering would have to be brought to the house in buckets and pails. If no water was immediately available, it was hauled in barrels on wagons. Again, the amount of wood needed for heating, cooking and maintaining the bonfires during this three-day ritual would be shocking by today's standards. This would be especially true if the death occurred during the winter.

On the morning of the third day after the death, the entire family would prepare to accompany the deceased to the church for the funeral mass. The *Penitentes* would arrive in time to carry the coffin in a horse-drawn wagon. They would sing yet more *alabados* and pray during the trip to the church. The family would travel in wagons following the one carrying the body. As these wagons went along, neighbors and friends would fall into line and by the time the body reached the church, the bell would have been tolling for some time. By then, community members coming from all directions would be in place to receive the body as it was carried into the church, followed by the immediate family. The bell would continue to toll until everyone was inside the church.

Prior to the Second Vatican Council (1962–65), the funeral mass was very stately, somber and very dramatic. If there were young boys in the family, they would be among the many altar boys serving the mass. The priest wore special vestments reserved for funeral masses. The pall would be placed over the casket while the priest blessed the body with holy water again. There was an incense burner which the priest also swung as he slowly moved around the body and prayed. The church choir would be in place on the balcony and the solemn mass would begin. Again, prior to the Second Vatican Council, this mass would have been in Latin, but it was not the ordinary mass. It would have been a requiem mass intended specifically for funerals. The family, all dressed in black, with the women wearing shawls and in some cases veils, would be served communion first, followed by rest of the community.

After the mass, the casket would again be loaded onto the *Penitentes'* wagon for its final journey along with a procession of other wagons. People on foot would slowly make their way to the *campo santo* (cemetery) and the grave site. In communities such as La Jara, where the cemetery is immediately adjacent to the church, the pall bearers would carry the casket to the grave site and no wagons would be involved. The entire procession would be accompanied by the *Hermanos Penitentes* singing more *alabados*.

After the burial ceremony and much sincere weeping, the family, some close friends and the priest would return home. There, the funeral meal had been prepared and was ready to be served by people who had stayed behind.

For seven days following the burial, the family would remain at home in a state of deep mourning. People would continue to come to give condolences if they had not been available during the time of the services. Friends, neighbors and extended family members would continue to take care of the daily chores such as attending to animals, hauling water and cutting wood. On the morning of the seventh day, the whole family would attend *la misa de siete dias* (the seventh-day mass). After this mass, the family would officially begin their period of *luto* (a period of personal mourning) which minimally lasted six months but more generally lasted an entire year.

Luto was the period in which women continued to wear black; their heads were shawled in black when they attended church. During this period of *luto* the family did not attend any public events, weddings, baptismal receptions or festivities of any kind. On the first anniversary of the death, the family again gathered and, still dressed in black with the women shawled, attended *la misa de acabo de año* (the mass of the end of the year of mourning). This mass was also called *la misa de tumba* (the mass of the tomb). This mass was basically a replication of the funeral mass. There was even a replica of the mantled casket in the middle of the aisle in the front of the church. It is my understanding that this mass, along with the Latin-language mass, were among the practices done away with following the Second Vatican Council. Today some families still arrange special masses or arrange for the mention of names of the deceased in prayers on the anniversary of a death.

Following the anniversary mass, the family had done their duty according to local tradition. They had paid their respect to their dead and they could now return to a more normal life while still feeling the pain of their loss. According to local folklore, one of the mothers who lost her son in World War II wore black and continued to cover her head with a black shawl for the rest of her life. The women here held this mother in high esteem for honoring the memory of her son until her own death.

Cuba's practices related to death have changed dramatically over time. There are several reasons for these changes, some of them determined by events very far away. Among the most significant causes for some of the changes had to do with World War II.

Of tremendous importance was the number of people who moved

out of Cuba during and since the war and never came back. The absence of these family members left huge voids in our family structure and in the dynamics between those who moved away and the few that remained. Those who moved away had different life styles. They also had different demands on their time, such as full-time jobs and family commitments in their own communities. Attending extended death rituals is often impractical or impossible for our distant cousins. Furthermore, moving away loosened the family bonds we once shared in our closely-knit families. Interestingly, the only time we see many of our cousins and other relatives today is at funeral services. We all comment on how great it is to see each other and how we should try to visit more often. In fact it very well might not be until the next funeral or wedding that we do see each other.

Another truly significant cause for change in our death rituals occurred with the changes within the Catholic Church. The Second Vatican Council, convened by Pope John XXIII between 1962 and 1965 redefined many of the ceremonies of the church. As the church changed, religious practices here and elsewhere also changed.

Of course, all the other changes that occurred in our communities have had their impact on death rituals as well. People can read of deaths in newspaper obituaries, hear about them by telephone or read about them on the internet. They can travel back to Cuba for services much more easily than before and return home instead of staying with relatives for days. Food preparation also changed with the advent of running water, electricity and natural gas. Bonfires were replaced by outdoor electric lighting. It is still frequently the case that friends and relatives of a bereaved family provide food for funeral meals as well as for the family for days after the funeral rituals have ended. Similarly, help is often provided to the family to take care of animals and do other chores that the family is not yet ready to resume. This is an instance of behaviors from *antes* carrying over into our modern lives.

For those of us who experienced *antes*, we were taught from early childhood that death and dying were a part of living. Our sorrow notwithstanding, we have continued to take care of our family graves and visit them often. Although we no longer practice the strictly prescribed rituals of the past, we continue to honor the memory of our dead with love, dignity and respect.

Nuestro Convento de Antes
Our Early Convent

Nuestro convento de antes left a positive and indelible footprint on several generations in the community of Cuba and surrounding settlements. The impressive, three-story convent was situated next to the beautiful 1915 Catholic church, where they both commanded attention and defined the heart and soul of this community for five decades.

Sister Raphaela and Sister Euphemia arrived in Cuba on August 27, 1916. Incidentally, this would have been shortly after the church had been completed and construction of the convent would already have been in progress. The Franciscan priest in residence at the time of the sisters' arrival was Father Camillus Fangmann who was referred to locally as *el padre Camilo.* Also in residence were at least three Franciscan Brothers: Julian, Liberius and Livor.

According to archived materials (Immaculate Conception Convent School [1980], 2), the priest and the brothers moved out of the rooms behind the church sanctuary to accommodate the sisters. In spite of their unfinished quarters, school opened on the first Monday in September, 1916, with an enrollment of about ninety pupils. Sister Euphemia taught the more advanced pupils in one of the sacristies, while Sister Raphaela taught the little ones in the old public school some distance away. There is no indication of where in town this old public school was located. However, what is reported in the convent archive is that "thus passed the first happy year in Cuba." Incidentally, local Hispanic people never referred to the Franciscan Sisters as "nuns" (*monjas*). They were always referred to as *"las hermanas"* (the sisters), a title of respect and substantial authority.

The priests and the brothers had started working on the new convent building but, given our infamous lack of roads for transporting building materials, there were delays. In 1917, Sister Walburg was sent to cook for the teaching sisters, but she contracted influenza in that winter's epidemic and was sent back to Albuquerque. In the winter of 1918, when the influenza epidemic was at its worst here in Cuba (and the rest of the world), Sister Generosa came to help nurse the sick and dying. Besides having the epidemic to cope with, apparently Father Camillus' building fund was also running low. In a letter written from the Archbishop's House to Father Camillus in November 1919, the Santa Fé office had given approval for $5000 in additional funding to get the roof on the convent building. This task alone would have taken another year to complete. Delays and epidemics notwithstanding, in September of 1920 both Sister Euphemia and Sister Raphaela taught in the new building while continuing to live in the rooms behind the church.

It was not until September of 1921 that the sisters moved into their new home. At that time Sister Bridget joined them as a teacher and school opened for day students as well as for forty boarding students. No total enrollment is given for that first year following the completion of the building but there must have been over a hundred students. Regardless of the number of students, what people recall was how the status of this community rose in the eyes of neighboring towns and villages. The convent easily rivaled Our Lady of Sorrows Convent in Bernalillo or even the Convent of Loretto in Santa Fé. There was nothing anywhere near here as imposing and well-built as our convent school.

Given the size and the quality of the construction of *el convento de Cuba,* it was obvious that the building was expertly designed. Also, given the time it took to construct the building, it was neither haphazardly built nor built in the local traditional style. Yet there seems to be little information passed down about either the designer or the builders. There are several references that imply that the Franciscan Brothers in residence, as well as Father Camillus and his successors, were instrumental in the actual construction of this convent.

The interior of the convent reflected skilled workmanship throughout. The wide hallways on all three floors had beautiful, varnished wainscoting. The flooring and stairs were all oiled hardwood. The doors to every room were solid wood, varnished and polished to a high gloss. The wide banisters were also highly polished hardwood. Although it was strictly forbidden, it was difficult for students to resist sliding down the wide banister to the first floor.

The first floor of the building included the sisters' living quarters. This area, taking up the entire south half of the first floor, was off limits to everyone except the sisters. The north and east sides of this first floor consisted of two spacious, airy classrooms with large sash windows that were kept open in warm weather. There was also a smaller classroom and a beautiful formal dining room where the priests were served their meals. There was a central hallway with two wide staircases going up to the second floor.

The second floor was made up of classrooms similar to the large, airy ones of the first floor, situated on both sides of a wide, central hallway. Unlike the first floor, there was only one staircase going up to the third floor.

On the third floor there was a chapel for the use of the sisters which was also off limits to the rest of the school population. The remaining part of the third floor was used as a dormitory during those years the convent school had boarding students.

In the huge basement of the building was a very large laundry for the use of the sisters. In the laundry there was a coal-burning boiler for heating water. There was also a large, ancient washing machine that looked like an oversized wooden barrel positioned on its side. It had legs beneath the barrel and what appeared to be a crank for turning the loads of washing. There were large, deep sinks with hand-driven pumps for drawing water. There was an equally large kitchen in which meals were prepared for students, a student dining area, one classroom and an abundance of storage space. There were water pumps in the sisters' kitchen as well as in the student kitchen similar to those in the laundry. Since Cuba did not have running water until after World War II, the convent must have had a well. This well would have supplied all the water for the convent as well as for the rectory next door.

Remarkable as it may seem to us today, the only sources of heat for the school portion of this immense building were the wood-burning stoves in each classroom. As for the sisters' living area, perhaps there was a way in which that part of the building was heated from the coal-burning boiler that they used to heat water in the laundry. As big as the convent building was and as much activity as went on within its walls, it is difficult to imagine how much wood and coal were burned each winter to keep everyone warm. This question is especially relevant given Cuba's reputation for long, hard winters.

Among the unique qualities the convent building exhibited was its cement plaster exterior. At the time this building was constructed, cement plastering of structures was unheard of in this community. What is interesting is that the church next door was plastered with *adobe* (mud plaster) and traditionally was plastered every year by the congregation just before *la fiesta* (the feast day), as described elsewhere. Apparently, when the school was finished, it was plastered in the new, modern fashion, with cement. It remained so until its destruction in the 1960s.

Another unheard of feature on this building was its shingled roof. This was a construction feature that was simply not used here. Recall that $5000 had been approved by the Archbishop's office in Santa Fé specifically to put the roof on this mammoth building. These features, along with many that have been described in its interior, imply that whoever designed this building was not from here. Perhaps even those who actually constructed or supervised the construction of this exceptional convent brought a very unconventional, non-Southwestern world view into our midst. Whoever these people were, they certainly succeeded in providing the Franciscan religious order and the Catholic community with an impressive venue in which to accomplish their mission.

The status of the community related to the convent and the services it provided motivated families from this community, as well as surrounding areas, to bring their children to school in Cuba. Many of the families from the outlying areas who brought children to school here did so at tremendous sacrifice. However, that did not seem to matter. What was important was that their children came to *el convento en Cuba* to get their education. *El convento* was seen as a place of learning, prestige and discipline and thereby a place of status.

On May 22, 1936, our convent school held Cuba's first twelfth-grade graduation. The graduates were Susana Montoya, Antonio Montoya, Bessie Young, Donald Young, Felix Gurulé, Merejildo Gurulé, Eric Holz and Rudy Gutierrez.

There are many other stories to tell related to the era of *el convento*. However, those stories will have to wait for another time.

The Franciscan convent building in 1929. The orchard that appears in this photograph later became a bare playground. Courtesy of Judy Gutierrez Casaus and Sadie Martinez Ochoa.

High school students at the convent school, circa 1932–33. Bottom row, left to right: Billy Young, Manuel Crespín, Augustin Eichwald, Rudy Gutierrez, Esequiel Salazar. Row #2: Unidentified boy, Eric Holz, Donald Young, Juan Isidro Maestas, Antonio Montoya, Felix Gurulé, Sarafine Loomis, Merejildo Gurulé. Row #3, girls, left to right: Christina Casaus, Carolina Gurulé, Theresa Cordova, Bessie Young, Susana Montoya, Dolores Montoya, Sister Odda, Tomasita Montoya, Eursinia DeLaO, Alejandra Padilla?, Atilana Gurulé, Ermerlinda Gallegos and Margaret Sanchez. Photograph gift from Eursinia DeLaO Cordova.

One generation later, Sister Flora's 4th Grade class, 1946–47. This class would become Cuba High School's Class of 1955. Top Row, left to right: Manuel ___, Eddie Montaño, Herbert Wilson, Feliciano Valdez, Marcelino Montaño, Pedro Cebada, Epitacio Salas. Second Row: Luis Casaus, Leonardo Valdez, Alice Sandoval, Lillie Blecher, Gladys Jefcoat, Julia Maestas, Rosarito Herrera, Felix Atencio. Third Row: Rosalio Jaramillo, Ferminia Casaus, Rosella Apodaca, Esther Cordova, Gloria Montoya, Irene DeLaO. Front Row: Rita Sanchez, Erminda Lucero, Magdelena Mora, Laura Montoya, Rafaela Crespín, Helen Montoya, Bernice Cordova, Grace Sandoval, Mary Elizabeth Young. Photo taken on the west steps of *el convento*. Courtesy of Herbert Wilson.

Santos de Devoción Sincera
Santos Given Sincere Devotion

Antes, our *santos* were regarded with deep and sincere devotion. These *santos* and *retablos* were to the early settlers of northern New Mexico and southern Colorado a source of religious inspiration, comfort and love. *Santo* is a generic name in Spanish for any carved sacred image but typically the image of a saint. A *retablo* usually refers to an altar screen, but may be any painted flat image of a saint. In practice, the term generally refers to pine panels coated with *gesso* (plaster) painted in the same way as *santos*.

These *santos* provided the link between people and their faith. When the isolation of the northern frontier and the lack of resources deprived these faithful Catholics of any other means of securing sacred images, their Christian experience and devotion compelled the people in this area to make their own. These images were simple but meaningful representations of the people's saints. The artisans' primary motive was to convey the message of Christianity as they had known and remembered it in those far off places from which they originated.

According to scholarly and other reliable sources, the most prolific age of *santo* making in New Mexico was from about 1795 to about 1860. After 1860, the art declined until it faded out completely in the last decade of the nineteenth century.

There are historical reasons for the golden age of the making of *santos*. It was nearly one hundred years between the re-conquest and re-colonization by *Don* Diego de Vargas in 1692 and the beginning of home-crafted *santos*. During that century, people here had been totally dependent on what could be brought by caravan from Mexico. These supply caravans could take as long as two or three years before reaching the more remote settlements. These supply caravans were also primarily meant to serve the needs of the Franciscan priests in their efforts to Christianize the Native people and provided little if any supplies to the Hispanic settlers. As a result, the local artisans began crafting *santos*. There was little inclination to transport from Mexico religious symbols that could be manufactured here, especially when there was little money to buy such items.

There is ample evidence that from the beginning of the colonial period well into territorial times the shortage of priests was acute. The few priests who were sent to northern New Mexico from Mexico were normally assigned to minister at the Pueblos and not to the remote mountain villages settled by Hispanics.

By 1833, when Bishop Zubiría of Durango, Mexico finally visited New Mexico, he found the village churches under the leadership of New Mexican secular priests. These young men had studied at the seminary in Durango, Mexico since early in the nineteenth century to become secular priests and return to New Mexico to serve in their own communities. Many of them had been students of Bishop Zubiría and included individuals such as *Padre* Antonio José Martinez of Taos, *Padre* Manuel Gallegos of Albuquerque and Vicar *Don* Juan Felipe Ortiz of Santa Fé. As secular priests, these individuals were still bound by canon law which required them to be celibate and obedient to their bishops. Different from ordained priests, secular priests were not members of religious orders, such as the Franciscan or Jesuit orders.

Along with the shortage of priests and the colonists' dependency on supplies from Mexico, there was a substantial lack of hands-on leadership in the church in this area. Scholars record that when Bishop Zubiría made his Episcopal visitation to New Mexico, it had been 73 years since the last Episcopal visit to the churches of the northern frontier. One can understand how the poor, isolated colonists of northern New Mexico might have felt abandoned and on their own.

Bishop Zubiría also found that the village churches had their own *patrones* (patron saints) along with other *santos* to which the villagers were fully devoted. In almost all the villages Bishop Zubiría visited, he also found well-organized, active societies of religious laymen known as *La Sociedad de Nuestro Padre Jesús Nazareno* or *Los Hermanos Penitentes* (The Brotherhood of Penitents). At Santa Cruz, the Bishop issued a strong condemnation of this brotherhood of *Penitentes* and urged his priests to discourage further spread of these unauthorized groups of religious laymen. He also discouraged the proliferation of the *santos* used by the *Penitentes* during their Lenten and Holy Week ceremonies.

There were two important factors that Bishop Zubiría didn't understand regarding his condemnation of the *Penitentes* and the *santos* in 1833. The first thing he didn't understand was that by the time he became aware of the *Penitentes* and their role in their communities, the *Penitentes* had built *moradas* (meeting houses) and *oratorios* (chapels) in nearly every Spanish-speaking community in northern New Mexico and southern Colorado. Furthermore, during all those years that the people had been without priests attending to the needs of their villages, it was the devoted *Penitentes* who had comforted the dying and buried the dead. It was the *Penitentes* who gave charitable aid to widows and orphans and maintained the faith in general in those difficult times.

The other thing the visiting Bishop did not take into account was that his parish priests were members of the communities in which the *Penitentes* had been held in high esteem. It was also likely that these priests were related to every *Penitente* for miles around. Ultimately, the priests would merely warn the brotherhoods of the Bishop's displeasure.

With the passing of control of northern New Mexico and southern Colorado to the United States in 1848, control of local churches eventually passed from the Mexican diocese of Durango to the American diocese of Cincinnati. When Bishop Lamy first came on the scene from Cincinnati in 1851, he issued even harsher condemnations of the *Penitentes* and *santos*. These same priests tried to protect the *Penitentes* in their parishes until Bishop Lamy succeeded in excommunicating most of the Spanish-speaking priests and replacing them with priests from France, Germany and elsewhere in Europe.

The beginning of the decline of the beloved *santos* coincided with the arrival of Bishop Jean Batiste Lamy and his associate, Father Joseph Machebeaf. During the time that Bishop Lamy and Father Machebeaf were busy creating reasons to remove the Spanish-speaking priests from their churches; the *Penitentes* for all practical purposes went underground and retreated to their *moradas*. As the old *santos* were replaced in the official churches by the plaster statues imported from Europe and the eastern

United States, the old wooden *santos* were also taken to the *moradas* or to private family chapels. In many churches, such as the one here in Cuba, only the patron saint was left to dwell among the plaster statues of the other saints. It should be said that the Penitentes were later recognized by the Catholic church and are now, at least locally, an important part of the Catholic church community.

Records show that Americans coming into New Mexico during the early days of the territorial period demonstrated little if any interest in the *santos* or other religious art. In fact the few records that exist of Americans coming in contact with *santos* reflect extreme negativity, using such words as "grotesque" and "laughable."(Espinosa 1960, 29) An American who wandered into San Miguel Chapel in Santa Fé during mass said the church was decorated with a great number of the most miserable paintings and hundreds of crosses.

We must assume that the race to take possession of these "grotesque" and "miserable" artifacts began somewhere around 1900, when American folk art came into vogue. By the early twentieth century people were traveling more by train and in so doing were discovering the unique attractions of the great Southwest, which included all the Native Americans in the area as well as the small, predominantly Hispanic settlements.

By the 1920s, there were prominent collectors and dealers in native arts and crafts. These collectors would go around from village to village asking the local grocer or teacher if they ever came across old *santos* or native *frezadas* (the Rio Grande style wool blankets). The collectors said they would be prepared to offer a good price for such items. In fact, the prices they were willing to offer were tiny in relation to the value of the artifacts they collected. Flagrant as this greed seems to have been, the collecting and trading in *santos* and other religious objects had now become a very lucrative business. *Moradas* and *oratorios* were stripped of their *santos*, as were people's homes. Families would be offered a few dollars for their *santos* at a time when they had no money at all. Remember, this was the time when people in northern New Mexico were either self-sufficient or got what they needed by barter. The money economy did not really get going here for another decade.

There is an incident reported where three old *Penitentes* in a village refused to sell their *santos*. A collector wanted them badly but he had to wait twelve years for the last of the three *Hermanos* (brothers) to pass away before he could get those *santos!*

With each passing decade the better specimens were harder to find, yet the price kept going up. In the mean time, the museums got into the race to enhance their own collections. The result was that, unbeknownst to the local people, our humble (or "grotesque") *santos* had now become extremely valuable and highly desired.

In 1969, a writer for an exhibition of New Mexico *santos* at the Taylor Museum in the Colorado Springs Fine Arts Center described the situation in this area in the 1930s. This writer states that by the 1930s the *moradas* and private chapels in a particular place in New Mexico had begun to make their *santos* available. Interestingly, the writer says that in 1936, at the time of its opening, the Taylor Museum found itself in a position to salvage many of the religious artifacts from this village.

The writer does not explain how the museum came to be in this position. What is reported is that eventually the entire content of two *moradas* and a family chapel became part of the Taylor Museum collection. This huge collection contains over 900 New Mexico *santos*. The writer goes on to say that panels from the original altar screen from the local church were also "salvaged" from the *morada*. This altar screen contained more than forty *retablos* and sculptures along with auxiliary items, including tin chandeliers and *Penitente* ritual equipment. This collection is so large that only a small part of it can be displayed at any one time.

Personally, I still find it difficult to figure out why all of these religious items needed "salvaging," or protecting back in the 1930s or why they had to be moved all the way to the Taylor Museum in Colorado from what had been private or communal places of worship.

This is not the end of the pitiful plunder of poor villages and lack of respect for what the local people of these villages held sacred and dear. In 1961, a *morada* was bought by a "movie-maker and collector of primitive art". (This is how this person is described in a 1970 issue of a popular, trendy home-decorating magazine) (Hahn 1970, 56-59). The Taylor

Museum writer, on the other hand, describes the buyer of the *morada* as having left it not greatly changed in exterior appearance. Inside, the new owner and family have tried to preserve most of the architectural elements and some of the atmosphere of the past. It is also pointed out that in the main room the family now houses their personal collection of New Mexico *santos*. In the 1970 article referred to before, the house is featured in splashy, full-page color photographs of the interior.

In a photograph of the main room, one can see no fewer than twenty-five *retablos* simply hung side-by-side from one end of the room to the other, as if they were strips of jerky hung up to dry. There are also countless *santos* shown lined up on a plain wooden shelf in no particular order. Along with all the *santos* and *retablos*, there are also several large crucifixes and a *Santo Entierro* (a very special piece used in the *Penitente* Holy Week ceremonies). Such a piece would never have been seen outside of the traditional *oratorio* but in this house it is displayed as a show piece rather than a religious relic. A question one might ask is how this kind of insatiable glut and exploitation of what belonged to communities and had been held sacred by them was allowed to happen?

By the 1970s, this obscene and overly ambitious buying, selling and trading of New Mexico's religious artifacts reached a climax. In the summer of 1972, thieves broke into Santa Fé's San Miguel Chapel, believed to be the oldest church in the United States. This chapel sits just off Santa Fé's plaza and is visited by thousands of tourists every year. The thieves not only took the wooden statue of San Miguel, the *patrone* of the chapel, which dates back to the 1700s but also took a three-hundred-year-old painting of Our Lady of Guadalupe. In addition, they took other *santos*, *retablos* and other miscellaneous religious objects including a two-hundred-year-old mass book and an equally old missal.

Santa Fé and the rest of northern New Mexico were shocked by this blatant act of crime and lack of respect. In August of 1972, then governor Bruce King declared a state of emergency with regard to preservation and security of New Mexico's historical art. According to the *Albuquerque Journal*, the governor issued a proclamation. Fifteen churches, chapels and *moradas* in New Mexico had been robbed of Spanish colonial religious art in the previous two years. Only a few of these objects have ever been recovered. However, among the *santos* recovered was San Miguel, who is back on his altar in his chapel.

The governor's efforts notwithstanding, in 1973 Santa Fé and the whole of New Mexico received a further shocking blow. The famed statue of *La Conquistadora* was stolen from Santa Fé's Saint Francis Cathedral. *La Conquistadora* is for all practical purposed the patron saint of New Mexico. This statue was brought from Mexico City around Christmas, 1625. It survived the Pueblo Revolt of 1680, going with the retreating Spanish colonists back to El Paso. In 1692, Governor *Don* Diego de Vargas chose the statue as a symbol for the re-conquest of New Mexico. It has been here ever since. Eventually the famed statue of *La Conquistadora* was found in a cave somewhere near Los Lunas, New Mexico, about one hundred miles south of Santa Fé. However, during the many weeks that this *santo* was missing, it was feared by many that it might never be found; thereby leaving a great void in the religious culture of the people of New Mexico and a fear that it could never be replaced.

In the forward (p. x) to Dr. José E. Espinosa's book, *Saints In The Valley*, Fray Angelico Chavez, O.F.M., explains best the religious role of New Mexico's *santos*. He says, "To him (Espinosa) and to me they are not queer fetishes for an ethnological alcove in a museum, nor yet objects of art to lend atmosphere to a southwest fireplace. They are dear relics of a Faith and a People in a certain time and place, a dimension to which our blood and faith can transfer us at will, and as legitimate and touching as those first attempts to portray the Savior and His saints on the walls of the catacombs."

While few of the rest of us could possibly describe our feelings so eloquently, this is very much the way most of the Hispanic people of northern New Mexico feel about their *santos* and the rest of their religious and cultural heritage.

The patron saint of Cuba, New Mexico, *La Virgin de la Immaculada Concepción y el Niño Jesús,* by the local *santero* (carver of *santos*) *Don* Manuel Aragon y Lucero. According to *Don* Rafael Aragon, son of *Don* Manuel Aragon y Lucero, these two *santos* were finished circa 1883–1884.

Nuestro Padre Jesús Nazareno, the patron saint of the local *Penitentes*. This *santo* was also carved by *Don* Manuel Aragon y Lucero, date unknown.

Christ on the cross. A traditional crucifix, this is the largest of the Cuba *santos*. This piece is fifty-nine inches from the base of the cross to the top. It was also carved by *Don* Manuel Aragon y Lucero, date unknown.
Held by the late David Casaus.

7

~ The End of Antes ~

Nuestra Historia en las Fotografías
Photographs as a Source of History

Like other snapshots, photographs taken in the Cuba area show brief, but highly detailed, pieces of our history. Some of these, particularly when set into their proper context, may be quite touching and emotionally charged and many of them help to validate portions of the history of the people who have lived in this little hamlet. Photographs that have been shared by families for generations help to document the many changes that have occurred in our surroundings over the years. Furthermore, some of these photographs can document the pride, progress and humor in the lives of our ancestors.

The following historical accounts are related to photographs that record significant moments in time in our community. The four photographs document the changes and the development that occurred in what has become Main Street, Cuba, between 1910 and 1960.

In the first picture following this article, we see what was very likely the first Catholic Church built in our community. This photograph is dated 1910 and clearly labeled "Adobe Church, Nacimiento, New Mexico, 1910." Up to now, no record has been found to tell us when the church was built or by whom. This church was here before statehood and possibly before the name of our community was changed from Nacimiento to Cuba in 1887. Long after the name was changed, people still referred to the town as Nacimiento and the church as the Nacimiento church. According to local sources, this church was located very close to the center of what became the village of Cuba. This information is confirmed by the fact that in the picture there is a fence around the sanctuary that also encloses a cemetery which was located in front of the church. Today, the ruins of that old cemetery are still visible across the street from the old jail. This church must have faced eastward since the mountains are visible in the background, as are the trees along the river, visible to the west of the building. Note also that this church had a bell tower and must have had a bell. Whether or not that bell became a part of the 1915 church is not known, but it probably did. Today there are still people here who, although they are not old enough to remember the church itself, do recall very clearly the cemetery and the ruins of this church in the location described above.

What is dramatically significant about this photograph is the absence of any buildings around the church, except two small structures in the distance along the river. Given the location of this church, it appears that what became the town of Cuba was nothing but flat, vacant land in 1910.

Another photograph, too blurry to be included in this presentation, shows the Main Street of Cuba, probably in the early- or mid-1920s. In this photograph one can make out the finished convent school which was completed and occupied in 1921. This blurry old photograph also shows what appears to be the remains of the old church shown in the 1910 photograph. A substantial number of new buildings had been built along what had become Main Street after the 1910 photograph was taken. In this blurry photograph, there were two motor cars and one truck in evidence, along with horse-drawn wagons, saddled horses and what appears to be a donkey, all sharing our Main Street.

The next picture was taken at the south end of town looking north. The steeple of the 1915 church is in view on the right side of the photograph. Unfortunately, the convent building is not shown in this picture. That would have helped as a point of reference in determining when Main Street appeared as it does in this picture. What seems to be the roof on the Eichwald mansion is visible directly across the road from the church. We know from family sources that the Eichwald home burned down in December, 1923. Therefore, it can be reasonably inferred that this photograph was taken in the early 1920s. Note the many buildings on the west side of the road which appear to be businesses. There is a very legible sign on one of the buildings that indicates that there was even a hotel on our Main Street at that time. Even though Young's Hotel was built in 1916, the hotel in this photograph is not Young's. There is only one car in the middle of this picture and, ironically, it is stopped right next to a horse-drawn covered wagon.

The third photograph is unusual in that it was taken looking westward toward Cuba Mesa. Again, given the landmark buildings, it would have been taken between 1921 and 1923. This picture clearly shows the convent building, and the church. The edge of the Eichwald mansion is visible at the right edge of the picture.

These historical photographs serve to document what had definitely become Cuba's Main Street by the early 1920s. These pictures also serve to show the tremendous amount of growth and development that took place in the ten years between 1910 and 1920.

Today's readers will very likely want to know why Cuba's Main Street development occurred as it did at this particular place and at this particular time. There are several major factors that contributed to this: the lack of economic success in the surrounding area and "location, location, location." First, as to location, at this early time, travelers coming into town from the south could have passed along this part of Main Street, coming from La Ventana and beyond. Travelers coming from the southwest would likely have stayed close to Cuba Mesa a little farther north than the current highway does. This would have allowed them to cross the Rio Puerco in a less marshy area. Then, they would have come into town along what is now Miera Road. (The Mieras were important early businessmen in Cuba.) Travelers coming to town from Gallina, La Jara, San José (Regina), or Vallecito Los Pinos would have crossed the Rio Puerco just north of town and would have gotten to what is now Main Street at its northernmost end.

Travelers coming down from the mountains to the east and possibly also from San Miguel, San Pablo and Señorito would have entered town more or less along along *Rito de Leche* or *Rito Nacimiento* Thus the early town grew up between the intersections of Main Street with Miera Road to the south and the Rio Puerco bridge at the north end of what is now Reed Road. Both the earliest church and the earliest post office were situated between these two intersections and other businesses and family residences came to fill in this area.

It is also important to remember that substantial parts of what is now downtown Cuba was subject to flooding during spring runoffs and summer flash floods. As early as the 1880s or 1890s, irrigation systems began to be developed which would serve to control much of the water that had previously flooded the current downtown area. This combination of the location of the early church, the post office, the intersection of roads and the improvements in flood control accounted for the gradual migration of people and businesses in from El Alto (near Nacimiento), Copar and other small hamlets into what became modern Cuba.

As to the lack of economic success, by the late 1920s mining both in Copar and La Ventana had pretty well played out and there was little reason for merchants to remain in those communities. Many of those people brought their businesses into Cuba. There was hope of making money in the then-prosperous sheep and wool industries that were well established here by that time.

The last picture is dated September, 1960. Its primary historical importance is that it shows a portion of Main Street right about in the middle of present-day Cuba. As one looks at this photograph, one is made aware of the Del Rio Hall, a very old building which was one of the two halls in town where dances were held for many years. The building next to the hall, Del Rio Bar and Café, continued to be a bar until the early 1980s when it burned down completely. That building was also very old and it is not surprising that there was nothing left of it following the fire. Note the towering television antenna and the many cars parked along the street.

The main focus of this picture is a float representing the *Penistaja* Club in what appears to be a parade. The float consists of a horse-drawn wagon with people in it that appear to be dressed in nineteenth century clothing. The costumes correspond to the sign on the side of the wagon which reads, "Pioneers of the West." Ironically, in the 1920s photographs mentioned earlier in this article, automobiles were a novelty. Some thirty-five years later, the horse-drawn wagon is unusual and distinguished enough to be a part of a parade.

Given that the photograph is dated September, 1960, perhaps this wagon was part of a Cuba Fiesta parade or perhaps a high school homecoming parade. This particular photograph does help to document the dramatic changes that have occurred in the appearance of our Main Street. Taken together, these photographs help illustrate the tremendous changes that occurred in our town over a relatively short period of time. The town continued to look much like the 1920s pictures through the 1930s and looked much like the 1960 picture by the mid-1950s.

Although many of us are aware of the countless changes and challenges the community and its people have endured, perhaps it is good to look back at some of the evidence as shown in these few photographs. If for no other reason, we should do so in order to gain an appreciation for how far we have come.

Adobe Church, Nacimiento, New Mexico, 1910.

Cuba's Main Street in the early 1920s. Contributed to the Sandoval County Historical Society by Thomas F. Ball. Courtesy of the Sandoval County Historical Society.

Cuba's convent, 1915 Catholic church and part of Main Street, circa 1921–23. Contributed to the Sandoval County Historical Society by Thomas F. Ball. Courtesy of the Sandoval County Historical Society.

Main Street, Cuba New Mexico, September, 1960 showing part of a parade
and various buildings and contemporary automobiles.

El CCC y el WPA
The CCC and the WPA

Toward the end of *antes*, real paying jobs came to the young men
of Cuba, first through the Civilian Conservation Corps (CCC) and later
through other programs. Congress passed legislation for these badly needed
jobs on March 31, 1933. The CCC was part of the first phase of the New
Deal initiated by the newly elected president, Franklin Delano Roosevelt.
This piece of legislation was passed as an immediate unemployment relief
measure during the Great Depression. The CCC was authorized to provide
work for 250,000 jobless male citizens between the ages of 18 and 25. The
jobs consisted of reforestation, road construction, prevention of soil erosion,
park development and flood control projects. All of the projects would be

under the direction of army officers. The men would live in camps, and be provided with food, shelter and clothing appropriate to their work. Each man would be paid thirty dollars per month. Twenty-five dollars would be sent to the workers' dependents at home and the other five dollars would be paid to the worker for incidentals. Modern readers might find it hard to imagine that a young man could get along on five dollars for an entire month, but in those days it tended to be sufficient.

Even in today's sagging economy, it is difficult to appreciate the difference those thirty dollars meant each month to the families of these workers. Northern New Mexico had been so depleted of cash money that even the most vital necessities were out of reach. With this money, families could begin to buy basic provisions such as food and clothing.

The CCC was a virtual army of generally willing and enthusiastic workers, spread from coast to coast. These men literally changed the face of our nation with their picks, axes, shovels and dedication. In New Mexico and specifically here in Cuba, young men and their families benefitted greatly from the money they earned. As well, men from here profited from the work experiences and travel opportunities offered to them through these vital projects.

Cuba and surrounding communities gained enormously from reforestation of some areas that had been heavily logged, from the building of erosion control dams and improvements in range lands. The winter of 1933 was among the hardest times ever endured by the people of Cuba. Families had no money, there were no jobs and the herds and flocks of livestock had diminished to an all-time low. The people were desperately poor. Therefore when the opportunity to join the CCC was presented to young men, they did not hesitate to register and join the Corps.

The young workers registered at what were called Flag Camps and from there they were assigned to projects. One of these Flag Camps was at La Cueva, another seems to have been located at El Rito and there were many others throughout the state. All of the camps throughout the nation were identified by numbers.

In a map of New Mexico showing the locations of CCC camps between 1933 and 1942, there are at least eighty-four camps (Meltzer no date, no page). There is a large cluster of these camps in north-central New Mexico and another large cluster in the southwestern part of the state. In Sandoval County alone, there were eight camps and there were an additional six in southern Rio Arriba County, including Coyote, Abiquiu and El Rito. Two camps were located just south of Cuba. One, located at *el Rito de Semilla*, was known as Camp #8. Parts of the adobe long-house ruins are still visible today. They are located on the east side of Highway 550 very close to mile marker 40. (A Zia Pueblo tribal corral is located on the other side of the highway at this point.) According to Mr. Dirk Vanhart (pers. comm., 26 October, 2010), the other nearby camp, located about eight miles closer to Cuba, was west of the highway and is now in ruins. It was referred to as Camp #7.

Men from here might have gone to either of these camps or anywhere else in the nation, depending on when they registered and where they were needed. For instance, now ninety-two year old Mr. George Casaus (pers. comm.) worked at Camp #8 while his brother Perfecto worked out of a camp at Elephant Butte. Perfecto Casaus worked there during the time that Elephant Butte Dam was being built. Others from here went to work in the development of Carlsbad Caverns National Park and at Bandelier National Monument. Among the many young men Mr. George Casaus recalls joining the CCC around the time he did were Sarafín Loomis, Facundo Garcia, Miguel C de Baca, Casimiro Dominguez and Decidedio Madrid. Others who joined were Ruben Cordova, Eliseo Valdez and Jim Curry. Although Mr. Curry was older than twenty-five at the time, he was hired to supervise the construction of the stone bridge at *Señorito*.

According to Mr. Curry's own account, written in about 1967 in the *Cuba News*, he said he was assigned twenty of the young men out of the Flag Camp at *La Cueva*. He was given one truck and permission to set up a Fly Camp at *Señorito* to build the bridge. Mr. George Casaus says that his father, *Don* Pedro Casaus, even though he was also well beyond the age of twenty-five, had worked on the *Señorito* bridge. According to Mr. Curry's account, he hired a man with a team of horses to skid large rocks into a loading place. This man could very well have been *Don* Pedro Casaus. The Casaus family has always been known to have good horses and given the times and the lack of money, *Don* Pedro Casaus would likely have been very pleased to have been hired by Mr. Curry. He would also have had the skills necessary to manage a team of horses in a job like skidding large boulders into place.

The second major stimulus came in 1935 when Congress passed the Emergency Relief Appropriations Act. A major part of this legislation was the establishment of the Works Progress Administration (WPA). Under this legislation, the economic relief program expanded well beyond the specific kinds of work that the CCC had provided. The CCC was intentionally designed to provide low-skilled work only for men. The WPA was far more comprehensive in scope and allowed for many more kinds of jobs that both men and women could perform and be paid for.

Between 1935 and 1938 there were six major WPA projects in Cuba and three more in La Jara. Sources indicate that in the same period of time, there were ninety-seven WPA projects going on in Sandoval County alone (Meltzer, no date, no page). Similar projects were going on all over the country. The Cuba projects consisted primarily of road repairs and improvements. This included the construction of the road from Cuba to Los Pinos in 1938. Beside the road work, there was also a sewing room operation in town. Sewing rooms hired women who knew how to sew or wanted to learn how to sew. WPA provided the machines, the materials and an instructor/supervisor to head the program. The women made clothing for needy families as well as quilts and other household items that families needed. The finished products were then distributed to families in need.

The three projects in La Jara included constructing roads and building La Jara School. That seventy-four-year-old building, with some renovations, now serves as La Jara's Community Center. The people of La Jara were wise in their decision to renovate it and modify its function to fill the needs of the community after children from La Jara started attending school in Cuba. That building is a local landmark for many of the people who attended school there during its original service.

Throughout Sandoval County, there were dozens of school rooms added to existing schools under the WPA. Other schools were remodeled and modernized in ways that made the schools more attractive and functional for students and teachers alike. Additionally, approximately ten entirely new schools were built in our county by WPA workers. According to my sources, there must have been a couple of hundred new schools built across the state by WPA workers between 1935 and 1942. Across the county, roads were built or improved, bridges were erected, dams were constructed and gophers and prairie dogs were controlled to improve pasture land.

While most of the WPA projects were geared to employment of manual laborers such as road building crews, provisions had also been made for projects dealing with the arts. This part of the WPA employed writers who conducted oral history projects in various communities. For example, Mrs. Lou Sage Balchen wrote about how the people of Placitas used to live: their customs and folklore. There is also a wonderful collection about the generations of people in such northern New Mexico communities as Taos, Truchas and *Pueblo Quemado* (now called Cordova) written by Lorin W. Brown as part of the WPA writers' program. Artists painted murals in and on public buildings and musicians operated community recreational and educational programs along with their actor and artist counterparts. The famous Santa Clara Pueblo artist, Pablita Velarde, was commissioned to paint scenes of Pueblo life under a WPA grant. She worked at Bandelier National Monument under the direction of the National Park Service.

By June 30, 1943, when the WPA was officially terminated, it had employed over eight million people and managed over a million and a half individual projects. Among these projects were those that benefitted our local communities such as the road to Los Pinos, the school at La Jara and a bridge over the Rio Puerco at La Ventana.

Politics being as it is, there were people who were critical of what the WPA was doing. These critics claimed that the program had been too extravagant. However, for the people of this region, the one dollar a day for ten to twelve hours of demanding physical work did not seem extravagant at all, especially for those families who had not seen anything like thirty dollars in a single month for a very long time, if ever.

Of all the New Deal programs, the CCC and the WPA were by far the most successful and effective. Thanks to these programs, those of us born during the Great Depression were assured a much higher quality of life than our parents and grandparents had endured in their youth. Even with all these improvements, however, the basic style of life did not substantially change. People continued their same traditions and practices, but did so with a little more security than they had in previous times. It would take yet one more event to materially change the *antes* lifestyle of this community. World War II began on the heels of the Great Depression and brought many of the New Deal programs to an end as the nation's focus turned to war and unemployment ceased to be the central concern of either the people or the government. It was only after World War II that the lifestyle changed and the new schools and new roads and bridges became so very important.

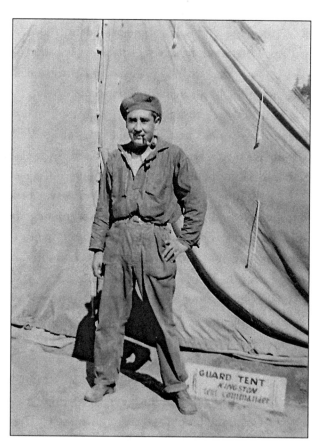

Twenty-five-year-old Ruben Cordova in his CCC-issue uniform. The sign at the bottom reads, "Guard Tent, Kingston Tent Commander." According to Mr. Dirk Vanhart (pers. comm.), Kingston was the name of a camp located in the Gila National Forest in southern New Mexico.

A CCC work crew ready to go to a job. Location unknown but probably Kingston Camp.
Ruben Cordova is in the truck directly above the man in the light colored pants on the left.

La Guerra y Antes
World War II and Antes

    La Guerra, meaning World War II, collided head on with *antes* on December 7, 1941. *La Guerra* struck the fatal blow to life as the people of Cuba had known it to be. During the period between 1942 and *circa* 1948, those who remained here maintained a semblance of what life had been like before the war began. But it was during the war years that some of the major and most lasting changes began to occur in our society.

    During the war, Cuba's economy improved greatly. Despite having to cope with ration books, the unavailability or shortages of certain products, the standard of living for everyone who remained here was enriched. Having been used to bartering and sharing, the people shared the ration stamps or traded them. In many cases, people simply gave their unused stamps to other members of their families or to their neighbors. For instance, there were so few cars in those days; very few people had any use for gasoline or tire ration stamps. These stamps could be given to someone who did have a car or truck and in return the owner of the vehicle would agree to take someone to Albuquerque and back on their next trip to the city. People here had always lived with shortages of all kinds. During the war, they accommodated the shortages as they had done before: simply by doing without.

The most important and lasting changes that occurred during the war were the role of women and the role of money. Many of the men from this area enlisted in the Armed services or left for other parts of the country to work in the defense industry. For the first time in the history of Cuba, women had money and had control of how that money would be used. The most obvious source of money came in the monthly allotment checks from the government to the dependents of all the service men. These checks were not large, but the impact that this steady income stream had on local women was profound and permanent. Women could now have checking accounts or open savings accounts and they could decide how the money would be spent. Prior to this economic change, if a woman earned any money, especially a single woman such as a teacher or a clerk, she would immediately turn the money over to her father as soon as she received it. If married, she would turn her earnings over to her husband to manage. During the war the husbands and fathers were gone and women learned very quickly how able they were at managing money. Furthermore, they liked being in control of their own resources.

Local women also left here to work in the defense plants in California, Arizona or Utah. Some also went to Albuquerque where there were plenty of jobs that paid well. These women learned more than how to manage their handsome salaries. They also learned how competent they were at learning new skills and holding a job outside of the home.

Among the new skills women learned was driving a vehicle. Few as these old trucks and cars were before the war, when the men left to fight the war, many of the vehicles were simply parked and stored away. Some of the local women figured out rather soon after the men left that they and the rest of the family would have to walk where they went while the old GMC truck was stored in the *fuerte* (storage shed) surrounded with fodder. This situation did not make sense to them so they got what little instruction they could from someone who did know how to drive, took the tarps off the trucks and started driving. Many a gate got bent and the *fuerte* suffered from the trials and errors of learning to drive in reverse, but the rest is history. The women learned to drive out of necessity, but having done so, vowed never to relinquish this privilege.

There was a real change in world view among the local people as a result of the war. This change was brought about by three major factors. The first of these had to do with the improved economy. People had more money to spend. The second factor involved a deep concern about the war and wanting to learn about where the local service men might be fighting. These concerns resulted in people buying battery-operated radios and buying and reading newspapers and magazines. Prior to the war, magazines had been items of such luxury that no one ever bought them. During the war years, people bought such publications as *Life Magazine* or *Look Magazine*. The readers were exposed to much more than news of the war. The same was true of listening to the radio. During the 1940s, radio was at its peak, not only in news broadcasting but in music, entertainment, soap operas, and, of course, advertising. With such exposure to the world at large, the people of Cuba became connected to the rest of the nation. We were no longer an isolated backwater village in the mountains of New Mexico. We had learned what J-E-L-L-O was all about. And there were those among us, even then, who thought that "the J stuff" was better than *cuajada* (curds and whey).

The third major factor that contributed to widening the local people's world view was travel. This too became possible with an improved economy. It was encouraged by the awareness gained from the media brought into our homes. Ironically, it was during these critical war years that people here began to explore the world beyond Bernalillo. This new ability to travel was in large measure the result of the war itself. The war effort demanded that some people move from one place to another. There were the service men who had to leave home to be part of the military and go where they were sent. Secondly, there were those who went to places where defense plants, such as shipyards, ammunition factories, etc. were located and where workers were needed. Many people from Cuba travelled to and from these places because there were still family members here to visit or to care for. Other people travelled to the military bases to visit the men stationed there or whose furloughs did not allow them to come home. All of these ventures involved travel far beyond the confines of almost anyone from the time before the war. With more money available, local people also travelled into Albuquerque more frequently than they had before the war.

Because there were few private automobiles and gasoline was rationed, most of this travel was by public transportation, mainly buses and trains. These experiences alone exposed our local citizens to multitudes of people different from themselves. These new encounters may have been with people who not only spoke different languages but who may have preferred foods different from our own. These experiences not only broadened the world view of the travelers, but also of those who waited patiently at home for their return so they could hear all the stories and thereby share in the experience. It was through these adventures outside of Cuba that place names such as California, Seattle, Fort Bliss (El Paso, Texas) and Long Beach, California became household names. These places could be located on maps just as easily as Berlin, Italy, Japan, France or the Aleutian Islands. Without a doubt, World War II was the single most significant event in the lives of the population of Cuba during that period of time.

Following the end of the war, there was no going back to life as it had been *antes,* before that day in early December, 1941. Given the catastrophic events of the war itself, such as the atomic bomb, there would be many reasons why people, even as tightly bonded as we had been, could not simply pick up life where they had left off in 1941.

The exodus during the war had been huge for a community of our size and the homecoming was never totally complete. There were those who happily chose to come home following their military duties or from whatever other adventures had taken them away from here. On the other hand, there were many people whose travels had shown them a world they very much preferred to the place they had come from and they never looked back. Others continued to visit for a while, until they simply couldn't relate to this place anymore. By the end of the war, others had made commitments through jobs or marriage that prevented their return. Moreover, people here slowly forgot who these former residents were, or barely remembered them from their own *antes*.

Another group could not return home, even if they had wanted to. These were the men whose lives were sacrificed fighting in far-away places. These are Cuba's World War II heroes. Nine of our soldiers never returned; a large number for a community as small as ours. Alfonso Sandoval was on the USS Arizona, docked at Pearl Harbor on December 7, 1941, and was probably our first casualty. Anselmo Gutierrez died somewhere in the Pacific arena and Leandro Montoya died fighting in Europe. Juanito Casaus, Fermin Montoya, Frank Maestas, Luciano Salaz, Ricardo Montoya and Ray Kimbel also died on battlefields far away from home.

Not all of the news we got was so sad. On January 30, 1943, there appeared in the *Albuquerque Journal* two small pictures of soldiers in uniform, along with a short article about these men. Unfortunately, the quality of the newspaper photographs is not good enough to reproduce in this book. The soldiers pictured in the *Journal* were from right here in Cuba. They were Sergeant J. Aparcio Gurulé and his brother, Corporal Merejildo Gurulé. The story stated that both brothers were stationed with the Allied Expeditionary Forces in North Africa. The article also reported that Aparcio Gurulé had been with the forces that landed at Casablanca, Morocco, early in the African campaign and that his brother was serving in a tank destroyer battalion that arrived somewhat later. At the time, neither the family here nor Aparcio had any idea where Merejildo might have been. This incident was not at all uncommon during that war.

Nineteen forty-three was a deadly time for all Allied Forces everywhere. Europe was still under the tight grip of a strong Nazi German army which, at that time, appeared to be winning the war. Yet amid all the chaos, death and destruction that was going on, our very own Gurulé brothers happened to be in the same place at the same time, somewhere in

North Africa. According to the *Journal* article, the two brothers met there and were able to visit with each other for about five minutes. Following that fleeting visit, they each went their separate ways to attend to the crucial business of war.

Today's readers must simply try to imagine the excitement and the jubilation of the local people as word began to get out into the street that the *Albuquerque Journal* had pictures of these two well-known and beloved members of our community. Furthermore, the news that they were both alive and had miraculously gotten to see each other in the battlefields of North Africa was astounding.

These two little pictures and the story that accompanied them were, for Cuba's citizens during World War II, not only a topic of joyous conversation and great pride but a historical event. Despite the fact that not many people bought the newspaper in those days, those who did shared their papers or read the story of this miraculous meeting to their neighbors and family members. History had been made for the people of Cuba in some far-away place called North Africa. Ultimately, both of the Gurulé brothers returned to live out their lives here in Cuba.

As for the children *y la Guerra*, we spent years without chewing gum. We also spent a lot of time pretending to be B-29's in our mothers' kitchens or trying to build an airplane out of a cardboard tube that some linoleum had come in. Like children all over the country, we were involved in the war effort. We collected scrap iron so it could be recycled to help win the war. We scoured every hillside and river bank for scrap metal with great success. By the end of the war, there was not a rusty nail, bolt, metal buckle or wheel rim in sight for miles around. We bought defense stamps at school, which cost a dime each. These stamps went into a little book that, when filled, we could turn in to buy a $10.00 Savings Bond. That too, we were told, would help to win the war. Ten years later, we could cash in our bonds and collect our ten dollars.

Our mothers and grandmothers made us pray a lot. Depending on how scared everyone was for the safety of our relatives in the war, we might have to pray on our knees for long periods of time.

By the time our fathers returned from fighting the war, the children were as much as four or five years older than when they had last seen them. Everyone else seemed to have changed as well. Given what we had all gone through, whether away at war or here in the safety of our village and mountains, one thing was certain: it would never be the same again. This reality is what divides *antes* from the present.

Tres Amigos queridos de Cuba. (Three dear friends from Cuba) Roberto Gurulé, Ruben Cordova and Manuel Montoya. Mr. Gurulé and Mr. Montoya had gone to southern California to work in the defense industry, while Mr. Cordova had enlisted in the Navy. Here they are shown bidding farewell to Mr. Cordova as he is about to be shipped off to some unknown place in the Pacific, 1942–43.

Casorios de Antes al Estilo Moderno
Local Weddings in Modern Style

Antes, dramatic changes occurred in weddings over a short period of time following 1939. Not only did the style of the weddings change, but so did the protocol and most especially the paraphernalia. These changes put weddings through the late 1940s into a completely different era from those that preceded them or followed World War II.

As early as 1940 the war in Europe had become a major threat to the world at large. Even in our quiet hamlet war seemed inevitable. The old order of doing things was rapidly changing, including wedding practices. The traditional way of having an honorable wedding, as described elsewhere, with predictable steps and formalities seemed inappropriate for a generation in a hurry to marry before the approaching war.

Furthermore, the economic changes brought about by the New Deal programs of the 1930s had actually brought money into our community. Through programs such as the CCC and WPA, Cuba had become part of the money economy and could now afford to have fancier weddings. Weddings could be conducted in what was perceived to be more main stream in style and could include more people than just the bride and groom and their *padrinos* (best man and matron of honor). Granted, there were cultural consequences from having more money and making these changes. However, these were issues that young people getting married after 1939 were very likely not concerned about.

During the short interval between 1939 and the late 1940s, wedding parties became bigger, as can be seen in two of the photographs that follow. These wedding parties usually involved the bride, bridegroom and *padrinos*, along with six bride's maids without male escorts. At this time it became common to include small children in weddings as flower girls and a boy as ring bearer, as can be noted in the third picture that follow. These children were so young that they had to be rehearsed for the occasion and led through the ceremony, perhaps unwillingly, but always gently.

The next major change that occurred in wedding parties and

community practices was the addition of male escorts for the bride's maids. Conveniently, this change began in the early to mid 1940s. By this time almost all of the young, eligible and handsome young men were in the armed services but if they were available they were generally wearing impressive-looking uniforms. These young men, while proudly serving our country, also provided a rather dashing image in what had become by now a huge wedding party, as can be seen in the fourth photograph.

One can see there is very little similarity between the *antes* weddings, as seen in the first photograph and what became the modern, larger and more choreographed weddings, we have become accustomed to following World War II.

Another change was that whole wedding parties would drive to Albuquerque to have studio pictures taken to mark the event. This practice was a direct result of people having more money and another sign that Cuba had become a part of the money economy of the nation as a whole. Although there were still snapshot pictures taken at weddings, these were not the only pictures a family would have of the wedding day. There were exceptions. Corine Chavez Gurulé (pers. comm.) recalled that she and Merejildo Gurulé had been married in 1948, on January 26th. The night before their wedding, we had a major snowstorm, making it difficult even to get around town, let alone get to Albuquerque to get pictures taken. When the time came to leave for Albuquerque, to keep their appointment with the photographer, only she and Merejildo and their *padrinos* were able to go,. According to Corine, the rest of her wedding party stayed behind and enjoyed the wedding reception while waiting for the dance.

Corine also confirmed (pers. comm.) that she had six adult bride's maids without escorts. There were also two teenaged flower girls, Rosemary Martinez and Gloria Montoya, and Corine's four-year-old niece, Marcella Atencio, also a flower girl. However, due to the snow storm, there is no studio picture of this grand wedding party or even any snapshots. Corine does have a studio picture of herself, Merejildo and their *padrinos*, Isabel Gurulé and Fabian Gutierrez.

By today's standards, the weddings that took place in our community during the decade of the forties seem far more subdued than those that followed in the 1950s and into modern times. Those reserved, shy wedding couples in our *antes* pictures before 1939 would very likely be shocked if they were to witness the scale and pageantry (and expense) of what evolved from their humble but sincere ceremonies into present day weddings here in Cuba.

A beautiful example of an *antes* wedding. Bride and groom are *Don* Elizardo Gallegos and *Doña* Genoveva Montoya, married in 1918. The most significant aspect of this picture is the lack of frills, such as flowers. All of the emphasis seems to be focused on the bride's attire, including her beautiful white satin shoes and lace gloves.

It is believed that the bride is Eva Lovato who married Lorenzo Gutierrez around 1946. Left to right are bride's maids Ferminia Lovato, Lydia DeLaO, Lucilla Garcia, the bride, an unidentified bride's maid, Velma Cordova, another unidentified bride's maid and an unidentified flower girl. Notice the bride's maids are wearing unmatched dresses without fancy head pieces, except for the two flowers each of them is wearing in their hair. This picture was taken behind the rectory of the old Catholic Church where there used to be a small patch of lawn and a blue spruce tree. This served as a backdrop for many wedding pictures as well as countless First Holy Communion pictures.

This photograph is of two of the six adult bride's maids and the children involved in the wedding of Manuelita Casaus and Gabriel Maestas in October, 1947. The bride's maids are Lydia De La O and Frances Aragon. The flower girl is Vangie Mora and the ring bearer is Herbert Montoya. It is said that Herbert's entire outfit, including the top hat, was hand made by his godmother, a well-known seamstress in Bernalillo. Note that by 1947, at least in this wedding party, the two bride's maids are wearing matching dresses and hats.

This photograph records the wedding of Rebeca Montoya and Sotero Montoya. In the back row, from left to right are Ramon Gurulé, Elfidese Montoya (groom's sister), Antonio Lucero, Dora Montoya (bride's sister), José Gallegos, Marcia Gurulé, Eulalio de Herrera, Manuel Montoya, Lena Martinez Gutierrez and Rudy Gutierrez. In the front row, left to right, are Josephine DeLaO, the bride (Rebeca), and groom (Sotero) and Ermalinda Sandoval. The date of the wedding is uncertain. Courtesy of Judy Gutierrez Casaus.

No Había Servicios de Salud
Health Services were Scarce

Antes, there were very limited health or medical services available to the people of Cuba or those in the surrounding areas. Finally, on December 11, 1949, after much effort from a small group of people, the Cuba Health Center was dedicated and opened for service. In retrospect, we can see that there was a shameful irony associated with this tragic lack of medical services for the people of rural New Mexico compared to what was available elsewhere to those who could afford care. Almost immediately after the arrival of the railroad in New Mexico in 1880, the railroad companies began a country-wide advertising campaign aimed at sickly Midwesterners and others calling them to come to New Mexico to be cured of their ailments. The railroad companies, in order to promote travel by rail, published brochures claiming that the dry, sunny New Mexico climate, along with the countless therapeutic mineral springs, was a good environment in which to regain one's health.

These advertising campaigns worked. Soon there was wave after wave of sick people from the Eastern and Midwestern parts of the United States migrating westward by train to be cured. There were hundreds of people who came here with tuberculosis, malaria, asthma and other diseases. Keep in mind that tuberculosis had been the leading cause of death in the nineteenth century and these people were literally flocking into New Mexico for "the cure."

The result of this huge influx of Anglo, middle class and educated people was astounding. A whole industry developed in New Mexico to serve the needs of these sick strangers while the railroads continued to make money by bringing them here. Dozens of spas were built around major mineral springs such as Ojo Caliente, Las Palomas (later Hot Springs and today called Truth or Consequences) as well as Jemez Springs and Sulfur Springs right here in our own Jemez Mountains. Jemez Springs and Sulfur Springs were not connected to Albuquerque by railroad, but in 1903 a stage line took people to enjoy the bath houses and sweat rooms. They could also stay in small cottages at these springs. Most of the other hot springs facilities were near railroads and extended from Taos County in the north all the way to Deming and Las Cruces near the Mexican border.

In addition to the spas, there was a boom in the building of sanatoria. These were facilities for people suffering mostly from tuberculosis and other respiratory problems. Later still, sanatoria were created for soldiers who had been gassed on World War I battle fields.

In Jerry L. Williams' *New Mexico in Maps*,(Williams 1986, 129-131) there is a chart listing over one hundred facilities including sanatoria, health homes, ranches, camps, mineral springs and spas. Ojo Caliente, located near Española, was among the oldest. The map that accompanies

Williams' chart also shows the railroad lines leading directly to the facilities or the nearest place that the infirmed could reach by railroad.

Sources show that more than half of the tuberculosis patients who came here died within their first year in New Mexico. Apparently the advertising campaigns were so intense and so persuasive that, despite the death rate, people from the east kept coming. The railroad companies were not alone in this campaign. For instance, by the turn of the century, the Commercial Club (forerunner of the Chamber of Commerce) in Albuquerque donated land for a sanatorium and office space for the publication of a monthly magazine for and by health seekers.

Herein lies the irony of the prosperity and publicity activity. All the time that care was being provided to terminally ill people from all over the country, our own people, especially those in rural communities, were dying from lack of medical care. Of course there is no mystery as to where the few doctors working in New Mexico at the time were located. These health facilities offered far more opportunities and money for doctors than the rural towns and villages could ever afford. Furthermore, the attitude seems to have been that the *rusticos* (rustic, rural poor) were going to die anyway. (Today we should be very happy that there are some doctors who are willing to work in communities such as ours.)

There is in our history *de mucho mas antes* (from very long ago), an important example from 1804 of the impact a single doctor had on the population of Santa Fé. As most people know, smallpox used to be a deadly, very contagious disease. Those who did survive were marked with deeply pitted scars, most prominently on their faces. Most of those who survived the disease were left blind for the rest of their lives.

During Governor Juan Bautista de Anza's term in office in the winter of 1780–81, there was a smallpox epidemic in the area around Santa Fé. Many Pueblo people and Spanish villagers died of the disease. In Santa Fé alone, it was reported that one hundred forty-two residents, mostly children, died that winter. Ten years later, in 1791, more than one hundred soldiers, along with their families and some servants, moved into the newly constructed *Presidio de Santa Fé* along with a surgeon, a chaplain, the usual scouts and some interpreters. Fearing another smallpox epidemic, the new

Presidio army surgeon vaccinated hundreds of Santa Fé children against the disease in 1804.(Abbink 2007, 62; Jones 1979, 140)

Apparently, the surgeon was aware that Doctor Edward Jenner had successfully vaccinated against smallpox in 1796 in England. Up to that time, no effective treatment had been developed. A question that should arise at this point has to do with how a vaccine could be gotten to Santa Fé to inoculate all those children. According to reliable sources, the live vaccine came from Mexico over *El Camino Real*. It came in the arms of Mexican children who had been inoculated for the purpose of transporting the vaccine to Santa Fé. Once there, pus from the Mexican children's arms was transferred to the local children so that they would also be spared from the disease and perhaps another epidemic would be avoided. Interestingly, there is no mention of whether the Mexican children were ever returned to their homes. Certainly one hopes that they were, having played such an important role in preventing an epidemic.

At the local level, people in Cuba used to get *viruela* (smallpox). As a matter of fact, approximately one hundred years after Doctor Jenner began inoculating people against this deadly disease, my own grandmother, Genara C de Baca, survived smallpox. She did so with deep facial scars, but luckily did not go blind. As contagious as the disease was, one has to assume grandma Genara was not the only one who was exposed or who survived the disease at that time. There is no record of other members of the immediate family catching the disease but there must have been other members of the community who were affected.

Besides smallpox, some people here actually survived other deadly communicable diseases as well. One such disease was called *diteria* (diphtheria). This was a respiratory disease transmitted by close respiratory or physical contact. In the pre-vaccination era, younger children were most often affected and severe cases resulted in death. This untreatable disease was not uncommon, but at the turn of the century a fair number of children lived to tell their stories about the experience.

Prior to having safe drinking water, people were perpetually exposed to typhoid fever. This is a life-threatening disease caused by a bacterium that is closely related to the strain of *Salmonella* associated with many food-poisoning cases today. Since people were not accustomed to boiling drinking water, it is very likely that the people who got typhoid fever got it from contaminated drinking water. Today we know that typhoid fever can be prevented by treating water, by good sanitation systems and by the proper treatment of foods. Today, people who do get this disease can be treated with antibiotics but *antes*, those who got *tifoidea* often died for lack of medication.

There were several other deadly diseases people suffered from before the appearance of the Cuba Clinic and modern medicine. The influenza pandemic of 1918 had a terrible impact on this community as described in other parts of this book.

Probably the most direct and shameful irony related to New Mexico being advertised as the place to go to cure tuberculosis, also called "consumption" in earlier times, is that our own rural populations, both Spanish and Native people, were suffering from this highly infectious disease. Tuberculosis usually attacks the lungs and is spread through the air when people who have the disease cough, sneeze or spit. When left untreated, TB kills more than fifty percent of its victims. Very few people from here ever went to a sanatorium, especially early on. There was no one to advise people that rest and improved nutrition could make the patient stronger, better able to resist the disease and perhaps even able to recover. There were no lounge chairs or sunrooms in our homes where a victim could rest. Furthermore, transportation was always such an issue that a person from here would not even have been able to get to Jemez Springs to spend a few days at the mineral baths. There would also have been the question of how the bill for such a treatment could be paid by any local family to enjoy "the cure" at a spa.

It is part of our history and reality that prior to the opening of the Cuba Health Center we had very limited access to dental or eye care or a preventative physical exam unless we went to Albuquerque. Again, there were such issues as transportation and the fact that there were no telephones to call and make an appointment. If someone in our town had the good fortune to have been to a doctor they liked and had been effective, the person would recommend that doctor or dentist to others in town wishing such services. Referrals were basically by word of mouth.

As far as mental health services are concerned, people simply endured or were taken care of by their families and others in the community. If the situation became dangerous, there was only one option. Somehow, the mentally impaired person had to be gotten to the State Mental Hospital at Las Vegas, New Mexico about one hundred fifty miles away. Once there, the individual usually remained for the rest of his or her life. Families knew this and avoided this option if at all possible.

Prior to the mid-twentieth century there were only two kinds of limited medical providers in our community. The first type of health providers included the trusted *curanderas* (traditional healers, practitioners using herbal remedies), the *sobadores* (individuals who performed therapeutic massages) and the trusted *parteras* (midwives) who delivered many of our babies and provided a certain amount of postnatal care when needed. Two of these women, *Doña* Gregorita Sanchez and *Doña* Victoria Aragon delivered a large portion of the population of Cuba. Both were well known and highly respected for the service they provided our community.

The other kind of medical providers were people like "Doctor" F. E. Bird and "Doctor" Robert Taylor. Records show that Doctor Bird came to Cuba around 1919 (Immaculate Conception Convent School [1980], 3) and was referred to as a physician. However, the folklore claims that he was not a licensed physician. Doctor Bird lived and practiced here well into the 1930s. It was rumored that Doctor Bird performed several appendectomies on people's kitchen tables and the patients survived to tell the story. Doctor Bird lived in a house on the east edge of modern-day Cuba. Given when he came to Cuba, he must have been quite elderly when he left the area. People seem to have liked him and trusted him. It is unclear how long Doctor Bird's and Doctor Taylor's practices overlapped but it seems that they were both here for a number of years, given the ages of people known to have been delivered by one or the other of them. (According to my parents, I was delivered by Doctor Bird.) Doctor Taylor was still delivering babies, sewing up cuts and setting bones well into the 1940s.

Doctor Taylor was a very sensitive, respected gentleman , a very good medical practitioner, but like Doctor Bird, not licensed. He exercised a tremendous amount of caution and knew and understood his limitations. He was very straight-forward about letting families know when a situation was beyond his expertise. Doctor Taylor, like our midwives, delivered many babies during his career in La Jara and Cuba.

One of the problems for residents of Cuba was that Doctor Taylor lived in La Jara. Although La Jara is only a few miles away, when mom was about to deliver the baby, someone had to get to La Jara and bring Doctor Taylor back to Cuba. In the time Doctor Taylor worked, this was not a quick or easy task. In some cases, especially in winter, the baby might have arrived before the emissary could get back with the doctor.

Finally, I would like to relate an incident of true hardship due to the lack of medical services before the Health Center opened. The woman involved in this story survived to tell her story and is still alive today. I want to retell this story because there are people who simply do not appreciate the immense impact the Cuba Health Center has had on the health and well-being of the people of Cuba and the surrounding areas. As well, many people do not recall or do not know of the tremendous efforts of the citizens who made the Health Center a reality despite countless obstacles they had to overcome. This story illustrates what it is like to be without any local medical services.

Sometime in the late 1930s, this woman developed what turned out to be an acute case of nephritis, a severe inflammation of a kidney. This condition is extremely painful. This woman and her husband did not own a vehicle but he managed to get her into town, where they took the bus to Albuquerque and somehow got to a hospital. At the hospital, the husband was told that his wife was extremely sick and would have to remain in the hospital. She was diagnosed quickly and they were told that she would have to have surgery.

Due to obligations at home, the husband had to leave his wife at the hospital and come home. Kidney surgery in those days was high-risk surgery, even under the best of conditions, but our friend had the surgery done and her kidney was removed. These were the days without antibiotics and the risk of infection was extremely high.

This woman does not recall how long she was in the hospital but it might have been weeks. When the time came for her to come home, she somehow got to the bus depot in Albuquerque and rode to Cuba. Her husband was waiting for her and had arranged for someone with a car to take her home a few miles away from the bus depot. What is amazing about this story is not only the resilience of this woman but it shows the pain and the limitations they had to work under just to get her to a hospital and back following such a serious ordeal (pers. comm.).

Very early on, if a person were very badly injured or ill, their family might try to take them to Albuquerque in a wagon, a trip of about five days in good weather. The story above describes a journey that took the better part of a day. Today, we have ambulance service that can get a person to Albuquerque in just less than an hour and helicopter service that is even faster. Cuba has not moved, nor has Albuquerque but this is a good illustration of the progress that has been made in the days since *antes*.

First Board of Directors of Cuba Health Center. Front Row, Left to right: Martha Casey, Leonor Hoch, Betty Jane Curry, Nancy Childress, Sally Montoya, Esther Hampton, Genevieve Casaus, Johnnie Smith. Standing, left to right: Uvaldo Martinez, Rudy Velarde, Walter Hernandez, Eric Freelove, Ruben Cordova, Rudy Gutierrez.

La Última Generación de Antes
The Last *Antes* Generation

Those born in the decade between 1930 and 1940 actually are the last generation who truly experienced *antes* and who remember what life was like before electricity, without running water or indoor plumbing or life without telephones, radios or television. With few exceptions, we are now the elderly members of our community. Our parents' generation, "The Greatest Generation," as Tom Brokaw called them, are almost all gone. This generation lived and survived the Great Depression as young adults. Many of them went away from this area during World War II to serve in the military and to work in defense plants. Most of them never got over the poverty and indignities they endured during that time, nor were they ever going to let us, their children, forget the hardships that had shaped their lives forever.

The generation born after World War II (1941–1945) has little if any recollection or experience of what *antes* was like. Following World War II, life in Cuba changed so fast and so radically that there is little to lead us to believe we all lived in the same place. But *antes* is engraved in the memories of those of us born in the 1930s. Remembering that humble, simpler way of life is important. Having lived in the immense shadow of The Greatest Generation, we were known for years as "The Silent Generation." There was built into that description the implication that we would become "The Do-Nothing Generation." Fortunately, that implication would prove to be mistaken.

The stock market crash of 1929 had already occurred and the country was well on the path into the Great Depression that would last for the entire decade. In 1930, Herbert Hoover was still president and was literally without understanding of how to stop the complete collapse of the entire American economy. In Europe, war was looming everywhere by the middle of the decade and war was already in progress between Japan and China. Ironically, amidst this world-wide mess, it was only in 1931 the *The Star Spangled Banner* was designated by Congress to become the national anthem of the United States.

In January of 1933, Franklin Delano Roosevelt was inaugurated as the thirty-second president of the United States. He would remain president until he died on April 13, 1945. Interestingly, 1933 not only marked the beginning of the presidency of Franklin D. Roosevelt but was also the year that Adolf Hitler was appointed Chancellor of Germany. Later that same year, Hitler was granted dictatorial powers over the entire German nation.

However, even for many urban Americans, Europe was very far away and, whoever this Hitler fellow was, there were far more pressing issues, such as how to survive the Depression, to worry about right here at home. For people in the cities, even as bad as the Depression was, there were still islands of escape that they could flee to. For instance, they might watch *King Kong* in one of their new air-conditioned movie theaters. This, along with *Dr. Jekyll and Mr. Hyde* was one of the more popular movies of 1933. Although these were not exactly feel-good movies, at least the viewers didn't have to think about how poor they were or about the looming war in Europe.

Here in Cuba, the people had neither *King Kong* nor *Dr. Jekyll* for escape or distraction. What people here had was the full reality of the worst winter of the Depression. Even by 1933, none of the government's New Deal programs had yet been implemented and there were no jobs, no money and very little hope. The Civilian Conservation Corps (CCC) legislation did not pass Congress until the end of March, 1933 and the Federal Emergency Relief Act was even slower to be enacted.

Once these and the other relief programs did reach Cuba, many people from here were able to go to work. However small the salaries were from these New Deal programs, they were better than nothing. Remember from earlier stories that ours had been basically a barter economy before the late nineteenth century. Stores had begun to come in and a money-based economy had started to grow before the depression. People sold crops and livestock to make money and mortgaged their property when they could not cover their bills. As a result, a lot of property changed hands during the early part of the twentieth century. The Depression only made this problem worse until people started bringing home paychecks from these federal programs.

It was our young parents and grandparents who suffered the full impact of the Depression. The hardships became so ingrained in them that for the rest of their lives they lived with what became known as "The Depression Era Mentality." Furthermore, they passed these attitudes down to their children. Even well after the end of the Depression, when resources were much more plentiful, we were never allowed to waste food. We had to wear out our clothes and shoes or pass them on to someone who could wear them before we got new ones. Most interesting of all, our mothers kept great stores of food, way beyond a family's needs at any particular time. This practice lasted well into modern times. It was our parents' way of assuring themselves that neither they nor their children would ever go hungry again.

The CCC and WPA (Works Project Administration) jobs only paid a dollar a day but they were much sought after and widely talked about for years after they had come and gone. By the time those of us born in the middle to late 1930s were old enough to appreciate the stories, our needs were well beyond simple survival.

Unfortunately, this new state of affairs did not last long. On September 1, 1939, Germany attacked Poland with such force that the rest of Europe was left stunned and helpless. With the fall of Poland, everyone knew that a wider war was to come. The United States resisted getting involved for over two years as more and more of Europe became involved. Ultimately, following the attack on Pearl Harbor, Hawaii in December, 1941, the United States entered the war. After the struggles of the Depression, this war also became a part of the legacy of The Greatest Generation.

Those who went off to war fought bravely and honorably and, despite the many casualties, most returned home as heroes. These new heroes had been exposed to an entirely new way of life in the larger world and were now determined to build a new kind of world for their children. They accomplished their goals, project by project and would never accept "No" for an answer to their efforts to improve and modernize their towns and villages. They believed they could improve the quality of life all over America, including our little village of Cuba. After all, hadn't they been told that this was what all the sacrifice endured during World War II was all about?

Not surprisingly, in post-World War II Cuba, the number one priority for our new heroes was clean, safe, running water. The Cuba Water Users Association was organized in early 1946. Eventually, Reed Road and Main Street had running water. The source of this water was the Rio Puerco, well to the north of town. The supply line ran down Reed Road and Main Street and on to the other end of town.

After even more hard work, countless meetings and a lot of persistence, the Rural Electric Association finally got electricity to Cuba. Although we only had one light bulb in each room and wiring was generally exposed inside houses, we all soon had refrigerators, washing machines, electric irons and even large chest-style freezers. (My own mother's chest freezer lasted fifty years!)

Electrical appliances and other goods that would have been considered unobtainable luxuries just a few years earlier were now in great demand. These were truly durable, useful and "big ticket" items. But by now the community's economy had changed once and for all. Much of the money paid to people in the military was sent to their families throughout the war and, except for food and a few other essentials, there was nothing to spend the money on and so it was saved until after the war.

It was no wonder that the national economy was booming and sounding like a well-oiled machine. By 1949, Southern Union Gas Company had brought a natural gas line through Cuba and we had natural gas stoves, water heaters and room heaters. *Don* Manuel Sandoval was one of the local agents in Cuba for Southern Union and, since people were unfamiliar with gas appliances, every time a pilot light went out or a stove or heater failed to work, our mothers would send the children out to look for *Don* Manuel to please come to light the stove or heater. Eventually, everyone learned to light their own pilot lights without blowing up anything or anyone. *Don* Manuel was so patient and kind to all the people, especially the elderly, who were afraid of modern gas appliances.

Just as *Don* Manuel Sandoval helped us learn the intricacies of gas appliances, *Don* Virginio Sandoval helped to wire all the houses for electricity and helped us learn how to use our new electric-powered marvels. (You have to unplug the heater if you are going to use the iron or you will blow a fuse.)

Along with gas, water and electricity coming to Cuba, the Ingram family started the Lindrith Telephone Company. This was not anything like a modern telephone service, but for the first time in the history of Cuba there was more than one telephone in our village. Even back during World War II, there had been only one telephone at Young's Hotel. People would have to be called from all over town to come to that phone or messages were taken and delivered to people about events happening in the wider world that affected local families.

Cuba was stepping into main stream America. By 1950, the Health Center had been completed. The Cuba Health Center was originally a six- to ten-bed hospital with a doctor and nurse in residence twenty-four hours a day. Many a baby born in the early 1950s from Cuba or surrounding communities were delivered at the Cuba Health Center by Dr. Elizabeth Howe, MD.

There were many other changes that occurred in very short order following World War II but perhaps one of the most important had to do with the schools. You may recall from an earlier story that a 1949 court decision made it illegal for church-related schools to serve as public schools. The problem for Cuba at that time was that the convent school belonged to the Franciscan Order and the sisters who taught there were the only teachers in town. The convent school became the Parochial school that is still affiliated with the Catholic church but the state of New Mexico had to build and support a separate school system. This was the case in all the other communities around the state where the public school function had been housed on property belonging to a church. There were also teachers to hire, lunch rooms to provision and staff and athletic programs to organize. When the first public school in Cuba was built a whole new era began in the education of the students of Cuba. The schools moved to the current location in the late 1950s. The old school was finally torn down just a few years ago.

By 1950, the 1930s generation was coming of age in a community that we had never dreamed could have emerged, even while we watched its changes. Furthermore, our parents were anxious for us to take full advantage of this Brave New World we were being thrust into. Even though our parents knew very well that we had no experience to guide us, they continued to urge us on. Given the encouragement we were getting, the so-called silent generation was to set a new pace. Our values changed, our styles were largely taken from the media and our music and dances were ours and not those of our parents.

In 1953, Cuba High School put out its first yearbook, called *The Yucca*. Fifteen of the seventeen students who graduated that year are shown in a photograph that follow, taken from that yearbook. According to the yearbook, there were school dances and basketball and even a senior class trip to Juarez, Mexico. The basketball team won seven out of its twelve games that year even though it had no gymnasium in which to practice or to host its games. At that time, basketball was an outdoor sport played on a concrete slab constructed by the coach and the players.

By 1954, Cuba was on the march. We were not going to be left behind in a rapidly changing world. The 1954 yearbook, still called *The Yucca*, has a full page of photographs showing progress of construction on the new gymnasium. It is obvious that the building of that structure was no small matter. On March 13, 1954, the *Albuquerque Journal* ran an article titled "Cuba To Dedicate $80,000 Gym On Wednesday." The article goes on to say that a St. Patrick's Day parade and dedication ceremony were to take place. This was an event that included floats, speakers and the crowning of the Gym Queen, who was then seventeen-year-old senior Precilla Herrera. Naturally, there was also a basketball game. The crowning of the Gym Queen took place during half time. Unfortunately, the paper does not tell us who won the game but it does say that the building would serve as a combination gymnasium and auditorium and that it had a seating capacity of one thousand people.

By 1955, the high school yearbook, now called *The Rambler*, had twelve pages of advertisers and business sponsors. That yearbook was easily twice the size of the previous ones and was filled with photographs of all kinds of student activities, including a concert by the Cuba High

School band. There were majorettes, cheerleaders, a glee club, a student newspaper and dances for many occasions. That year it appears that the Valentine's Day dance was one of the highlight activities and senior student Ferminia Casaus was crowned Valentine Queen. There are also several pages of "class favorites" and "students most likely to succeed.

Without a doubt, the Cuba schools in the 1950s were expanding and offering their students almost unlimited opportunities. One thing that was lacking was a football team. Football did not begin until after the school moved to its current location in 1958–1959. The class of 1959 was the first class to graduate from the new high school. Apparently in the fall of 1959, Cuba had its first football team. Along with football came the traditional homecoming activities and the first Homecoming Queen, Frances Arellano.

By 1960, not only had the last *antes* generation grown up, but the whole world was changing. We were in a whole new era. Ultimately, the so-called Silent Generation was not silent at all. Various movements that occurred in the 1960s caused many of us to become a generation of service to others. We became teachers, lawyers, social workers, nurses, counselors and political activists against the injustices we had inherited. Some of us also served our nation with honor and bravery in the military. Those from the earliest part of the 1930s generation fought in Korea and those from the end of that era fought in Viet Nam.

Some of us, both veterans and those who resisted war, were active in the civil rights movement, the Peace Corps and the women's movement. Some were also active in the efforts to restore land rights to communities across northern New Mexico. As we were growing up, our songs started out as far back as Frank Sinatra and Nat "King" Cole, then passed through Elvis Presley and Richie Valens and matured in the time of *We Shall Overcome* and *De Colores*.

Not everyone from our generation passed along the same journey. In our parents' generation, people went off to other states to work in World War II defense plants or in other jobs and, even though they dreamed of doing so some day, they never came back. Some of our own generation did much the same. Some of our generation simply dropped out and became hippies and never came back.

We are getting older now, but we have not forgotten that it was our generation that proved that people are capable of changing the way we think about our fellow men, women and children. Our parents changed the world we lived in but we helped to change the way people think about that world and those who inhabit it.

All of this started from our having the experience of living humbly and simply in that now fading world of *antes*.

Graduating Class of 1953. Back row, left to right: Frank Archuleta, José Maria Lucero, Eustacio Casaus, Eustacio Chavez. Middle row: Vangie Chavez, Tex Ann Cantrell, Louis Jefcoat, Annie de Herrera Trinnie Casaus, Lucy Montoya. Front row: Jacobo de Herrera, Virginia Sandoval, Bessie Crespín, Josephine Garcia, Camilo Vigil.
Not shown: Matilde Casaus and John Browning.
Photograph from the 1953 Cuba High School yearbook called *The Yucca*.

Basketball team, 1951–1952. Back row, left to right: Eustacio Casaus, José Maria Lucero, Joe Peña, Alex Maestas, Jacobo de Herrera. Front row: Bill Pace, Camilo Vigil, Eddie Montaño, Isaac Aragon, Eustacio Chavez. Courtesy of Eustacio and Eufemia Garcia Chavez.

Cuba High School's first Homecoming Queen, Frances Arellano. Courtesy of Antonia Amie Chavez Aguilar and Frances Arellano Chavez.

In Memoriam
Memorial to Those Who Did Not Come Back

This book, with the collective efforts of the readers and the community as a whole, is dedicated with reverence to those servicemen from Cuba and La Jara who died during World War II. These young men went off to war and through no fault of their own did not return to the womb of our beloved mountains or to the world of *antes*. Lest we forget them or their sacrifice, they were:

1. Alfonso Sandoval, son of *Don* Fernando and *Doña* Pablita Sandoval of Cuba,
2. Anselmo Gutierrez, son of *Don* Epifanio and *Doña* Agapita Aragon Gutierrez of La Jara,
3. Fermin Montoya, son of *Don* Juan Montoya and *Doña* Victoria Romero Montoya of Cuba,
4. Frank Maestas, son of *Don* Andres Maestas and *Doña* Merencia Gurulé Maestas of La Jara,
5. Leandro Montoya, son of *Don* Jesús Maria Montoya and *Doña* Teodorita Garcia Montoya of Cuba,
6. Luciano Salaz, son of *Don* Abel Salaz Sr. and *Doña* Celestina Gonzales Salaz of Cuba,
7. Ricardo Montoya, son of *Don* Marcos Montoya and *Doña* Ferminia Montoya of La Jara,
8. Juan Casaus, son of *Don* Juan Casaus Sr. and *Doña* Angelita Lobato Casaus of Cuba,
9. Ray Kimble. (Information about this young man's family seems to have been lost, except that he was from Lindrith.)

On Sunday, December 11, 1949, the original Health Center in Cuba held its opening ceremony, with the building being dedicated to the memory of these nine young men, while their parents occupied the seats of honor at the ceremony. Today, the bronze plaque bearing the names of these young men is still in place within the part of the Health Center that used to be the original waiting room of our wonderful little hospital.

Dedication ceremony. The plaque is clearly visible behind some of the parents and three young men still in service uniforms. Those shown in this photograph are (back row, left to right) are *Don* Marcos Montoya, Gilberto Morales, Gabriel Montoya, Jr. and Reynaldo Lovato, *Don* Jesús Maria Montoya and *Don* Epifanio Gutierrez. In the front row, left to right are *Doña* Teodorita Montoya, *Doña* Ferminia Montoya, *Doña* Agapita Gutierrez and *Doña* Victoria Montoya. Courtesy of Judy Gutierrez Casaus.

~ Epilogue ~

The world of *antes* has been gone for more than fifty years now. Today, Cuba looks like many other small towns across the American Southwest. A four-lane highway cuts through the middle of town, flanked by fast-food restaurants and gas stations. Since our town is so far from major population centers, people frequently stop to refuel their cars, to get a snack or a meal, or just to take a break in an otherwise very long trip from one place to another.

When people stop, they may hear a bit of a conversation in Spanish or in *Diné bizaad* (the Navajo language) but English is spoken in all the businesses in town and by nearly all the people who live here. What do people think of our town as they pass through? Do they wonder about how this town came to be here? In part, this book is written to answer their questions.

Our visitors will see business people about their work, ranchers hauling cattle or hay and young people glued to the latest versions of electronic entertainment. One might see a tractor on the streets but never a horse. Throughout town, there are satellite antennas on nearly every roof and computers in almost every home. Businesses use internet connections to process credit card transactions and order goods and even cowboys on horseback (or ATV's) carry cell phones. While it is a quiet town, it is relatively modern and definitely in touch with the rest of the world.

Cuba has grown over the past few decades, particularly with recent improvements in communication with the wider world. Artists of every sort have moved into the area because of its beauty and tranquility. Other professionals who can work out of their homes and a fair number of retirees have chosen to live around Cuba as well. Certainly these people are curious about the community and its history and this book is also written in part to help them understand the richness of the place they have chosen as their new home.

But the world of *antes* has not really gone away. It still lives in the minds and hearts of those who were a part of it. Whenever a couple of people of a certain age meet at the Post Office or the grocery store and visit for a few minutes, some story from *antes* or a *dicho* (a proverb) we learned as children will arise in the conversation. When a few people get together at a local coffee shop for a break from their work, reflections on *antes* will arise as well.

Some of our people share lunch together at the local Senior Center and inevitably stories from *antes* are a part of their conversation. But the time of *antes* was so long ago that stories are remembered dimly or with gaps in them. There are as many questions as there are details well-remembered by these story-tellers. It might take four of five people to fill in all the parts of some shared experience from long ago. But the reliving of the experience is the important thing, not the smoothness of the narrative. In part, this book has been put together to help flesh out some of those partially-remembered stories.

Perhaps the richest exchanges concerning our past happen at weddings and at funerals. These occasions are somewhat different because people return to Cuba from far away to join their families for these events. These are occasions when *antes* really comes back to life. Weddings are almost always followed by receptions. While the stated purpose of these receptions is to honor the bride and groom and their parents, this is also a time for family and other community members to interact with each other and spend an afternoon or evening reminiscing about their shared past. Again, as many questions are asked about details as are given by any particular story-teller. Relatives from out of town may hear stories on these occasions that they have never heard before. Children and young adults may find out things about their families that they have never known. People may even come to discover that they are related to other families in the community that they did not know about and go away realizing that they have a whole new set of cousins to try to keep up with!

Most of these weddings are followed by dances as in the *antes* period but they likely do not end with *La Raspa* and *Home, Sweet Home.* Certainly *Don* Sambrano does not quietly step into the hall at the end of the evening to see that everyone gets on their way home safely and without incident. Actually, those of us who lived in the time when that really happened have likely gone home to sleep well before the end of the dance.

Like weddings, funerals are not as formal as they used to be. It is often the case, however, that there is a service the evening before the funeral itself. In the Catholic church, this is a time for the Rosary to be recited and eulogies presented. Other churches offer families the opportunity to gather to pray and sing and to eulogize the departed. In either case, this service and condolences are followed by a gathering involving fellowship and food. (As always, food and conversation continue to be at the center of any gathering.) As with weddings, these are opportunities for people from far away to return and join their friends and families for the events.

Funerals are also followed by social gatherings, involving even more food. While some of these are catered, most are supported by donations of food from the homes of the friends and family of the departed out of respect for that person and for the immediate family. While the occasion of a funeral is a sad one, the sadness and melancholy of the moment is frequently lightened by the interjection of some funny story, often from the days of *antes.*

In these times, a funeral often represents the breaking of yet one more link with the world of *antes.* As we gather at these events, we are all made conscious of how long ago that really was and how few of us are still left. Before the last of us who remember this unique, always busy, sometimes funny, sometimes sad period are gone, this story should be told. It is really for that reason that this book has been written at this time.

For every story in this book, there are several others that could be told. On some topics, perhaps there are dozens. Some have been left out because this account is long enough as it is. Others have been left out for reasons of discretion. (Some stories are better left untold!) As well, there are very many other stories about how Cuba passed through the transition from an isolated colonial village into a modern rural community in a matter of a very few years.

In the newspaper version of this material, each article ended with the expression, *¡Hasta Luego!* This expression can mean "Good bye" or "See you later." Literally it means something more like "Until later" or "Until we meet again." Perhaps there will be more stories to follow the ones in the present volume.

¡Hasta Luego!

- Bibliography -

Books:

Abbink, Emily. *New Mexico's Palace of the Governors: History of an American Treasure.* Santa Fé: Museum of New Mexico Press, 2007.

Andrade, José Manuel Pita, trans. Patricia S. Parrent. *Goya.* Madrid: SILEX, 1975.

Batchen, Lou Sage. *Las Placitas: Historical Facts and Legends.* Placitas, NM: The Friends of Placitas, Inc., 2000.

Borderlands and the Arts Program. *The Art of the Spanish Southwest: An Exhibition of Water-Color Renderings from the Index of American Design, National Gallery of Art.* Washington, D.C.: United States-Mexico Commission for Border Development and Friendship, no date.

Brokaw, Tom. *The Greatest Generation.* New York: Random House, Inc., 1998.

Brown, Lorin W., with Charles L. Briggs, Marta Weigle. *Hispano Folklore of New Mexico: The Lorin W. Brown Federal Writers' Manuscripts.* Albuquerque: University of New Mexico Press, 1978.

Bustamante, Adrian H., Cordelia Thomas Snow, Sandra Jaramillo, Joseph P. Sánchez, Gerald T. E. González, and Orlando Romero (Four Hundredth Anniversary of Santa Fé Book Committee) eds. *All Trails Lead to Santa Fé.* Santa Fé: Sunstone Press, 2010.

Chávez, Fray Angélico. *But Time and Chance: The Story of Padre Martinez of Taos, 1793-1867.* Santa Fé: Sunstone Press, 1981.

— — —. *La Conquistadora: The Autobiography of an Ancient Statue, Revised Edition.* Santa Fé: Sunstone Press, 1983.

— — —. *Origins of New Mexico Families.* Santa Fé: The Historical Society of New Mexico, 1954.

Cobos, Rubén. *A Dictionary of New Mexico and Southern Colorado Spanish.* Santa Fé: Museum of New Mexico Press, 1983.

Eichwald, Alex H. *Don Augustin, 1862-1927: An Immigrant, a Merchant, and a Rancher.* Self published, no date.

Espinosa, José E. *Saints in the Valleys: Christian Sacred Images in the History, Life and Folk Art of Spanish New Mexico.* Albuquerque: University of New Mexico Press, 1960.

García, Nasario. *Más Antes: Hispanic Folklore of the Rio Puerco Valley.* Santa Fé: Museum of New Mexico Press, 1997.

Gonzales, Dolores, ed. *Canciones y Juegos de Nuevo México (Songs and Games of New Mexico).* New York: A. S. Barnes and Company, 1974.

Jaramillo, Cleofas M. *Shadows of the Past.* Santa Fé: Ancient City Press, 1972.

Jones, Jr., Oakah L. *Los Paisanos: Spanish Settlements of the Northern Frontier of New Spain.* Norman, Oklahoma: University of Oklahoma Press, 1979.

Julyan, Robert. *The Place Names of New Mexico,* rev. ed. Albuquerque: Univerity of New Mexico Press, 1998.

Lapesa, Rafael. *Historia de la Lengua Español, Septima Edición.* Madrid: Escelicer S.A., 1968.

Luna, Hilario. *San Joaquin del Nacimiento.* Albuquerque: Hilario Luna, 1975.

Market House Books Ltd. (Eds.), *Oxford Encyclopedia of World History.* New York: Oxford University Press, 1998.

Meyer, Michael, and William L. Sherman. *The Course of Mexican History.* New York: Oxford University Press, 1983.

Moore, Michael. *Los Remedios: Traditional Herbal Remedies of the Southwest.* Santa Fé: Museum of New Mexico Press, 1990.

Morris, Richard B. and Jeffrey B. Morris. *Encyclopedia of American History, 6th Ed.* New York: Harper and Row, 1982.

New Mexico Land Resources Association. *Land Resources of New Mexico.* Publisher uncertain, 1957.

Olibama López Tushar. *The People of "El Valle:" A History of the Colonials in the San Luis Valley.* Denver: Olibama López Tushar, 1975.

Pearce, T. M., ed. *The Place Names of New Mexico.* Albuquerque: University of New Mexico Press, 1965.

Real Academia Española (eds.). *Diccionario de la Lengua Española.* Madrid, Espasa-Calpe, S.A., 1970.

Roberts, Susan A. and Calvin A. Roberts. *A History of New Mexico.*
Albuquerque: University of New Mexico Press, 1986.

Shalkop, Robert L. *Arroyo Hondo: The Folk Art of a New Mexico Village.*
Colorado Springs: The Taylor Museum of the Colorado Springs Fine
Arts Center, 1969.

Simmons, Mark. *Albuquerque, A Narrative History.* Albuquerque: University
of New Mexico Press, 1982.

— — — . *New Mexico: An Interpretive History.* Albuquerque: University of New
Mexico Press, 1988.

Sisneros, Francisco and Joe H. Torres. *Nobres: Nombres de Pila en Nuevo
Mexico.* Bernalillo, New Mexico: Las Campanas Publications, 1982.

Smith, William, revised by Rev. F. N. and M. A. Peloubet. *A Dictionary of the
Bible.*
Philadelphia: John C. Winston Co., 1884.

Swadesh, Frances Leon. *Los Primeros Pobladores: Hispanic Americans of the Ute
Frontier.* Notre Dame, Ind.: University of Notre Dame Press, 1974.

Vásquez, Jane Atkins and Carolyn Atkins, *Remembering Presbyterian Mission
in the Southwest: 25th. Anniversary of the Menaul Historical Society.*
Albuquerque: Menaul Historical Library, 1999.

Velarde, Pablita. Old Father Story Teller. Santa Fé: Clear Light Publishers,
1989.

Williams, Jerry L. *New Mexico in Maps, 2nd Ed.* Albuquerque: University of
New Mexico Press, 1986.

Wilson, Chris and David Kammer. *La Tierra Amarilla: Its History, Architecture
and Cultural Landscape.* Santa Fé: Museum of New Mexico Press, 1989.

Periodicals:

Coulter, Lane. "New Mexican Tinwork History." *Antiques* (October, 1991):
606-617.

Dean, Florence. "Seventy-fifth Anniversary, The New Deal Program,
1993–2001." *Enchantment Magazine,* (Publication of the Jemez Mountain
Electric Cooperative), Vol. 60, No. 3, (March, 2008): 12-15.

Guest, John. *"Cinco Santo." New Mexico Magazine* (August, 1961): 32-34.

Hahn, Vera D. "Lively Living In A Sanctuary." *American Home, Vol. 73, No. 3.*
(March, 1970.): 56-59.

"La Ventana." *New Mexico Magazine* (April, 1965): 2-5.

Lilly, Marjorie. "Richness of the *Pastorela* Play." *Enchantment Magazine*, (Publication of the Jemez Mountain Electric Cooperative), Vol. 59, No. 12, (December, 2007): 12-14.

Schein, Maureen. "History." *La Luz de Jemez*, (Publication of the Jemez Mountain Electric Cooperative), Vol. 11, Issue 12, (December, 2007).

Newspapers:

"Burglars Strip Santa Fe Mission of Priceless Art." *Albuquerque Journal*, July 7, 1972.

Calloway, Larry. "Stolen Statue Had Role in History." *Albuquerque Journal*, March 25, 1973.

"Cuba to Dedicate $80,000 Gym on Wednesday." *Albuquerque Journal*, March 15, 1954.

Curry, Jim. "Señorito Bridge." *Cuba News*, [1967].

Fisher, Betty. "Changes At Health Center." *Cuba News*, April 21, 1972.

"King Takes Action on Religious Art Thefts." *Albuquerque Journal*, August 9, 1972.

Steinberg, David. "Mountain Search Recovers Famous *La Conquistadora.*" *Albuquerque Journal*, August, 1972.

"State seeks to protect art objects." *Daily Review* (Hayward, California), October 15, 1972.

Miscellaneous and unpublished materials:

Familia y Fé. Diseño por Motley, Michael and Michael Picón. Santa Fé: Museo de Nuevo Mexico, En conmemoración des Quintocentenario Colombiano. 1992.

Goya: Reproducciones de obras maestras del Museo del Prado (post card collection, plate 801). Madrid: Ediciones de Arte OFFO los Mesejo [1975].

Immaculate Conception Convent School. *Convent School Journal, 1916–1980.* Cuba, New
Mexico: Immacuate Conception Convent, unpublished manuscript, [1980].

Lucero, Manuel Reyes (transcribed by Doloritas Lucero). *Registro de Manuel Reyes Lucero.*Cuba, New Mexico: unpublished, 1914.

Rambler, The (Cuba High School Yearbook). Cuba, New Mexico: Cuba High School, 1955.

Meltzer, Richard. *Coming of Age in the Great Depression.* Publisher unknown, date unknown. (This is a small, loose-leaf collection of maps and lists of CCC and WPA projects in New Mexico attributed to Meltzer.)

Session of the Capulín Spanish Presbyterian Church. *Minutes of the Session, 1887–1940.* Capulín, New Mexico: unpublished manuscript, [1940].

Session of the Cuba Spanish Presbyterian Church. *Minutes of the Session, 1940–77.* Cuba, New Mexico: unpublished manuscript, [1977].

U.S. Post Office, unpublished internal newsletter, no date.

Yucca, The (Cuba High School Yearbook). Cuba, New Mexico: Cuba High School, 1953.

– Index –

NOTE: In order to avoid repetition, Spanish words are translated in this index instead of a separate glossary. Page numbers followed by the letter p indicate a photograph.

CPSIA information can be obtained at www.ICGtesting.com
Printed in the USA
LVOW061044181111

255539LV00005B/1/P